DAVID CRANE's first book, *Lord* [...]
of Edward Trelawny, was publishe [...]
Until recently he taught English [...] don. He
now lives in north-west Scotland [...]

ALSO BY DAVID CRANE

Lord Byron's Jackal: A Life of Edward Trelawny

THE KINDNESS
OF SISTERS

*Annabella Milbanke
and the Destruction of the Byrons*

DAVID CRANE

Flamingo
An Imprint of HarperCollinsPublishers

Flamingo
An Imprint of HarperCollins*Publishers*
77–85 Fulham Palace Road,
Hammersmith, London w6 8jb

Flamingo is a registered trade mark of
HarperCollins Publishers Limited

www.**fire**and**water**.com

Published by Flamingo 2003
9 8 7 6 5 4 3 2 1

First published in Great Britain by
HarperCollins*Publishers* 2002

Copyright © David Crane 2002

David Crane asserts the moral right to
be identified as the author of this work

isbn 0 00 655159 9

Set in PostScript Monotype Baskerville by
Rowland Phototypesetting Ltd, Bury St Edmunds, Suffolk

Printed and bound in Great Britain by
Clays Ltd, St Ives plc

CONTENTS

LIST OF ILLUSTRATIONS

The Milbanke and Melbourne Families. *Courtesy of the National Gallery, London.*
Annabella Milbanke as a child © *Ferens Art Gallery/Bridgeman Art Gallery.*
Miss Milbanke by Hayter. *Courtesy of the National Portrait Gallery, London.*
Lady Byron, 1833. *Courtesy of the National Portrait Gallery, London.*
Lady Byron by Newton. *Courtesy of the National Portrait Gallery, London.*
Lady Byron in her old age. *Courtesy of the National Gallery, London.*
Augusta Leigh by Hayter. *Courtesy of the British Museum, London.*
Newstead Abbey © *Mary Evans Picture Library.*
Newstead Abbey.
Lord Byron by Thomas Phillips. *Courtesy of the National Portrait Gallery, London.*
Manfred on the Jungfrau © *Bridgeman Art Library.*
Lady Melbourne by John Hoppner. *Courtesy of the National Portrait Gallery, London.*
Jane Elizabeth, Countess of Oxford. *Courtesy of the Tate Gallery, London.*
Lady Caroline Lamb by Thomas Phillips © *Devonshire Collection, Chatsworth. Reproduced by the courtesy of the Duke of Devonshire and the Chatsworth Settlement Trustees.*

Milbanke Pew.
Fare Thee Well © *The British Museum, London.*
The Separation © *The British Museum, London.*
Ada Byron from a miniature. *Courtesy of the National Portrait Gallery, London.*
Ada, Countess of Lovelace © *Queen's Printer and Controller of HMSO, November 1992. UK Government Art Collection.*

Ada on her deathbed © *Bodleian Library, University of Oxford. MS. Dep. Lovelace Byron 118, fol. 108 r. Reproduced by courtesy of Laurence Pollinger Limited and the Earl of Lytton.*

Medora Leigh. *Reproduced from Moore, Doris Langley: Ada: Countess of Lovelace, John Murray, London 1997.*

Lapeyre, Medora's final home.

Lapeyre from above.

Lapeyre centre.

Reverend Fredrick William Robertson. *Courtesy of the National Portrait Gallery, London.*

Coffins and Augusta George Leigh.

Byron and Ada's tomb. *Reproduced from Barber, Thomas Gerard, Byron and Where he is Buried, Henry Morley and Sons, Hucknall 1991.*

Grave of Annabella.

All photographs without credits are from the author's own collection.

ACKNOWLEDGEMENTS

No one can write about Byron without first acknowledging a debt to the vast mass of literature on the subject that has gone before. From the moment that Byron died in 1824 the biographers and memoirists went to work on him, and if two major biographies in the last five years – and a third on the way – are anything to go by, the search is by no means over.

With so much written on Byron's life and posthumous reputation, it would be impossible to acknowledge every influence, but certain debts incurred here will be obvious. Like everyone else who writes on Byron the scholarship of Professor Leslie Marchand provides an indispensable framework, but given the particular emphasis of this book the work of Malcolm Elwin and Doris Langley Moore in disentangling the massive archive in the Bodleian Library known as the Lovelace Byron Papers has been of equal importance. I have often disagreed with their conclusions, but could not have begun without their scholarship, and am very grateful. Quotations from the Lovelace Byron Papers are included with the permission of the Earl of Lytton and Laurence Pollinger Ltd.

On a more personal note, it is a pleasure to thank all those who have helped with the writing of this book: Haidee Jackson, for her time and kindness on more than one visit to Newstead; Ryan Davis for the photographs of the catacombs at Kensal Green Cemetery; Perran Wood for hours of conversation on the Byrons and the photographs of Medora Leigh's last home in the south of France; Derek Johns for his encouragement and suggestions; Catherine Eldridge for her attempts to provide a scientific answer to the issue of Medora's paternity. I am also especially grateful to Alan Petty, Stella Tillyard and Elisabeth Green who read all or parts of this in manuscript, and to Min Stacpoole who waded through it more than once to help make it a better book than it would otherwise have been.

I would also like to thank everyone at Harper Collins who has worked on this, but especially Arabella Pike, whose enthusiasm and commitment has survived some fairly radical changes of direction since the first draft was stolen by some very disappointed burglars. Finally, this book is for Honor, who has helped at every stage, and whose unfailing support has made it possible.

PROLOGUE

> The glory of mankind has been to produce lives, to pro-
> vide vivid, independent, individual men, not buildings
> or engineering works or art, not even the public good.
>
> D. H. Lawrence[1]

> You should not have warred with the World – it will
> not do – it is too strong always for any individual.
>
> Madame de Stael to Byron[2]

In the late afternoon of 15 June 1938, a small group of men
stood at a gaping hole at the south-west corner of the chancel
of St Mary Magdalen, Hucknall. Beneath their feet a short
flight of steps led down to a low, cramped vault, and by the glare
of a photographer's lamp they could make out a pile of coffins
heaped on top of each other in a mouldering jumble of wood
and bone and twisted lead that had lain undisturbed for over fifty
years.

They had converged on the church in some secrecy. Earlier in
the day a lorry had brought builders' tools and planks to the
north door, and one by one through the afternoon a surveyor,
antiquarian and doctor had appeared. Finally a mason and three
labourers arrived and began lifting the massive, cracked slab of
York stone that now lay beside the open crypt.

It took them two hours to raise the stone, but by six o'clock in
the evening it was done. During the course of the work there

were other visitors in the church, but once the vault was open most of these, and all the women, were asked to leave.

Even by English standards, those who remained were a curiously prosaic lot to be indulging a taste in literary necrophilia. There was clearly a generous streak of romance in the character of Canon Barber, the Vicar of Hucknall, but if a brace of churchwardens and half the professional classes of the county were not ballast enough to steady the most extravagant imagination, he had also co-opted the Diocesan Surveyor and local MP in a bid for respectability.

A miner's lamp was swung into the vault to test the air, a ladder lowered to avoid the shallow, awkward steps, and Canon Barber climbed down, followed in turn by the surveyor, photographer and antiquarian. The purpose of the meeting, if the Canon is to be believed, was to establish the existence of a lost medieval crypt, and although it was soon plain that any such hopes were misplaced, measurements were duly taken and recorded, leaving the way clear for the real, if unacknowledged, business of the day.

The labourers were dismissed until the next morning, and the party adjourned to the church hall, only returning at the dead of night. Again, Canon Barber was the first down. Alone in the vault, lit now only by the photographer's lamps, he had time for a more careful inspection. It was a cramped, rectangular chamber six feet wide, just over seven feet long, and no more than eight feet beneath the floor of the nave. Its walls were of plastered brick, with two sloping slabs of stone making the vaulted roof. In three piles, running north to south rested the more or less intact shells of about half a dozen coffins, with the crushed debris of others beneath them. Round his feet lay the dust and bones of three centuries.

There seemed to be no order to anything. At the foot of the stairs, though, he identified the seventeenth century coffin of a baby, its lead lining buckled and twisted under the weight of a double-cube funerary chest, to which scraps of faded purple velvet still clung. On the lid was a brass plate with the following inscription:

Within the Urn
are deposited
the heart and the brain
of the deceased
Lord Noel Byron

The lid was loose, and inside was a sealed lead case, with a second inscription adding an oddly casual 'etc' to the contents of the urn. Beyond the chest, Barber could now distinguish more easily the coffin for which he was searching. It was made of well-preserved oak and ornately decorated. Further shreds of purple material – faded since to crimson – clung to the brass headed coffin nails. On the lid rested the remains of a Baron's coronet. The velvet and ermine had rotted away, and the pearls had been wrenched from their finials. Only the simple rim survived to identify the rank and probable identity of the dead.

There was no coffin plate to confirm Barber's guess, but the lid was loose and he could see that the lead casing had already been cut open. 'Somebody', he recalled with an endearing disingenuousness, 'had deliberately opened the coffin.

A horrible thought came over me that souvenirs might have been taken from the coffin. The idea was revolting, but I could not dismiss it. Had the body itself been removed? Terrible thought! From time to time visitors to the church had asserted in my hearing that the body of the Poet was not in the Vault. I wondered now on what ground this assertion could have been made. Had they known of the opening of the coffin, and received some secret information that the body had been removed? The more I thought about it, the more fearful I became of the possibility of the coffin being empty. There was the coffin before me – the lid was loose and easily raised – the leaden case within torn open. Within the case was another coffin of wood – the lid had never been fastened. What was beneath it? If I raised it, what should I discover? Dare I look within? Yes, the world should know the truth – that the body of the great poet was there – or that the coffin was empty. Reverently, very reverently, I raised the lid, and before my eyes there lay the embalmed body of Byron in as perfect a condition as when it was placed in the coffin one hundred and fourteen years ago. His features and hair were easily recognisable from the portraits with which I was so familiar. The serene, almost happy expression on his face made a profound impression upon me. The feet and ankles were uncovered, and I was able to establish the fact that his lameness had been that of the right foot. But enough – I gently lowered the lid of the coffin and as I did so, breathed a prayer for the peace of his soul.[3]

'Close thy Byron and open thy Goethe', that renegade Byronist Thomas Carlyle demanded in *Sartor Resartus*, but Barber's vandalism is only the most literal example of England's refusal to bend to the Sage of Ecclefechan. From the moment in July 1824 when Byron's black servant struggled for one last view of his master's coffin as it was lowered into the Hucknall vault, a defiant nation has shared his reluctance to let its most notorious poet go, a complex mix of curiosity and guilt driving it to re-stake its claim in the man it had once forced into exile.

It is as hard to exaggerate the impact of Byron's death on England as it is that of his life. In the orthodox histories of the nineteenth century the two seminal figures of his age are Coleridge and Bentham, but both men were pre-eminently 'sires of sires', their influence disseminated through disciples until it was simply part of the zeitgeist – lived and breathed by men and women who would have been hard pressed to identify the source of their beliefs.

With Byron it is the opposite, and there is in this sense no English writer like him, no one who has stamped his image so firmly on the phenomenon that bears his name, no one who has so completely made his life the measure of his art. It is difficult to imagine that anybody in their right mind has ever allowed a dislike of Wordsworth to stand in the way of his *Prelude* for instance, but from the first triumph of *Childe Harold*, Byron and his art have been inseparable, his personality and life validating or threatening the poetry in ways that have no obvious parallel. 'We shall, like all others who say anything about Lord Byron', Blackwood's declared, begin, *sans apologie,* with his personal character. This is the great object of attack, the constant theme of open vitupera-tion to one set, and the established mark for all the petty but deadly sneers, shrugs, groans to another . . . Is there a noble sentiment, a lofty thought, a sublime conception in the book? 'Ah yes!' is the answer. 'But what of that? It is only the roué Byron that speaks!' Is a kind, a generous action of the man mentioned? 'Yes, yes!' comments the sage; 'but only remember the atrocities of "Don Juan".' Salvation is thus shut out at either entrance: the poet damns the man, and the man the poet.[4]

With the solitary exception of Milton, no English writer has so polarised opinion or posthumously stirred such visceral responses as Byron. In the wake of Shelley's death off the coast at Lerici the Tory press might lash him with a cruel and casual contempt that still has the power to shock, but the entrenched battle lines that formed around Byron's memory are of another order altogether, scars that define not just a world of coterie politics but the permanent cultural life of a whole nation.

It is notable, in fact, that it is not with other literary reputations that the posthumous cult of Byron can be compared, but with those deaths that seem to reveal some crisis of confidence or national identity. In more recent times the great state funeral of Sir Winston Churchill patently belonged to an order of its own, but if the sombre mood of that week was of an empire mourning its own passing, one only needs to think of other such funerals – Wellington's, Nelson's, the torch-lit procession of the old, mad George III – to recognise the context in which Byron's needs to be seen. 'We have been stunned from another quarter', Sir Walter Scott wrote,

> by one of those deaths . . . as from an archangel's trumpet to awaken the soul of a whole people at once.[5]

'Hark! forth from the abyss a voice proceeds,' Byron himself wrote of Princess Caroline – lines doubly prophetic of the mood that would greet his own death and that of another thirty-six year old aristocratic exile whose funeral cortege followed the almost identical journey northwards through the streets of London,

> A long low distant murmur of dread sound,
> Such as arises when a nation bleeds
> With some deep and immedicable wound . . .
>
> Scion of chiefs and monarchs, where art thou?
> Fond hope of many nations art thou dead?
> Could not the grave forget thee, and lay low
> Some less majestic and less beloved head?[6]

There was something else about Byron's death, however, something alien and atavistic, that not even the politicised guilt and pseudo-Catholic trappings of Princess Diana's funeral can quite match. Some years ago there was a documentary film of a Bengali village terrorised by a man-eating tiger, and in the ritual celebrations that greeted its killing, the frenzy of hands that stretched up in a bizarre mixture of fear and reverence to touch the garlanded corpse, we probably come as close as we can to the mood in which England awaited the return of Byron's body.

For Byron *was* that tiger (an image he used of himself – for that matter an image his mother-in-law used of him) – Blake's tiger, a thing of 'fearful symmetry', an elemental force, beyond comprehension – too dangerous to be allowed to live and too vital to live without. 'Alas poor Byron,' Carlyle wrote in the flush of pentecostal panic that greeted the news from Greece,

> The news of his death came down on my heart like a mass of lead; and yet, the thought of it sends a painful twinge thr' all my being, as if I had lost a brother! O God! That so many souls of mud and clay should fill up their base existence to the utmost bound, and this, the noblest spirit in Europe, should sink before half his course was run! . . . We shall hear his voice no more: I dreamed of seeing him and knowing him; but the curtain of everlasting night has hid him from our eyes. We shall go to him, he shall not return to us. Adieu my dear Jane. There is a blank in your heart, and a blank in mine, since this man passed away.[7]

With his looks and glamour, his aristocratic pedigree, and the scandals that clung to his name, it is no surprise that Byron excited this attention in life, but the oddity is that death only intensified the cult of personality that surrounded him. For Jane Welsh the blank in creation his death left could have been no greater if the sun or moon had fallen from the skies, and it was as if no one could quite believe the enormity of their loss without the evidence of the body. 'Don't look at him, he is dangerous'[8], a horror-struck Lady Liddell had warned her daughter, covering her eyes when she saw the exiled Byron in Rome, but in death that was just what everyone wanted to do. In Missolonghi the wretched Julius Millingen and the rest of Byron's doctors had hacked at his corpse in a brutal parody of an autopsy, measuring his skull and weighing his brain, slapping vital organs on their scales as if the mystery of genius and personality was there to be found in his remains. In the same room, only days later, his companion and biographer, Edward Trelawny, pulled back the burial sheet to stare down on Byron's body with a similar confidence – 'the great mystery was solved', he later wrote with a ruthless disregard for truth; 'Both his feet were clubbed, and his legs withered to the knee – the form and features of an Apollo, with the feet and legs of a sylvan satyr.'[9]

Back in England, it was little different when after almost six weeks at sea the *Florida* docked with his coffin just below London Bridge. While Byron's old friend Hobhouse waited on deck for the undertakers to drain the preserving spirit off the corpse, crowds lined the banks and watched from the flotilla of small boats that bobbed around the ship, as eager to glimpse his return as they had been to watch his departure from Dover eight years earlier.

A French officer from Le Havre delivered Hobhouse a request from General Lafayette asking to see the body. Down in the hold, a boy was caught cutting a relic from Byron's shroud. Over the next days, as the sense of loss sank in, the crowds only grew, men and women queuing in their thousands to pass the coffin as it lay in state in Great George Street, cramming the pavements and windows along the route of the funeral cortege and packing the church at Hucknall so full that there was scarcely room for the coffin.

Nor was this just the morbid excitement of a season, as the

Parish Clerk's Album at Hucknall, placed there by John Bowring more than a year after the funeral, underlines. The church was then a more modest structure than the building which Victorian improvers bequeathed to Canon Barber, but for the mass of visitors who made the pilgrimage, the intimacy of the old St Mary's ministered to their grief in ways that Westminster Abbey or St Paul's could never have done. 'So should it be', Bowring had written in the front of the album,

> let o'er this grave
> No monumental banners wave;
> Let no word speak – no trophy tell
> Aught that may break the charming spell
> By which, as on the sacred ground
> He kneels, the pilgrim's heart is bound.
> A still, resistless influence,
> Unseen, but felt, binds up the sense;
> While every whisper seems to breathe
> Of the mighty dead who rests beneath.[10]

The extravagant grief of the young Tennyson, the maudlin reflections of Mary Shelley as she watched the funeral cortege from her Kentish Town window, the lecture extemporised by Coleridge as it passed up Highgate Hill – all these quite properly belong to literary history, but skimming down the lists of names below Bowring's poem the most striking thing as ever with Byron is the sheer breadth and cosmopolitanism of his appeal. The two names that head the album, for instance, are those of the royal Duke of Sussex and of Pietro Gamba, brother of Byron's last Italian mistress, who visited Hucknall before sailing for Greece to die in the cause that Byron had made Europe's. There are visitors here, too, from New Orleans and Baltimore, representatives from the Spanish Cortes and the American Congress, comedians and Grenadier guardsmen, writers, theatre managers and clergymen, school parties, ships' crews, and – in 1832 – a John de Bracken, home from Calcutta, where eight years earlier prayers for the repose of Byron's soul rose from a Greek chapel on the banks of the Hoogly.

After the seismic convulsion of grief that greeted Byron's death, these quieter after-shocks recorded in the Hucknall Album might come as no surprise, but they still raise teasing questions about his place in English cultural life. Among those hundreds of visitors many might have been hard pressed to say what had brought them, and yet in a curious sense it is the presence of the 'common man' – the great battle cry of Diana's funeral – rather than of Washington Irving or the Duke of Sussex that is the most intriguing aspect of the Byron cult.

For a man of Sussex's liberal pretensions, the pilgrimage carried clear and deliberate political overtones, but precisely what kind of 'fane' did those hundreds of obscure admirers imagine they were visiting at Hucknall? What were parents doing, signing the visitors' book with their daughters, paying homage at the shrine of a man who had publicly ridiculed every tie of family life? Why were army or naval officers at the tomb of a poet who took such pride in sharing Napoleon Bonaparte's initials? What did good protestant Englishmen think they were up to, leaving messages that would not look out of place at the foot of the Bambino in Rome's Aracoeli? What was it that brought so many clergymen to the grave of a writer the Bishop of Calcutta had labelled the 'systematic poet of seduction, adultery and incest; the contemner of patriotism, the insulter of piety, the raker into every sink of vice and wretchedness to disgust and degrade and harden the hearts of his fellow-creatures'?[11] What was nineteenth century England doing longing after 'a perfected idol . . . as the Israelites longed for the calf in Horeb'?[12]

The most exciting answer to these questions is that Byron had come to represent a subversive element in the national character for which the encroaching morality of the nineteenth century allowed less and less expression. In his wonderfully contrary study of the Byrons, A.L. Rowse once went so far as to claim that Byron was scarcely English at all, and if this is a characteristic over-statement, Rowse is right that the values Byron embodied have always prospered on the margins of English life rather than at its centre, a source of equal fascination and fear to a country reluctant to recognise its own complex identity.

'Into what dangers would you lead me, Cassius', a nervous Brutus asks in *Julius Caesar,*

> That you would have me seek into myself
> For that which is not in me?'

and the fear that accompanied Byron to the grave was the fear of what he had shown them in themselves.* 'Every high thought that was ever kindled in our breast by the muse of Byron', *Black-wood's* protested, expressing the sense of outrage and almost self-disgust that his readers came to feel as the full implications of their 'idolatry' were brought home to them,

> every pure and lofty feeling . . . is up in arms against him.
> We look back with a mixture of wrath and scorn to the
> delight with which we suffered ourselves to be filled.[13]

It is this that gives the history – and the posthumous history – of Byron its continuing importance because he raised demons that no community could afford to acknowledge or allow to live. In a wonderful sequence near the beginning of Stanley Donen's *Charade* George Kennedy opens the west door of a church, strides down the aisle to where an open coffin rests between banks of candles on its bier, stares for a moment at the body, takes a pin out of his raincoat lapel, jabs it into the corpse to make sure it is dead, turns on his heel and strides out again.

There was something of *that* about Byron's funeral – the mood along the Tottenham Road seemed to George Borrow like that of an execution – because for all its beauty and fascination the tiger was safer dead. There was nothing feigned in the grief and loss of the young Tennyson or Carlyle, and yet from the notorious day that his closest friends burned his memoirs in John Murray's offices to the letters George Eliot sent Harriet Beecher Stowe, even Byron's most passionate admirers needed to deny or suppress the

---

* This was illustrated vividly by figures such as W.G. Whitcombe, who followed Byron to Greece. In 1825 the nineteen year old Whitcombe arrived in the town of Nauplia, assumed the name, identity and morals of the Byronic hero of a popular novel, *Anastasius*, attempted to assassinate Byron's friend Trelawny in an incident that might have come straight out of one of Byron's Eastern tales, and promptly went mad with fear and guilt when he realised what he had done.

truths that his life embodied. John Cam Hobhouse, that loyal 'bulldog', told Tom Moore in a conversation about the memoirs, that he knew more of Byron than anyone else, and much more than he should wish anyone else to know.

'Yet each man kills the thing he loves'[14] wrote a later exile from these shores, and along with the adulation, Byron has always inspired an anxiety that ranges from comic wariness to suspicion, fear and open hatred. Through the novels of the nineteenth century Byronic imitators would continue to stalk the Caucasus or the moors with all the misanthropic glamour of their original, but from *Persuasion* to *Jane Eyre*, from *Glenarvon* to *Dracula*, from Mary Shelley's Raymond to Polidori's Ruthven – the first vampire in English fiction – 'Byronism' is a physical threat to be feared, shunned, exiled, immolated, staked through the heart or – that most English of solutions, – blinded, crippled and then,'Dear Reader', married.

It is only too appropriate that Mary Shelley's name should feature on this list, because no one has so painfully united what D. H. Lawrence called the '*predilection d'artiste*'[15] for the aristocrat with a bourgeois fear of everything he stands for. 'For there does exist, after all,' Lawrence wrote in his great essay on Thomas Hardy – an essay characteristically less about Hardy than Lawrence himself –

> ... the great self-preservation scheme, and in it we must all live ... But there is the greater idea of self-preservation, which is formulated in the state, in the whole modelling of the community ... In the long run, the State, the Community, the established form of life remained, remained intact and impregnable, the individual, trying to break forth from it, died of fear, or of exhaustion, or of exposure to attacks from all sides, like men who have left the walled city to live outside in the precarious open. This is the tragedy of Hardy, always the same: the tragedy of those who, more or less pioneers, have died in the wilderness, whither they have escaped for free action, after having left the walled security, and the comparative imprisonment, of the established convention. This is the theme of novel after novel: remain quiet within the convention, and you are good, safe and happy in the long run, though you never have the vivid pang of

sympathy on your side; or, on the other hand, be passionate, individual, wilful, you will find the security of the convention a walled prison, you will escape, and you will die, either of your own lack of strength to bear the isolation and the exposure, or from direct revenge from the community, or from both. This is the tragedy, and only this.[16]

This book is the story of that tragedy, because supreme among the Lawrentian outsiders is Byron, an aristocrat in the conventional sense by a convoluted accident of inheritance, an aristocrat in the Lawrentian sense to the core. It has been plausibly argued that Byron was never in fact at ease with the chance that brought an impoverished Aberdeen schoolboy a title, but from that day in 1812 when, as the author of *Childe Harold*, he 'woke to find himself famous' his life became a paradigm of Lawrence's struggle between the individual and the community – the archetype of all those artists forced into exile, compromise or silence by the hostility of the crowd, of the men and women who have had to pay with their freedom or security for their integrity, the living victims of that same communal, English instinct for self-preservation that pushed Hardy to sacrifice his heroes and heroines on the altar of social convention.

Crippled with a deformity of his right foot, abandoned by his rake of a father, brought up in poverty by his violently possessive mother, alternately abused and terrified by his Calvinist nurse, Byron might have had little choice in the matter, but no psychological pleading can disguise the gusto with which he embraced his fate. In recent years it has become the fashion among biographers to present him as some kind of 'monster-victim' of this childhood, but the exhilarating truth about Byron is that he was an outsider by intelligence and will, an enemy by instinct, sensibility, temperament and politics of all that this 'tight little island'* stands for.

No major English poet – except perhaps his hero, Alexander Pope – has made such creative capital out of a sense of alienation

---

* Oh! what a snug little Island,
  A right little, tight little Island!
  Thomas John Dibdin 'The Snug Little Island' in *The British Raft*, 1797

and grievance. It would take most of his life before the combination of exile and technical mastery matured these feelings into the great verse of *Don Juan*, but from his first callow satire the poet fed ruthlessly off his sense of difference, transmuting all the social and physical insecurities of childhood into the antinomian hauteur of the Byronic hero.

And the key word there is 'Byronic', because it was the glee with which Byron seized on the idea of hereditary doom that has made his name synonymous with the rebel outsider. The more unstable elements of his character probably owed as much to his mother's Gordon blood as the paternal line, but it was exclusively through the history of crime and excess that was 'Mad Jack' Byron's bequest to his son that a perverted Calvinism and the curse of deformity coalesced into a single, liberating myth of predestined damnation and revolt.

From the moment when, as a nine year old child, after the successive deaths of father, cousin, uncle and the 'Wicked Lord', he came into the title and first saw the ruins of his ancestral home near Nottingham, the shape of this rebellion was set. Newstead had originally been founded as an Augustinian priory in the reign of Henry II, and for all the changes it was still the great west front of the former church that gave the house its special character, a soaring, pinnacled and traceried façade behind which nothing stood, a piece of history preserved as theatre as wonderfully and spuriously evocative as everything else about the child's bankrupt inheritance.

If it is impossible to imagine any nine-year old would be impervious to the romance of Newstead, no one but a Byron could have gloried so in its evidence of ancestral ruin. The priory had first come into the family in 1537 at the Dissolution of the Monasteries, but the ruthless transforming energies of Henrician England had long disappeared there, leaving house and lands mouldering in the same irreversible decay, the Byron name stained by murder, its deer slaughtered, woods felled, mining rights leased, rooms bare, its ruined east wing open to the skies.

Among the great English Romantics, Byron is unique in an almost complete absence of feel for his native landscape, and the cloistered world of Newstead quite literally set in stone a sense of physical alienation that had begun in his infancy. In his earliest verse there was a certain amount of Ossian-like posturing over the mountains of his childhood, but it was significantly the ruined priory that became what Pope's Twickenham grotto and garden had been to another crippled outsider – the emotional and physical context of his creative life, the 'other place' of the imagination where he could reinvent himself in the successive alter-egos with which he would take on the world. 'Newstead, fast falling, once resplendent dome', Byron saluted it in one of his juvenile poems,

> Religion's shrine! Repentant HENRY's pride!
> Of warriors, monks, and dames the cloister'd tomb,
> Whose pensive shades around thy ruins glide,
> Hail to the pile! More honour'd in the fall
> Than modern mansions in their pillar'd state;
> Proudly majestic frowns thy vaulted hall,
> Scowling defiance on the blasts of fate[17]

In his adult life Newstead would be more a financial burden than a retreat, but its blend of history and loss retained a central place in his imagination. As a boy at Harrow and then Cambridge his sense of identity was wrapped up with the Byronic inheritance it embodied, but even after he had been compelled to sell it, the lessons of pride and vulnerability he had learned under its roof always remained with him,

It influenced everything in his life, his strengths and weaknesses, his politics and social manner – the awkward mix of arrogance and uncertainty – and above all the poetry that can often seem an emanation of childhood alienation. In the last great poem of his life he returned to Newstead with a freshness that underlines its importance to him, but if it is impossible to imagine the satirist of *Don Juan* without acknowledging the role Newstead played in his development it is as hard not to see its influnece in the lack of 'place' that is such a glaring weakness of his descriptive verse.

Nothing is ever as simple as that with Byron, of course, but his deliberate, 'aristocratic' obtuseness about the *business* of poetry

that clouds the issue here was ultimately no more than a manifes-
tation of the same insecurity. One only has to think of the ease
with which Keats can move through an English landscape in dark-
ness and identify every scent and sound to see what is missing
from Byron's verse, but in some adolescent way it would have
seemed *beneath* him to look with that kind of particularity.
'"Where is the green your friend the Laker talks such fustian
about", Trelawny recalled in an anecdote which – true or not –
neatly brings Byron's hostility to a world with which he was at
odds and poetic sensibility into a single focus,

> "Who ever", asked Byron, "saw a green sky?"
> Shelley was silent, knowing that if he replied, Byron
> would give vent to his spleen. So I said, "The sky in England
> is oftener green than blue."
> "Black, you mean," rejoined Byron; and this discussion
> brought us to his door.[18]

This insensitivity to his surroundings might seem an odd criticism
of a poet whose evocation of the Greek landscape inspired a
generation to fight and die for its freedom, but even then it was
an *idea* of landscape rather than landscape itself that quickened
his creativity, a sense of decline and loss that was as much imaginative projection as classical association.

It is no coincidence, either, that the one place that could genuinely vie with Greece in Byron's mind was Venice, and again it
was the palpable air of decay that clung to the Serenissima in her
dotage that gripped his imagination. There are times in fact when
this almost reflex melancholy can strike an oddly adolescent note
in a writer of his wit and sophistication, and yet it is precisely this
quality of arrested growth that links boy and man, and – critically
– man and *poet* in a sense of alienation that found its first and
deepest expression in Newstead.

The greatness of D. H. Lawrence's novels, as F. R. Leavis remarked, was the proof they give that he *lived*, and the same could
be said with even more validity of Byron's poetry. In the wonderful satires of his last years he produced some of the finest
comic poetry in the English language, and yet for all its brilliance

and fun the ultimate fascination of his verse lies in the testament
it offers to the courage and defiance with which Byron lived his
life.

It was a defiance that darkened everything, from the wounded
bitterness with which he responded to rejection, to the reckless
and self-destructive exhibitionism with which he greeted success.
There are other outsiders for whom success comes as a kind of
belated membership card, but it was perhaps the defining hall-
mark of Byronic rebellion that triumph only propelled him from
the defence onto the attack, driving him in an ascending trajectory
from Newstead on an inevitable collision course with the community he despised.

This is not another biography of Byron – nor even of the
notorious marriage that led to his final rupture with England –
but an exploration of this timeless battle between the values he
stood for and those of the community. There are any number of
English authors around whose lives a similar argument might be
built, but the unity of his life and art and the fame which surrounded Byron make him the one writer whose history defines
in some permanent way what it means to be English.

At the height of the marriage crisis, it was claimed with a breathtaking simplicity that men and women's attitudes to him demon-
strated whether they were 'good' or 'bad', and nearly fifty years
after his death Harriet Beecher Stowe berated the English nation
for any softening in its attitude to him. It seemed to the American
novelist that the moral sinews of the nation had been radically
weakened by his verse and life, and while she was in some ways
a case apart, there was too much agreement on all sides of the
political spectrum to dismiss hers as the naïve voice of New England puritanism.

'England, England!'[19] she lamented, and if she was wrong in
her diagnosis, she was right that the threat Byron offered had not
died with him. For the dozen years which followed the triumph
of *Childe Harold*, his poetry and personality had sent his contemporaries scuttling for cover behind the city walls, and yet it was only
in death that his rebellion was revealed in its full destructiveness,
consuming and maiming lives with all the inexorable power of

Greek tragedy until it reached its final, savage climax in the 'High Noon' of Byronic Romanticism that forms the core of this book.

This was the first and last confrontation in twenty years between the two women who had been brought together by his marriage and fought over his corpse, the sister he had loved and the wife who had brought about his exile. It took place at the White Hart at Reigate, a small town some twenty miles south of London, on 8 April 1851, the year of the Great Exhibition, the year Victorian England gloried in its prosperity and moral superiority with a complacency Byron would have loathed.

Byron, though, had been dead for almost twenty-seven years. Of his great contemporaries, Shelley had been gone for twenty-nine, Keats thirty, Coleridge seventeen, even Wordsworth – the 'Wordswords' of *Don Juan* as he had long since become – one.

And thirteen years into Victoria's reign, it was a different world. Tennyson, who as a schoolboy had carved Byron's name into a rock on hearing the news from Missolonghi, had just been presented to the Queen as the new Poet Laureate, his tortured frame tightly trussed in the same court dress that Samuel Rogers had once lent his predecessor. Matthew Arnold – that other representative voice of the mid-century – had just become engaged. Trollope was wondering if he would ever make a novelist. Dickens, never one to be seduced by national prosperity, was beginning *Bleak House*, Mayhew publishing his *London Poor*. George Eliot was editing at the *Westminster Review*, Charlotte Bronte squabbling with Thackeray, her sisters Emily and Anne, already dead. Byron's half-sister, Augusta Leigh, was sixty seven; his widow, Annabella Byron, fifty-eight.

Byron had been dead for almost as long as he had lived, but for the two women who met at the White Hart his memory had all the sharpness of recent bereavement. For the best part of forty years his presence or legacy had alternately enriched and shattered their lives, and this Reigate meeting was the final testament to his dominance, one last dramatic demonstration of the fear and adulation that had convulsed a generation and for which in their polar antagonisms Annabella Byron and Augusta Leigh stand the perfect surrogates.

It is this that gives both the fascination and significance to this meeting, because the battle that climaxed at Reigate is also in miniature the archetypal struggle of the outsider and the community that had raged around Byron ever since the first publication of *Childe Harold.* The secret histories of these two women have a misery that no repetition can dim, and yet for all the melodrama of the story this book tells, it is the *representative* quality that gives a kind of Aeschylian grandeur to the history of incest, bastardy, betrayal, love and hate that in Byron's name and memory bound them together.

If this focus on the Reigate meeting needs no justifying, the form that has been adopted here requires some explanation. In the first and last parts of this book the methods are those of any conventional biography, but if there is a single episode in the whole Byron saga that *demands* a freer, more speculative approach, it is this last confrontation between Annabella and Augusta at the White Hart.

With that in mind, the form is that of an 'imaginary dialogue', and if this is in part because we do not *know* what was said, it is not necessity that has determined this option. There can be few lives or deaths that have ever been subjected to the same scrutiny as that of Byron's, and yet as so often with him the most compelling truths of this narrative lie in regions for which the traditional tools of history or biography are simply not enough.

It is not only that scholarship can never deliver the certainties to which it aspires, but that this meeting has less to do with 'objective truth' or ascertainable fact than with the kinds of subjective experience that gradually take on an independent and destructive life of their own. Within the restrictions of orthodox biography it would have been possible to chart the chronological path that took Annabella and Augusta from their first meeting to this last, but what biography could never do is dissolve the barriers between past and present or capture the distorting operations of memory, the co-existence of contradictory but equally valid 'truths'; could never re-open those avenues that, one by one, are closed by life but remain in the mind; could never, most important of all, do full justice to that sense of waste, that consciousness of other possibilities – other 'selves', resolutions, aspirations, untapped or thwarted potentialities of human growth – that was Byron's terrible gift not just to these two women but to his whole generation.

There is, too, another – entirely fortuitous – advantage to a dialogue of this kind, in that the inevitable whiff of Victorian melodrama about it, the sense of characters speaking out of 'role', of addressing not each other but the audience beyond, perfectly captures the way in which they spoke. In a letter written just before the meeting at Reigate, Annabella accused Augusta of never saying or writing anything without a third person in mind, and whether or not that is fair to her it certainly is to Annabella herself whose natural mode of address was the statement or deposition made and obsessively recorded with the judgement of posterity in her sights.

And if this reconstructed dialogue is essentially a fiction, it is a fiction that is strictly circumscribed by historical evidence. The old White Hart in Reigate had passed its Regency peak by the time that Annabella chose it and is now long since gone, and the setting here is essentially a theatrical rather than an historical space, its symbolism and props those of a Pre-Raphaelite painting – this after all is the year Ruskin championed the Brotherhood – rather than a Victorian coaching inn doomed by the advent of the train.

There has, too, been a compression of time to contain within the classical unities the final unfolding of these lives, but those are the only liberties taken. There is nothing here, otherwise, that does not have its source in the thousands of letters, statements, depositions, reminiscences and journals that document the relationship of the two women. Much of it, too, is in their own words, spoken, written or reported over a period of more than thirty years. We have the letters that they exchanged before Reigate, and the minutes taken after. We have the notes, written on a slip of paper in a nervous, almost indecipherable hand, that Byron's widow took with her to the meeting. We have the correspondence that followed. We know their state of health, how they looked, how they dressed, how they sounded, how they stood and walked, their physical responses to pain. Above all, though, in the mere presence of two elderly women – the one frail from chronic ill-health, the other dying – we have the ultimate proof of that obsession with the memory and influence of Byron that makes their story the story of the age itself.

A MEETING OF OPPOSITES

On a chill and blustery Tuesday in April 1851, an elderly woman, accompanied by a man in his early thirties, emerged from the entrance at the top of Trafalgar Street in Brighton to take the north-bound railway for Reigate. If anyone in the crowded terminus had noticed either of them it would almost certainly have been the man, a tall and striking figure, whose charismatic preaching at the Holy Trinity had made the names of 'Brighton' and 'Robertson' synonymous across the English-speaking protestant world.

With her air of genteel invalidism, and discreet, unassuming appearance, it is unlikely that the woman beside him would have attracted a second glance. She had never been more than five foot three in height and in her late fifties seemed scarcely that, a fragile, neat creature with a slight, 'almost infantine'[20] figure, fine delicate hands, deep and striking blue eyes, silver hair, high forehead, and the preternatural pallor of the permanent invalid.

To the circle of her friends, in fact, who watched over her prolonged decline with a complete and willing devotion, it seemed that Annabella Byron hardly belonged to this world at all. There was a calm certainty about her that struck a note of unearthly detachment, an ethereal refinement that seemed to the chosen 'soulmates' of these last years to be that of 'one of the spirits of the just made perfect ... hovering on the brink of the eternal world'[21].

If anyone had taken a closer look at this pair, however, as they made their way under the soaring gothic of Brighton's new terminus to the first-class carriages of the London train, there would have been little doubt where the balance of power lay. Thirty five years earlier the young Annabella Byron had appeared to her sister-in-law less as a visiting angel than an avenging spectre, and in the remote and concentrated self-possession of her bearing, it was as if all the frailties or pleasures of life had been purged away to leave behind only a pure, indomitable will.

And yet behind this 'miracle of mingled weakness and strength'[22], as Harriet Beecher Stowe called her, there was a nervousness, an emotional and physical excitability, that raged all the fiercer for its ruthless suppression. In a self-portrait she wrote in the last year of her life she spoke of the 'burning world within'[23] that so few ever saw, and as she took her place beside Robertson, and sat compulsively folding and refolding her scrap of paper with its illegible instructions to herself on it, she knew only too bitterly the cost at which any outward calm had been won.

If she had caught her reflection in the glass before it was swallowed up in the blackness of the Clayton tunnel, she would have been forced to recognise there the evidence of the same grim truth. Forty years earlier, in her second London season, Hayter had painted her with the louche abandon of some Regency Magdalene, but if she had looked now for the face of the young Annabella Milbanke in the reflection that stared back, searching for some trace of all those potentialities and hopes that were frozen when pain and humiliation petrified her strength into the obduracy of a long widowhood, she would have looked in vain.

There would have been something in its unyielding expression, however, in the set of the mouth, in the air of conviction, the concentration, that anyone who had seen her as a child would have had no difficulty recognising. Some years after her death Robertson's biographer, Frederick Arnold, remarked on the doctrine of 'personal infallibility' to which Annabella Byron subscribed in these late years, and if a lifetime of alternating sycophancy and hostility had done their worst to make her what she was, the foundations at least of her old age were laid in the cosseted, self-absorbed childhood of Annabella Milbanke.

*   *   *

To have any real sense of the woman in the train bound for Reigate, or the forces that had shaped her life, it is necessary to go back even further than that, to another generation and world that is best glimpsed in a family portrait by Stubbs that now hangs in the National Gallery in London. On the left of Stubbs's grouping a young woman of seventeen sits high in the seat of a light carriage, reins and whip competently and prophetically in hand, her face, simultaneously 'unfinished' and determined, framed by a white bonnet, her eyes boldly, almost immodestly, engaging with a future that seems in her control.

The girl, Elizabeth Lamb, is pregnant, although it is impossible to tell from the painting. At her side, her father, Sir Ralph Milbanke, his expression serious, leans against the carriage; in the centre, holding the reins of a dappled grey that matches her carriage pony, stands her brother, John; on the right, slightly apart, elegant in profile on a superb bay, is her husband of a year, Peniston Lamb, the future first Lord Melbourne.

There is a sense of calm to the piece, a reserve and unforced serenity that can only come of an unconscious collaboration of artist and sitters. In the distance a rocky outcrop looms over a stretch of water with some vague suggestion of domesticated wildness, but Stubbs's figures need no background, confidently filling their social and pictorial space, sufficient to themselves under the enveloping protection of a darkly spreading oak.

The oak and the girl, the past and the future, both linked in an unbroken chain to which the figures bear silent, unruffled witness. There is no conversation in this 'conversation piece', no interaction almost, just a shared strength that needs no articulating. From the side Peniston Lamb looks across – as well he might – to his formidable young wife, but the gaze is unreturned. Even the horses seem entirely self-contained, blinkered or cropping the grass, indifferent to each other, their owners, or the two dogs that, like a pair of attendant saints, stare up, in that eternal gesture of English portraiture, with unnoticed devotion at their masters.

There is none of the golden glow of other Stubbs paintings here, none of the bucolic ease of his *Haymakers*, but a cool silvery light warmed only by the pink of Elizabeth's dress and the answering tinge of the clouds. On a nearby wall an elderly couple also painted by Stubbs aboard their phaeton might be Jane Austen's Admiral and Mrs Croft, but this group is not about affection or fulfilment but hierarchy and power, about dynastic and cultural certainties, and about what David Piper memorably called that 'obscure but potent directive of fate' that gives Stubbs sitters their air of unchallenged and unchallengeable authority.

According to tradition, the Milbanke family traces itself back to a cup-bearer at the court of Mary Queen of Scots, who fled the country after a duel, settling in the north of England. Whatever the maverick promise of these origins, however, the next two hundred years saw a blameless decline into respectability, all taint of romance erased, in a family progress that took the Milbankes from Scottish exile by way of aldermanic and mayoral office in Newcastle to a baronetcy and a safe seat in Parliament.

It was Charles II who granted the title to the first Sir Mark Milbanke in 1661, and over the next century the Milbankes' influence was consolidated in the network of alliances and marriages that inevitably underpinned eighteenth-century political life. In generation after generation of Sir Marks or Sir Ralphs the same pattern emerged, as the Milbankes of Halnaby Hall married into other northern families, extending their land and connections across the north-east of England, augmenting agricultural interests in one marriage or mineral interests in another before, in the middle of the eighteenth century, forging the key alliance with the powerful Holderness family that gave Stubbs's 5th Baronet a place in the Commons.

There is something so reassuringly dull about the Milbankes' political careers, so entirely lacking in individuality, that one feels instinctively with them that one is in touch with the solid bedrock of Sir Lewis Namier's England. Sir Ralph had first entered parliament as one of two unopposed members for Scarborough in 1754, and at the first election of the new reign stood in the Holderness interest for Richmond, loyally and uncritically supporting successive administrations, before retiring in 1768 without having spoken a single word in fourteen years an MP.

Over twenty years were to pass before another Milbanke sat in Parliament, but through the 1770s and 80s Sir Ralph's son, another Ralph, continued the same process of family consolidation, hitching his political fortunes first to Lord Rockingham and then, on his death, to Charles James Fox. In 1790 after a ruinous campaign that is reckoned to have cost the family £15,000, he was finally returned in second place for Durham Co, and for the next twenty-two years remained its MP, a genial and ineffectual 'Uncle Toby' whose fidelity to the Whig cause, in his daughter's succinct phrase, was 'as little valued as doubted'.[24]

It was into this family and this world, on 17 May 1792, that Anne Isabella Milbanke was born. The future Lady Byron has always seemed to belong so completely to the nineteenth century that it is easy to forget that this is where her roots lie, that her moral and social being was shaped by the inherited virtues and limitations implicit in Stubbs's painting or her family's dilettante public service.

But if the young Annabella was brought up in a political milieu, behind the web of alliances and obligations that supported two generations in parliament lay realities of landed life that had a far more profound effect on her vision. From the middle of the seventeenth century the principal seat of the Milbankes had been Halnaby Hall, a red-bricked Jacobean manor house, now gone, that lay just off the Great North Road outside the village of Croft in Yorkshire. In the village church of St Peter's a wonderfully grandiose tomb and pew still evoke the dynastic ambitions of the early Milbankes, but Annabella's affections remained all her life with the modest estate at Seaham on the north-east coast where she grew up. 'If in a small village', she recalled many years later, in a passage that might have come from George Eliot,

> you cannot go out of the gates without seeing the children of a few Families playing on the Green, till they become 'familiar faces', you need not be *taught* to care for their well-being. A heart must be hard indeed that could be indifferent to little Jenny's having the Scarlet Fever, or to

> Johnny's having lost his mother . . . I did not think property
> could be possessed by any other tenure than that of being
> at the service of those in need.[25]

The Milbankes and Seaham may have given Annabella a sense of
the rooted interdependency of country life, but through her
mother she could lay claim to a more exotic strain of English history. Judith Noel was born in 1751, the eldest daughter of Sir
Edward Noel of Kirkby Mallory, first Viscount Wentworth and heir
through the contorted female line to the sixteenth century Wentworth barony. It would be dangerous to describe any title that has
survived with the tenacity of the Wentworths as 'doomed', but when
a family branch can provide a Lancastrian standard-bearer at
St Albans, a Governor of Calais under Mary Tudor, and the devoted
mistress to the Duke of Monmouth, it is at least guilty of the kind
of ill-luck that might pave the way to a marriage with Byron.

For someone so outwardly prosaic as Annabella, there was, too,
a curiously vivid streak of romanticism that fed directly off her sense
of history. In a self-portrait written as a woman of thirty-nine, she
looked back on her childhood self, on a miniature Dorothea
Brooke pulled backwards and forwards between the claims of the
imagination and the stern imperatives of a protestant conscience.
'Impressed from earliest childhood with a sense of duty, and sym-
pathising with the great and noble in human character', she wrote,

> my aspirations went beyond the ordinary occasions of life
> – I wasted virtuous energy on a visionary scene, and con-
> science was in danger of becoming detached from that
> before me. Few of my pleasures were connected with reali-
> ties – riding was the only one I can remember. When I
> climbed the rocks, or bounded over the sands with apparent
> delight, I was *not myself*. Perhaps I was shipwrecked or was
> trying to rescue other sufferers – some of my hours were
> spent in the Pass of Thermopylae, others with the Bishop
> of Marseilles in the midst of Pestilence, or with Howard in
> the cheerless dungeon . . .
>
> About the age of 13 . . . I began to throw my imagination
> into a home-sphere of action – to constrain myself, from

religious principle, to attend to what was irksome, and to
submit to what was irritating. I had great difficulties to
surmount from the impetuosity and sensitiveness of my
character ... It was this stage of my character which prepared me to sympathise unboundedly with the morbidly
susceptible – with those who felt themselves unknown ...[26]

It would clearly be absurd to try to define her exclusively in terms
of ancestry, but there is a sense in which the solidity of the Milbankes
and the romanticism of the Wentworth inheritance combined to
produce in Annabella something distinctly new, a kind of fierce
ordinariness, a strident centrality that raised the commonplace to
the realms of genius, orthodoxy to the stuff of crusade.

Along with this dual inheritance, the circumstances of her own
contented upbringing can only have sharpened the feeling of
singularity with which she coloured the most ordinary imaginative
experiences of childhood. In the same *Auto-Description* she
lamented a 'want of comparison' in her Seaham life that blinded
her to the advantages of birth, and yet of greater importance than
the inevitable isolation of a small Durham village was the simple
fact that she was the only child of parents who had waited fifteen
years for an heir.

Ralph Milbanke and Judith Noel had married in 1777, and
although they had brought up a niece as if she was their own
child, there is no mistaking the ferocious joy that greeted Annabella's birth. It is often admiringly noted that she was encouraged
in her opinions from her earliest days, but if her childhood self
can be back derived from her adult character, hers was the kind
of independence that might have flourished more safely in the
face of opposition than indulgence, her character one that would
have fared better outside the warmth and admiration of a family
that placed her firmly and uncritically at its centre. 'It was indeed
Calantha's misfortune to meet with too much kindness,' her
cousin Caroline Lamb wrote of herself in a passage in *Glenarvon*
that throws an unexpected light on this – a passage that sufficiently
stung Annabella when she read the novel to have her mark and
angrily refute its psychology in a criticism that survives still among
her papers,

or rather too much indulgence from all who surrounded her. The Duke, attentive solely to her health, watched her with the fondest solicitude, and the wildest wishes her fancy could invent, were heard with the most scrupulous attention, and gratified with the most unbounded compliance.[27]

This regime of indulgence was made more dangerous in Annabella's case by an intelligence that in and outside the home had little to challenge it. Even as a child she was conscious of being cleverer than most of those around her, but it was a cleverness dangerously at the service of unchallengeable moral certitudes, an intelligence that seems never to have broadened with reading or turned on itself in any genuine spirit of criticism. From the evidence of her letters and journals there was certainly a kind of scrupulousness about her, and yet even here her scruples and self-doubts were, like her shyness, the self-referential workings of an imagination that ultimately appealed to no other judgement but its own.

If Annabella Milbanke had simply married as Milbankes had traditionally married, none of this might have much mattered, and it is likely that she would have done no more than add one more name to history's forgotten roll of mute, inglorious husbands. From the earliest family descriptions one can glimpse the formidable chatelaine she should have been, but substitute the name Byron for that of George Eden or any of her earlier suitors, see that ten-year-old girl with the determined pout Hoppner painted as the future Lady Byron, and the warmth, the love, the privilege and security of her sheltered upbringing suddenly seem the laboratory conditions for breeding the disaster of the most notorious marriage in literary history.

It is the inevitable condition of biography to shape a life with the benefits of hindsight in this way, and yet it is only hindsight that casts a shadow over the prelapsarian happiness of Annabella's childhood. In her own eyes the memories of Seaham would always have the poignancy of blighted innocence, but the horror is that it could have ever equipped anyone so essentially limited in experience or culture to imagine that she could understand or tame a Byron.

It is often forgotten, in the feeding frenzy that invariably accompanies her name, how vulnerably young she was when she first met him in 1812, and yet nothing suggests that another summer or two would have made the difference. She had come up to London for her first season in the previous year, and although there were suitors enough to satisfy anyone's vanity, not even a future governor-general of India or Wellington's adjutant general in the Peninsula had been sufficient to jolt her out of the complacent certainties of her Seaham world. 'I met with one or two who, like myself, did not appear absorbed in the present scene', she later wrote of this period,

> and who interested me in a degree. I had a wish to find among men the character I had often imagined – but I found only parts of it. One gave proofs of worth, but had no sympathy for high aspirations – another seemed full of affection towards his family, and yet he valued the world. I was clear sighted in these cases – but I was to become blind.[28]

It was a misfortune, too, for a woman who could think like this to see her future husband for the first time in his *annus mirabilis*, because if there were far more interesting 'Byrons' than the triumphant author of *Childe Harold*, there was none more likely to appeal to a romantic moralist of Annabella's stamp. 'Lavater's [the phrenologist] system never asserted its truth more forcibly than in Byron's countenance', the portrait painter Sir Thomas Lawrence wrote at the height of Byron's fame, wonderfully capturing the mix of glamour and threat in the figure that seduced London's 'golden parallelogram' in the spring and summer of 1812,

> in which you see all the character: its ken and rapid genius, its pale intelligence, its profligacy, and its bitterness; its original symmetry distorted by the passions, his laugh of mingled merriment and scorn; the forehead clear and open, the brow boldly prominent, the eyes bright and dissimilar, the nose finely cut, and the nostril acutely formed; the mouth well made but wide and contemptuous even in

its smile, falling singularly at the corners, and its vindictive and disdainful expression heightened by the massive firmness of the chin, which springs at once from the centre of the full under-lip; the hair dark and curling but irregular in its growth; all this presents to you the poet and the man; and the general effect is heightened by a thin spare form, and, as you may have heard, by a deformity of limb.'[29]

Byron was just twenty-four when, after more than two years' travel across Europe and the east, the sudden and unprecedented success of *Childe Harold* changed his life and the course of Romantic literature. He had already produced some feeble juvenilia and a long and scabrous satire he had since come to regret, but nothing in his literary or private life, nothing in the intense and homoerotic friendships of his Harrow and Cambridge days or the bisexual philandering in the Levant had prepared him emotionally for the loneliness of fame that swamped him on his return, a poet without conviction, an aristocrat without a sense of belonging, a liberal without the stamina or will for political life, an icon with a morbid sensitivity to his lameness.

It would have been odd in fact if Annabella alone had not felt drawn to Byron that summer, and yet even in the privacy of her diary and letters she felt she owed her intelligence some more refined expression of her feelings than the general excitement that gripped Regency society. She had first seen him at a morning waltzing party given by Caroline Lamb on 25 March, and after filling her journal that night with her impressions, the next day reported back to her mother in Seaham. 'My curiosity was much gratified by seeing Lord Byron, the object at present of universal attention', she wrote,

> Lady Caroline has of course seized on him, notwithstanding the reluctance he manifests to be shackled by her ... It is said that he is an infidel, and I think it probable from the general character of his mind. His poem sufficiently proves that he *can* feel nobly, but he has discouraged his own goodness. His features are well formed – his upper lip is drawn towards the nose with an expression of impatient disgust. His eye is restlessly thoughtful. He talks much, and

I heard some of his conversation, which is very able, and sounds like the *true* sentiments of the Speaker.

I did not seek an introduction myself, for all the women were absurdly courting him, and trying to *deserve* the lash of his satire. I thought that *inoffensiveness* was the most secure conduct, as I am not desirous of a place in his lays. Besides, I cannot worship talents that are unconnected with the love of man, nor be captivated by that Genius which is barren in blessings – so I made no offering at the shrine of *Childe Harold*, though I shall not refuse the acquaintance if it comes.[30]

The acquaintance finally came the next month at a party of Lady Cowper's, and with it the note of ironic detachment became increasingly hard to sustain. In her letters home to her mother she continued to insist that 'calm benevolence'[31] alone could touch her heart, but no amount of dissembling to her parents or herself could disguise the fact that curiosity was rapidly turning into the crusade that would shape her whole life. 'Do you think there is one person here who dares to look into himself?', she later recalled the question that had inspired her first mute 'offering' at the shrine of *Childe Harold*,

> . . . I felt that he was the most attractive person; but I was not *bound* to him by any strong feeling of sympathy till he uttered these words, not to me, but in my hearing – 'I have not a friend in the world!' It is said that there is an instinct in the human heart which attaches us to the friendless. I did not pause – there was my error to enquire why he was friendless; but I vowed in secret to be a devoted friend to this lone being.[32]

There is something unsettling in the reveries of the young Annabella, or at least in her incapacity to see them for what they were. The descriptions of Byron that litter her diary and letters are as banal as those of anyone else that season, but running through them is that old and dangerous sense of election, the conviction of some private and silent understanding that set her apart in a city swept along on the rhythms of the waltz and the voyeuristic thrill of Caroline Lamb's pursuit of Byron.

If there was nobody to blame for these delusions but Annabella, however, it is clear that she had not just imagined Byron's interest in her. In the wreck of their marriage she once accused him of only ever wanting what he could not have, but if there is something in that, the more brutal truth is that he simply could not see her for what she was – could not see the provinciality that passed for independence, the rigidity latent in her strength, the narrowness which, with the nostalgia of the jaded sophisticate, he wistfully put down to moral superiority. 'I set you down as the most puzzling person there', he later told her of the first time he had seen her, across a room full of morning-visitors at Melbourne House,

> For there was a quiet contempt of all around you & the nothings they were saying & doing in your manner that was so much after my own heart. There was a simplicity – an innocence – a beauty in your deportment & appearance which although you hardly spoke – told me I was in company with no common being.[33]

As the spring of 1812 wore on, and Byron's life drifted dangerously and publicly into the chaos of his notorious affair with Caroline Lamb, it was not so much what Annabella was as what she was *not* that attracted Byron. The kinds of virtues and solidity with which he invested her would always hold a theoretical attraction for him, but it is hardly an exaggeration to say that if there had been no Caroline Lamb to escape then there would have been no marriage to her cousin, Annabella.

Byron had first come across Caro Lamb, the twenty-seven-year-old, fragile, androgynous-looking child wife of William Lamb, when she had written to him under a thin veil of anonymity after the triumph of *Childe Harold* in February 1812. Even before she had set eyes on him she had declared that she would know its author if he was 'as ugly as Aesop'[34], and within weeks of meeting she had made sure their affair was public property, played out with a kind of arriviste relish on his part and on hers with a reckless exhibitionism hovering on the edge of insanity.

There is not a moment of an affair that defined and caricatured the Romantic passion in all its delinquent intensity that has not been raked over a hundred times, but in the context of his relationship with Annabella it still has its place here. In later years Byron came to hate Caroline with a passion that only Claire Clairmont could otherwise inspire, but in its first weeks at least what attracted him to the maddest of all the Spencers was precisely the wayward and uncontrollable element in her that he eventually came to loathe.

There was a wonderfully sane and balanced side to Byron that would always in the end tire of romantic excess, and yet after the initial excitement had passed something more than boredom turned him against Caroline Lamb. An illicit element to some of his earlier, male relationships had sometimes unnerved him, but as he tried to distance himself from Caroline he found himself contending with a woman ready to call the Childe's bluff, to live out the implications of his Romanticism with a patrician contempt for convention that in his first year of success he had neither the courage nor the confidence of 'belonging' to match.

Even with the contrast of Caroline Lamb to concentrate his mind, it is unlikely that his interest in Annabella would ever have quickened into anything more important had it not been for the intervention of her aunt (Caroline Lamb's mother-in-law), Lady Melbourne. By the time that Annabella made her London debut, the girl in Stubbs's portrait had reigned as the 'spider queen' of Whig society for over a generation, 'a sort of modern Aspasia' with the brain and morals to match, tolerant, attractive, intelligent, cynical, corrupt and – to Byron at least – 'the best, the kindest, and ablest female I have ever known, old or young'. 'She was a charming person', he later told Lady Blessington,

> uniting the energy of a man's mind with the delicacy and tenderness of a woman's. She had all of philosophy, save its moroseness, and all of nature, save its defects and general *faiblesse* . . . I have often thought, that, with a little more youth Lady M. might have turned my head, at all events she often turned my heart, by bringing me back to mild feelings, when the demon passion was strong within me. Her mind and heart were as fresh as if only sixteen summers

had flown over her, instead of four times that number –
and the mind and heart always leave external marks of their
state of health. Goodness is the best cosmetic that has yet
been discovered . . . She was a captivating creature, *malgre*
her eleven or twelve lustres, and I shall always love her.[35]

Even in her early sixties, the 'spider' or the 'thorn' still retained
the power, desire and intelligence that had once made her the
mistress of Lord Egremont and the Prince of Wales. As a young
bride she had been forced to stand and watch her husband's
ludicrous pursuit of the actress Sophia Baddeley, but with the
ambition and purpose Stubbs caught so well, disappointment had
simply deflected her energies into the ruthless pursuit of family
influence that was to consume the rest of her life. 'The charms
of her person and the endowments of her mind were worthy of
a better fate than that she was preparing for herself', Caroline
Lamb wrote savagely of her in *Glenarvon*, the *roman à clef* with
which she took her revenge not just on Byron but on the Whig
world that had turned its back on her,

> But, under the semblance of youthful gaiety, she concealed
> a dark intriguing spirit, which could neither remain at rest,
> nor satisfy itself in the pursuit of great and noble objects.
> She had been hurried on by the evil activity of her own
> mind, until the habit of crime had overcome every scruple,
> and rendered her insensible to repentance, and almost to
> remorse. In this career she had improved to such a degree
> her natural talent of dissimulation, that, under its impen-
> etrable veil, she was able to carry on securely her darkest
> machinations; and her understanding had so adapted itself
> to her passion, that it was in her power to give, in her own
> eyes, a character of grandeur, to the vice and malignity,
> which afforded an inexplicable delight to her depraved
> imagination.[36]

With daughter and mother-in-law both living in Melbourne
House, a delicate balancing act was required, but from the
moment Byron tried to extricate himself from the affair with
Caroline, he found Lady Melbourne a subtle and determined ally.
To a woman who had charmed and slept her way to the top of

Whig society, her daughter-in-law's morals were of no great concern, but the one crime the lax Regency world would not forgive was indiscretion and as Caroline's antics began to threaten the dynastic ambitions 'the spider' held for her family, Lady Melbourne moved to neutralise her.

In spite of all her cynicism, though, it can no more have occurred to Lady Melbourne than it had to Byron that the solution to their mutual problem lay in her cool, self-contained country niece. For their different reasons both Caroline Lamb and her sister-in-law 'Caro George' had done their best to convince him that Annabella was already engaged, but he had hardly needed their warnings to keep a wary distance from a woman he instinctively recognised as his opposite. 'My dear Lady Caroline', he had written as early as 1 May, after reading some verses of Annabella's,

> I have read over the few poems of Miss Milbank with attention. – They display fancy, feeling, & a little practice would very soon induce facility of expression . . . She certainly is a very extraordinary girl, who would imagine so much strength & variety of thought under that placid countenance? You will say as much of this to Miss M. as you think proper. – I say all this very sincerely, I have no desire to be better acquainted with Miss Milbank, she is too good for a fallen spirit to know or wish to know, & I should like her more if she were less perfect.[37]

There is no reason to doubt Byron – Annabella is not mentioned in his letters for more than four months – but the *idea* of her had taken a dogged hold of his imagination. There was no pretence on his part that he was in love with her, or anyone else, but as over July and August the pressure from both the Lambs and Caroline's mother to end the affair grew, he was faced with the fundamental need of the outsider to assimilate or face destruction. 'I see nothing but marriage & a *speedy* one can save me', he wrote to Lady Melbourne on 28 September,

> if your niece is attainable I should prefer her – if not – the very first woman who does not look as if she would spit in my face.[38]

'You ask "if I am sure of myself"'' he had already written to Lady
Melbourne ten days earlier, after first hesitantly broaching the
idea of Annabella to her in a letter from Cheltenham on the 13th,

> I answer – no – but *you* are, which I take to be a much better
> thing. Miss M. I admire because she is a clever woman, an
> amiable woman & of high blood, for I still have a few Nor-
> man & Scotch inherited prejudices on the last score, were
> I to marry. As to *Love*, that is done in a week (provided the
> Lady has a reasonable share) besides marriage goes on
> better with esteem & confidence than romance, & she is
> quite pretty enough to be loved by her husband, without
> being so glaringly beautiful as to attract too many rivals.[39]

At the beginning of October Lady Melbourne approached her
niece on his behalf, and on the 12th received Annabella's refusal
from Richmond, complete with a 'Character' of Byron explaining
her decision. 'The passions have been his guide from childhood,'
she wrote, up on her 'high stilts' as her aunt described her,

> and have exercised a tyrannical power over his very superior
> intellect. Yet among his dispositions are many which deserve
> to be associated with Christian principles – his love of good-
> ness in its chastest form, and his abhorrence of all that
> degrades human nature, prove the uncorrupted purity of
> his moral sense.
>
> There is a chivalrous generosity in his ideas of love and
> friendship, and selfishness is totally absent from his charac-
> ter. In secret he is the zealous friend of all human feelings;
> but from the strangest perversion that pride ever created,
> he endeavours to disguise the best points of his character.
> When indignation takes possession of his mind – and it is
> easily excited – his disposition becomes malevolent. He
> hates with the bitterest contempt; but as soon as he has
> indulged those feelings, he regains the humanity which he
> had lost – from the immediate impulse of provocation –
> and repents deeply.[40]

It is difficult to be sure of Byron's real feelings at this rejection,
or even whether he knew himself, but whatever they were he
would never have dropped the tone of cool worldliness with Lady

Melbourne that had become their common language. '*Cut* her! My dear Ly. M. marry – Mahomet forbid!' – he wrote to her on receiving the news, anxious to allay any suspicion of resentment,

> I am sure we will be better friends than before & if I am not embarrassed by all this I cannot see for the soul of me why *she* should – assure *her* con tutto rispetto that The subject shall never be renewed in any shape whatever, & assure yourself my carissima (not Zia what then shall it be? Chuse your *own* name) that were it not for this embarras with C I would much rather remain as I am. – I have had so very little intercourse with the fair Philosopher that if when we meet I should endeavour to improve our acquaintance she must not *mistake* me, & assure her I never shall mistake her . . . She is perfectly right in every point of view, & during the slight suspense I felt something very like remorse for sundry reasons not at all connected with C nor with any occurrence since I knew you or her or hers; finding I must marry however on *that* score, I should have preferred a woman of birth & talents, but such a woman was not at all to blame for not preferring me; my *heart* never had an opportunity of being much interested in the business, further than that I should have very much liked to be *your relation*. – And now to conclude like Ld. Foppington, "I have lost a thousand women in my time but never had the ill manners to quarrel with them for such a trifle."[41]

The address on this letter – Cheltenham again – suggests, though, that Byron's good humour was not simply feigned for Lady Melbourne's benefit. He had gone to the fashionable spa town for the waters earlier in the summer, but long after it had been abandoned by most of London society he was still there, held by a growing fascination with that other 'Aspasia' of Regency England that he would have been reluctant to admit to Lady Melbourne, the beautiful, serially faithless forty-year-old Countess of Oxford, Jane Harley.

There is as much pseudo-psychological nonsense talked of Byron's predilection for older women – as if everyone over the age of thirty were somehow identical – as there is over his fastidious distaste at the sight of a woman eating.* In the wake of *Childe Harold* it was inevitable that he should gravitate towards the great hostesses who dominated Whig society, but among even that disparate group it would be hard to imagine two women with less in common than Lady Melbourne and Lady Oxford, the one all caution, cynicism, and dynastic ambition, the other generous, impulsive, radical and careless of the proprieties she had so successfully defied from the first loveless years of marriage.

The daughter of a clergyman, Jane Scott had been born in Inchin, and at the age of twenty-two 'sacrificed', as Byron later told Medwin, 'to one whose mind and body were equally contemptible in the scale of creation'[43]. If Lord Oxford had never been much of a match for his dazzling and ambitious wife, however, he was no gaoler either, and by the time that she began her affair with Byron the 'grande horizontale' of Whig political radicalism was already the mother of five children by as many fathers, 'a tarnished siren of uncertain age', as Lord David Cecil described her with patrician distaste,

> who pursued a life of promiscuous amours on the fringe of society, in an atmosphere of tawdry eroticism and tawdrier culture. Reclining on a sofa, with ringlets disposed about her neck in seductive disarray, she would rhapsodise to her lovers on the beauties of Pindar and the hypocrisy of the world.[44]

Byron had first met her during the London season, but it was at Cheltenham and then at Eywood, the Oxfords' country house in Herefordshire, that their friendship developed into the infatuation that absorbed him for the next six months. 'She resembled a landscape by Claude Lorraine', Lady Blessington – no ingenue herself – recalled him saying,

---

* Captain Gronow, who fought at Waterloo, recalled a dinner with Byron that the Psycho-analysts have carefully ignored. 'I recollect his saying', Gronow wrote, 'that he disliked seeing women eat, or to have their company at dinner, from a wish to believe, if possible, in their more ethereal nature; but he was rallied into avowing that his chief dislike to their presence at the festive board arose from the fact of their being helped first, and consequently getting all the wings of the chickens, whilst men had to be content with the legs or other parts.'[42]

'with a setting sun, her beauties enhanced by the knowledge that they were shedding their last dying beams, which threw a radiance around. A woman (continued Byron) is only grateful for her *first* and *last* conquest. The first of poor dear Lady [Oxford's] was achieved before I entered on this world of care, but the *last* I do flatter myself was reserved for me, and a *bonne bouche* it was.'[45]

It is impossible to imagine Byron speaking of Lady Melbourne in this tone, but if Lady Oxford never exerted the same dominance over him as the 'spider' had done, in the sensual and intellectual licence of the 'bowers of Armida'[46], as he labelled Eywood, he found a retreat from any fleeting disappointment at Annabella's rejection and the continuing assaults of Caroline Lamb. 'I mean (entre nous my dear Machiavel)', he had written to Lady Melbourne,

to play off Ly. O against her, who would have no objection *perchance* but she dreads her scenes and has asked me not to mention that we have met to C or that I am going to E.[47]

'I am no longer your lover', he wrote to Caroline herself, as good as his word, if the letter she reproduced in *Glenarvon* is the faithful copy of Byron's that she claimed it to be,

and since you oblige me to confess it, by this truly unfeminine persecution, – learn, that I am attached to another; whose name it would of course be dishonorable to mention. I shall ever remember with gratitude the predilection you have shewn in my favor. I shall ever continue as your friend, if your ladyship will permit me so to style myself; and as a first proof of my regard, I offer you this advice, correct your vanity, which is ridiculous; exert your absurd caprices upon others; and leave me in peace.[48]

In spite of the callousness of this letter – a cruelty that forms the counterpart to Byron's generosity – his relationship with Caroline had stirred him in ways that Lady Oxford never did. There is no disguising the sense of almost bloated content that runs through many of Byron's letters from Eywood, and yet at some level both he and Lady Oxford knew that the demons that drove him were not ones that could be contained within Armida's bowers or the boundaries of Whig politics she had marked out for him.

For all the sexual and intellectual freedom Byron enjoyed at Eywood, the affair with Lady Oxford was too tame ever fully to satisfy him. In all his most important relationships there had been an element of risk and social danger, but there was something almost institutional in the sexual abandon of Lady Oxford, a kind of *licensed* immorality that paradoxically took Byron closer to one branch of the Whig political establishment than he had ever been before.

And there was never a time, either, when Byron was more dangerous than when made aware of how little he wanted what English society had to offer him. 'I am going abroad again', he announced in March 1813, in the middle of his affair with Lady Oxford,

> . . . my parliamentary schemes are not much to my taste –
> I spoke twice last Session – & was told it was well enough
> – but I hate the thing altogether – & have no intention to
> 'strut another hour' on that stage.[49]

Byron was being partly disingenuous – for all the kind words that greeted his debut speech it had only had a limited impact – but his suppressed unease of this period was more than a defensive reflex to disappointment. It is clear from his own comments that he knew that he would never make a parliamentary orator, and yet it is hard to believe that success could any more have reconciled the creator of *Childe Harold* – still less the 'Titan battling with religion and virtue'[50] that Nietzsche admired in Byron – to the limitations of English public life and a career in politics.

If it seems inevitable that the young Nietzsche should be drawn to Byron – and in particular to the creator of the defiant Manfred – the quality that he most admired in him was the courage to follow his instincts that Lawrence also saw as the defining characteristic of the 'aristocrat'. In his Hardy essay Lawrence wrote that 'the final aim of every living thing . . . is the full achievement of itself'[51], but as Byron's affair with Lady Oxford guttered towards its untidy end, it was precisely that goal of self-realisation – the supreme ambition of the Romantic imagination – that he recog- nised with an ever increasing clarity he could never achieve in England.

In an age that is as ready to recognise the tyranny of sex as ours is, it is possibly enough to point out that for a man of Byron's sexual ambivalence a country that still sent homosexuals to the gallows was no place to be. From the publication of the spurious 'Don Leon' poems in the mid-nineteenth century, Byron has always been an icon and spokesman for homosexual freedom, and yet the vital thing in this context is not so much the question of his sexual identity *per se* – who now cares? – but the wider issues of creative fulfilment or frustration with which it was inevitably and intimately bound.

For Byron, as for Lawrence, the test of '*being*' was '*doing*', and as the year dragged on he was conscious of how little he had achieved as a poet. For all his aristocratic disdain for the business of versifying he was keenly aware that he had 'something within that "passeth show"' [52], and yet for a man whose lameness, child- hood and sexual ambiguities all supremely equipped him to chal- lenge political, moral, or physical injustice in every form he found it, he had precious little to show. The adolescent anger of *English Bards and Scotch Reviewers*, which he had long since repudiated? The stagey and harmless posturing of *Childe Harold*? A clutch of cautiously disguised tributes to the dead Cambridge chorister, Edleston? 'At five-and-twenty, when the better part of life is over', he wrote in his journal,

> one should be *something*; – and what am I? nothing but five-and-twenty – and the odd months. [53]

But if, in these early months of 1813, Byron still lacked what Lawrence called the 'courage to let go the security, and to *be*[54]', this sense of self-dissatisfaction and estrangement was gradually pushing him towards a crisis. As early as May he was writing to Lady Melbourne of the need to escape a world that was stifling him, and at the end of June he returned with increased irritation to the same theme. 'I am doing all I can to be ready to go with

your Russian' [Prince Koslovsky, a visiting Russian diplomat], he
told her,

> depend upon it I shall be *either* out of the country or nothing
> – very soon – all I like is now gone – & all I abhor (with
> some few exceptions) remains – viz – the R[egent] – his
> government – & most of his subjects – what a fool I was to
> come back – I shall be wiser next time.[55]

It is a curious, if somehow irrelevant, thought that Byron might
have gone abroad in the summer of 1813, either with the Oxfords
to Sicily as was planned at one time, or farther east to the Levant.
Byron himself had such a strong sense of his own destiny that
even with the benefit of hindsight it is hard to see his life in any
other shape than that which it finally took, and if this ignores
those elements of chance and sloth that right up to his death
might have disposed of him in a dozen different ways, one only
has to picture him for a moment harmlessly cruising the Mediter-
ranean to recognise the inherent implausibility of the vision.

Because if Byron was to grow as a man or a poet, he did not
need simply to *escape* England, but to smash with a complete and
final violence everything that held him to it. In his relationship
with Caroline Lamb during the previous year he had come dangerously close to doing this, and while he had pulled back from the
edge then it was only a matter of time before he recognised that
the conformist elements in his nature could never be squared with
the vocation for opposition he claimed as the Byron birthright.

'I have no choice' – Byron put the words in Manfred's mouth
– and it is this sense of necessity that attracted both Lawrence
and Nietzsche to the dramatic parabola of Byron's life and career.
There is of course a world of difference between the Lawrentian
'aristocrat' and the *übermensch* that Nietzsche hailed in the figure
of Manfred. Yet if Lawrence's ultimate concern was with *fulfilment*
in the deepest and most human sense of the word, he never
shirked the fact that for an outsider of Byron's stamp that inevitably meant war. 'This is the tragedy', Lawrence wrote,

> ... that the convention of the community is a prison to
> his natural, individual desire, a desire that compels him,

whether he feels justified or not, to break the bounds of
the community, lands him outside the pale, there to stand
alone, and say: 'I was right, my desire was real and inevitable; if I was to be myself I must fulfil it, convention or no
convention . . .'[56]

It is this sense of inevitability that gives the air of a 'phoney war'
to the period of Byron's affair with Lady Oxford. When at the
end of June she left England with her husband he confessed that
he felt more 'Carolinish'[57] about it than he had expected, despite
the fact that for all her attractions she could no more satisfy him
than Caroline Lamb herself had done before her.

Still less could one of the great *regnantes* of Whig society answer
his need for a rupture with everything that held him to England.
It did not, though, matter. By the time that Lady Oxford finally
sailed, on 28 June, the one woman had re-appeared in his life
who could fill both roles: a woman who by her birth and temperament was not only uniquely placed to define the full nature of
Byronic rebellion but also to meet with a peculiar psychological
and emotional fitness what Lawrence called 'the deepest desire'
of life,

a desire for consummation . . . a desire for completeness,
that completeness of being which will give completeness of
satisfaction and completeness of utterance.[58]

The woman in question was the Hon. Mrs Augusta Leigh, the
twenty-nine-year-old daughter of Byron's father by his first, scan-
dalous, marriage to Amelia Darcy, Baroness Conyers in her own
right and the wife of the heir to the Duke of Leeds, the Marquess
of Carmarthen.

The son of that famous sailor and womaniser, 'Foulweather
Jack', 'Mad Jack' Byron seemed 'born for his own ruin, and that
of the other sex.'[59] Six years before Augusta's birth, the dazzling
and wealthy Marchioness had met and fallen for him, picnicked

with him one day and abandoned her husband for him the next, living defiantly with him in a 'vortex of dissipation'[60] until a well-publicised divorce left her free to marry him and move to France.

Whatever fondness his son might retain for his memory, 'Mad Jack' was as callous a rake as eighteenth-century gossip portrayed him, with all the Byron charm and none of its generosity. For five years he lived off his wife's fortune in either Chantilly or Paris, but when shortly after Augusta's birth he lost wife and income together, Jack Byron abandoned the child to the first in a long succession of guardians and relatives, and set off on the predatory hunt for another heiress that finally led to Bath and Catherine Gordon.

For a few months, as a four-year-old, Augusta lived with her father and his pregnant new wife at Chantilly, but from the moment she was handed over to her grandmother, Lady Holderness, she left behind the depravation and uncertainty that was Jack Byron's only obvious legacy to his children. During the crucial years when Catherine Gordon and her son were struggling under the indignities of poverty and isolation, the orphaned Augusta was growing up among a clutch of aristocratic relations into a tall and graceful girl, 'light as a feather', with a long, slender neck and heavy mass of light brown hair, a fine complexion, large mouth, *retroussé* nose, beautiful eyes, gentle manner, and a pathological shyness that eclipsed even that of her unknown Byron half-brother.[61]

If these formative years among her Howard cousins and the half-brothers and sisters of her mother's first marriage gave Augusta an uncritical, aristocratic ease that Byron never matched, as a grounding in emotional subservience they had more corrosive consequences. There was a fundamental docility to her character that probably ran deeper than any social conditioning, but for a girl of such natural reticence and limited prospects, a childhood of gilded dependence in the great houses of her relations can only have compounded the instinct for self-surrender that was to mark her adult life.

It was an instinct confirmed, too, when after a six-year courtship she finally married her feckless cousin, George Leigh, and sank into a life of straitened domesticity from which she never escaped. Colonel George Leigh has always had one of those roles in the Byron story that never quite swells even to a walk-on part, but for his wife at least he was real enough, an irascible and incapable husband and father in equal measure, a cavalry officer whose career ended in financial scandal and a gambler whose sharpness, even in the world of Newmarket and the circles of the Prince of Wales, placed him on the wrong side of social acceptability.

It can seem at times as though Augusta only existed in and through other people, so it is little wonder that a woman with such a genius for self-effacement has always proved hard to pin down. From the first day that her character was dragged into the public domain it has been open season on her, but after a hundred and fifty years of legal and biographical prodding she remains as elusive and unknowable as ever, leaving behind only a kind of erotic charge that is as close as we can get to her, an impression of femininity so endlessly and placidly accommodating as to obliterate all individuality.

A 'fieldsman', Thomas Hardy wrote in *Tess*, is never anything more than a man in a field but a woman is continuous with the natural world, and something of that universality clings to the finest surviving image we have of Augusta Leigh. There is little contemporary evidence to suggest she ever looked like Hayter's lovely drawing of her, but in the languor and passivity of that face, the tilt of the head and the long curve of the neck, he has surely left us the essential Augusta – the 'sleepy Venus' of Byron's *Don Juan*, the Zuleika of *The Bride of Abydos*, the mother of seven children by a husband she hardly ever saw – the woman whose idle and easy sexuality could disturb and attract both men and women every bit as much as her half-brother's flagrant aggression.

Augusta had first met Byron when she was a girl of seventeen and he an awkward and overweight schoolboy of thirteen. From their first exchanges of letters the two were natural allies in his endless battles with his mother, but in spite of a protective – and on his side almost seigneurial – affection they saw very little of each other as children. At the age of seventeen Augusta was already infatuated with her Leigh cousin, and as Byron himself moved from Harrow to Cambridge and then on to his travels in the east she inevitably became more of an idea than a reality to him.

In the long run there could have been nothing more dangerous than this legacy of intimacy and distance, and no more vulnerable time for Augusta to re-enter his life than the summer of 1813, when his affair with Lady Oxford was petering out and Caroline Lamb was taking her last melodramatic revenge. The correspondence between Byron and Augusta for the preceding months is missing, but it seems almost certainly his idea that she should come up to London. She had written to him the previous January in need of money to meet her husband's gambling debts, and although financial troubles over Newstead left Byron in no position to help, his answer emphasises the sad hollowness she alone would fill. The 'estate is still on my hands', he began a long list of complaints, '& your brother not less embarrassed . . .

> I have but one *relative* & her I never see – I have no connections to domesticate with & for marriage I have neither the talent nor the inclination – I cannot fortune-hunt nor afford to marry without a fortune . . . I am thus wasting the best part of my life daily repenting and never amending . . . I am very well in health – but not happy nor even comfortable – but I will not bore you with complaints – I am a fool & deserve all the ills I have met or may meet with.[62]

There was something prophetic in that last line, because almost from the moment she arrived in London, Byron seems to have been bent on disaster. If 'form' is anything to go by, he would inevitably have turned to someone on the rebound from Caroline and Lady Oxford, but if anyone might have done, Augusta seemed to offer everything, the excitement of novelty and the comfort of familiarity, the danger of the forbidden with the guarantee of safety implicit in her name.

Because above all she was a *Byron*, and for someone so self-absorbed and yet utterly lacking in self-love as her brother that was an irresistible attraction. In the years since their childhoods he had formed some of the most intense friendships of his life, but it was only with a more attractive version of himself, as he now saw Augusta, a woman with so many of the same mannerisms and the same shyness, that he found his deepest, almost platonic desire for completion realised. 'For thee, my own sweet sister', he addressed her,

> in thy heart
> I know myself secure, as thou in mine;
> We were and are – I am, even as thou art –
> Beings who ne'er each other can resign;
> It is the same, together or apart,
> From life's commencement to its slow decline
> We are entwined – let death come slow or fast,
> The tie which bound the first endures the last![63]

With her endless good-humour and sense of fun, her charm and talent for nonsense – her 'damn'd crinkum-crankum'[64] as he called it – Augusta also represented a simple release from the tensions of London life. Almost immediately she became an integral part of his routines, included in his invitations and plans, the novel half of a double-act that was part spontaneous and part calculation. 'If you like to go with me to ye. Lady Davy's tonight', he wrote in a note that nicely captures the blend of pride and vanity with which he looked on her,

> I *have* an invitation for you – There will be the Stael – some people whom you know – & *me* whom you do *not* know & you can talk to which you please – & I will watch over you as if you were unmarried & in danger of always being so ... I think our being together before 3d. people will be a new *sensation* to *both*.[65]

With anyone except Augusta this might have led nowhere, but with her chronic habit of subservience, it was only a matter of time before affection and familiarity slid into something more perilous. It is impossible to know with any absolute certainty when brother and sister became lovers, but if the malicious gossip of Caroline Lamb – or Byron's own boast to Tom Moore that her seduction had cost him little trouble – has any substance it was probably only a matter of weeks or even days.

The mere use of the word 'seduction' in this context however – Byron at his coarsest – wilfully trivialises and misrepresents a relationship that he would always more honestly recognise as the most important of his life. If these things can ever be judged from the outside, it would seem that sex was always of secondary significance in their affair, on Augusta's side to a limitless capacity for self-surrender, and on Byron's to the expression of a kindness and generosity that was at the core of his personality.

And yet when that is said, his letters and verse make it clear that he inspired in the twenty-nine-year-old mother of three a passion that surprised them both with its violence and abandon. In the best known celebrations of their love it is always a platonic ideal of union that Byron is anxious to stress, but in Zuleika's language in *The Bride of Abydos* we are almost certainly taken closer to the earthier reality of its early days. 'To see thee, hear thee, near thee stay,' Zuleika tells the man she believes to be her brother, in a passage which unconsciously echoes the startled self-discovery of Shakespeare's Perdita in the great fourth act of *A Winter's Tale*

> And hate the night I know not why,
> Save that we meet not but by day,
> With thee to live, with thee to die,
> I dare not my hope deny:
> Thy cheek, thine eyes, thy lips to kiss,
> Like this – and this – no more than this;
> For, Allah! Sure thy lips are flame:
> What fever in thy veins is flushing?
> My own have nearly caught the same,
> At least I feel my cheek, too, blushing.[66]

Even when this is recognised, however, the seamless, almost inevitable transition from sister to lover was for Augusta only one stage in a more complete annihilation of self. 'Partager tous vos sentiments,' she wrote to him in November 1813, enclosing with the note a lock of her hair: 'Ne voir que par vos yeux' – 'to share in your feelings, to see only with your eyes, to act only on your advice, to live only for you, that is my only desire, my plan, the only destiny that could make me happy.'[67] 'To soothe thy sickness,' Zuleika continues in the same vein in the Bride,

watch thy health,
Partake, but never waste thy wealth,
Or stand with smiles unmurmuring by,
And lighten half thy poverty;
Do all but close thy dying eye,
For that I could not live to try;
For these alone my thoughts aspire:
More can I do, or thou require?[68]

The tragedy for Augusta, however, was that Byron *did* require more, because for him the affair was more complex and guilt-ridden than her simple devotion could comprehend. In reckless moments he might publicly ridicule the moral parochialism of an incest taboo, but at other times it could disturb him with a fear that stopped him naming Augusta even in the privacy of his journal. 'Dear sacred name, rest ever unreveal'd,' he quoted from Pope's *Eloisa* in his November 1813 journal, adding his own gloss: 'At least even here, my hand would tremble to write it.'[69]

Somewhere behind this fear lies the legacy of his Calvinist childhood, and yet as his deathbed shows, Byron was too intellectually and morally courageous to be cowed by the demons of the 'Scotch School'. Throughout his life he habitually dramatised himself in terms of Miltonic defiance, but for all the swagger of Cain or Heaven and Earth, Byron's sense of sin and exclusion was ultimately bound by this world rather than the next, his instinct for rebellion against man and not against God.

And this is perhaps the key to his behaviour with Augusta, because the fear he had of what they had done was less to do with a theological sense of sin than the growing recognition that he was prepared to push his defiance of convention to any limits. In his affair with Caroline Lamb the previous year, the courage or recklessness had seemed almost exclusively hers, but as he paraded Augusta in London and followed her to Newmarket and talked of exile together, as he trailed the affair in his letters and flaunted their incest in his poetry – as he pitted the Byrons against the world in the most public and symbolic way he could find – he discovered in Augusta not just his ideal refuge but his perfect weapon.

It would take the imaginative sympathy of a novelist to do justice to the complex and contradictory rhythms of Byron's life as it slid towards open rupture with the society that had embraced him only eighteen months earlier. If one simply believed the evidence of his journal for the winter of 1813–14, the frustrations of the previous year were as acute as ever, but as one turns from that to his verse, the contrasting boldness of the poetry suggests rather an artist and man growing into a defiant sense of his own power and vocation.

In the space of a few days in November 1813 he wrote *The Bride of Abydos*, and the following month, in another spasm of creative energy, threw off the third of his Eastern tales, *The Corsair*. In his letters and journals he was as dismissive as one would expect of these achievements, and yet no amount of Byronic self-mockery or defensive irony could deflect the central importance these poems had for him.

The Bride of Abydos, written with Augusta and the theme of incest constantly in mind, had been, in his own words, his first 'complete' poem but in its own harsher way *The Corsair* was every bit as subversive. He had written the *Bride* in the first place to keep himself sane, but with its violent and antisocial rage *The Corsair* was in itself a kind of deliberate public madness, brilliantly conceived simultaneously to alienate and seduce his public. 'Fear'd, shunn'd, belied, ere youth had lost her force,' Byron described his hero whom he must have known by now his readers would associate with himself.

> He hated man too much to feel remorse,
> And thought the voice of wrath a sacred call,
> To pay the injuries of some on all.
> He knew himself a villain – but he deem'd
> The rest no better than the thing he seem'd;
> And scorn'd the best as hypocrites who hid
> Those deeds the bolder spirits plainly did.
> He knew himself detested, but he knew
> The hearts that loath'd him, crouch'd and dreaded too.
> Lone, wild, and strange, he stood alike exempt
> From all affection and from all contempt:

His name could sadden, and his acts surprise;
But they that fear'd him dared not to despise:
Man spurns the worm, but pauses ere he wake
The slumbering venom of the folded snake:
The first may turn, but not avenge the blow;
The last expires, but leaves no living foe;
Fast to the doom'd offender's form it clings,
And he may crush – not conquer – still it stings![70]

'I have just finished the Corsair – am in the greatest admiration', Annabella Milbanke, wilting forgotten in the wings since her rejection of Byron's proposal, wrote to Lady Melbourne,

> In knowledge of the human heart & its most secret workings surely he may without exaggeration be compared to Shakespeare. He gives such wonderful life & individuality to character that from *that* cause, as well as from unjust prepossessions of his *own* disposition, the idea that he represents himself in his heroes may be partly accounted for. It is difficult to believe that he could have known these beings so thoroughly but from *introspection* ... I am afraid the compliment to his poetry will not repay him for the injury to his character.[71]

For a brief period in the autumn of 1813 – probably to placate Lady Melbourne – Byron did his best to draw back from the edge with his pursuit of the young, newly married Lady Frances Webster, but by the end of the year Augusta was pregnant with a child which the dates suggested might well be his. In the middle of the following January, with a crisis mounting, brother and sister drove north to Newstead, 'through more snows than ever opposed the Emperor's retreat.' Once arrived, there was no possibility of leaving. The roads beyond the Abbey were impassable, but their coals were excellent, he told his publisher, John Murray, the fireplaces large, the cellar full, his head empty, his only desire 'to shut my doors & let my beard grow.'[72]

For the moment, defiance and refuge were in perfect equilibrium. 'Never was such weather', Byron wrote contentedly after

ten days, 'one would imagine Heaven wanted to raise a Powder-tax
& had sent the snow to lay it on.'[73] Never had his ancestral home
seemed so all-sufficient as with Augusta. 'And what unto them is
the world beside,' Byron later demanded in *Parisina*, his drama
of incest and family doom that echoes the mood of these weeks,

> With all its change of time and tide
> Its living things, its earth and sky,
> Are nothing to their mind and eye.
> And heedless as the dead are they
> Of aught around, above, beneath;
> As if all else had pass'd away
> They only for each other breathe . . .
> Of guilt, of peril, do they deem
> In that tumultuous dream?[74]

There is something, in fact, of the magic of Pasternak's *Dr Zhivago*
about Byron's and Augusta's illicit exile at Newstead, isolated
from criticism and responsibilities by the impenetrable winter
landscape, as safe among the ruins of the abbey as Yuri and Lara in
the frozen wastes of Varykino. At the edge of Newstead's cloistered
world lurked the wolves, but like Zhivago watching their shadows
in the half-light of dusk, Byron could pretend for the moment
that they were merely dogs. To be alive, and to live in the present,
was enough. All his restless search after sensation was sunk in
'sluggish' content. Even the desire or need to write – for Byron
the 'lava of the imagination'[75] – was gone. Happy, he had neither
need nor urge to create. He felt, he told Murray in a revealing
metaphor for his poetic life, as he did when recovering from fever
in Patras – 'weak but in health and only afraid of a relapse.' 'I
shall keep this resolution', he wrote of his determination to give
up scribbling, 'for since I left London – though shut up – *snow*-
bound – *thaw*bound – & tempted with all kinds of paper – the
dirtiest of ink – and the bluntest of pens – I have not even been
haunted by a wish to put them to their combined uses.'[76]

The wolves, though, were not dogs, and with the Tory press in
full voice following the publication of his poetic squib against the
Prince of Wales, Caroline Lamb still primed for trouble and his

friends increasingly nervous, Byron was never going to be allowed
to forget it. Characteristically, just as the previous year Caroline's
antics had frightened him back from the abyss, his moods now
swung between defiance and compromise, between talk of the
exile he had been threatening for almost a year and a marriage
– any marriage – that might yet be his 'salvation' from the feelings
that he confessed to Lady Melbourne 'are a mixture of good and
diabolical'[77].

After his first impetuous talk of exile, Augusta too was beginning to look on the idea as the only way of averting catastrophe.
There is little doubt that she would have gone abroad with him
the previous summer if he had pressed her, but in the nature of
things she had more to lose than he did and for a mother as
indulgently devoted as Augusta, the thought of abandoning any
of her children – Georgiana, her eldest, had been born in the
first week of November 1808, Augusta Charlotte, a little over two
years later and a son, George, in June the next year – could never
have been a bearable option.

George was still only a baby when Byron first proposed exile
to Augusta, however, and it was probably her two daughters who
most exercised her concern. From an early age Augusta Charlotte
had begun to exhibit the symptoms of autism that would eventually lead her to an asylum in Kensal Green, and yet in her different
way the oldest, 'Georgey' – traditionally Byron's favourite – was
as much of a worry as her sister, constantly ill and as cripplingly
and elusively shy as Augusta herself had been as a child.

And even with Augusta's easy belief in the workings of a benev-
olent providence – virtually the only legacy from her pious Holderness grandmother – she must have felt that she had used up not
just her small stock of courage but her luck when the birth of a
third daughter in April passed without any gossip. It is impossible
to tell from the few elliptical comments in Byron's letters how
anxious they had been in advance, but whatever his thoughts on
the child he was certainly concerned enough for Augusta to journey up from London to the Leighs' home outside Newmarket in
the days before her confinement.

For all the space and time that has been expended on the

subject, the only thing that can be said with any certainty of the paternity of Elizabeth Medora Leigh, is that it cannot be known. It would seem likely that Byron and Augusta both initially believed that she was his child, and yet there is not a single scrap of evidence – not a remark or silence – that cannot be equally well interpreted to support either side of the argument. 'Oh! but it is worth while', Byron reported to Lady Melbourne – in the one notorious, throw-off paragraph on which a whole speculative industry has been raised,

> I can't tell you why – and it is *not* an '*Ape*' [an apparent reference to medieval incest superstitions] and if it is – that must be my fault – however I will positively reform – you must however allow – that it is utterly impossible I can ever be half as well liked elsewhere – and I have been all my life trying to make someone love me – & never got the sort I preferred before. But positively she and I will grow good – and all that – & so we are *now* and shall be these three weeks & more too.[78]

For all Byron's resolutions, however, the choice of the name Medora – the heroine of his *Corsair* – smacks of the kind of brinkmanship that threatened disaster at any moment. It has been argued, with some plausibility, that she was in fact called after the Oaks winning filly of 1813, but even if that is true Augusta – for all her 'goosiness' – was astute enough to know that in anything to do with Byron it was the perception rather than the reality of things that mattered.

She had, in fact, her own idea for Byron's wife, Lady Charlotte Leveson-Gower, but since the previous autumn an alarmed Lady Melbourne had been keeping a far more serious candidate waiting in the wings. For a time during his Eywood idyll there had been a slight froideur between her and Byron, but one of the great secrets of Lady Melbourne's influence was a talent for absorbing slights and from the first threatening appearance of Augusta in Byron's life she had been as ready to sacrifice her niece for his safety as she had been a year earlier for her own dynastic needs.

There are moments in the relationship of Byron and Annabella Milbanke that tilt the sympathies violently in one direction or another and the intervention of Lady Melbourne is one of these. There is no need to sentimentalise the broadly 'Austenish'attitudes to marriage of Annabella herself, but the machinations of her aunt over the next fifteen months belong to another league altogether, raising the cynicism of the Regency marriage market to levels for which *Glenarvon* or *Les Liaisons Dangereuses* – the constant point of reference among her family for Lady Melbourne – provide no real preparation.

Lady Melbourne's letters to Byron were always cooler, more discreetly circumspect, than his to her, and so it is difficult to be sure of her motives in this matter. It is clear that she was both genuinely fond of Byron and alarmed for him, but for a woman who only had to see a happy marriage, it was said, to want to destroy it, the appeal of the match must have been as much aesthetic as practical – the pure unalloyed pleasure of uniting two people so symmetrically ill-suited as Annabella and Byron, 'the spoilt child of seclusion, restraint and parental idolatry' and 'the spoilt child of genius, passion, and the world,'[79] as Mrs Stowe later described them.

Lady Melbourne's performance was one of dazzling cynicism as she brought them together again, interpreting one to the other, revealing or concealing as needed, playing equally on the weaknesses of Byron and Annabella until each imagined the initiative their own. There was a streak of passivity in Byron's nature that had always made him putty in Lady Melbourne's hands, but with her romantic high-mindedness and naivety her niece proved no less easy to manage.

After almost a year in which she had time to reflect on the loneliness of moral superiority and the dullness of domestic life without the *frisson* of Byron's attentions, Annabella was ripe for persuasion. 'I have received from Lady Melbourne an assurance of the satisfaction you feel in being remembered with interest by me,' her first direct letter to him had begun on cue on 22 August 1813 – midway between the beginning of his affair with Augusta and his half-hearted pursuit of Lady Frances Webster,

> Let me fully explain this interest, with the hope that the
> consciousness of possessing a friend whom neither Time
> nor Absence can estrange may impart some soothing feel-
> ing to your retrospective views.[80]

One of the supreme temptations of the novel, E.M. Forster once
confessed, is the desire to give characters the happiness that 'real
life' denies them, and this first letter of Annabella's can stir the
same kind of emotions. She was so much in the habit of regarding
herself in fictional terms that it would be hard not to follow suit
anyway, but the cruelty of her fate now was to find herself less
the heroine of her own shaping than the dupe of a Leclos plot
over which she had no control. 'You have remarked the serenity
of my countenance,' she went on,

> but mine is not the serenity of one who is a stranger to
> care, nor are the prospects of my future untroubled. It is my
> nature to feel long, deeply, and secretly, and the strongest
> affections of my heart are without hope. I disclose to you
> what I conceal even from those who have most claim to
> my confidence, because it will be the surest basis of that
> unreserved friendship which I wish to establish between us
> . . . Early in our acquaintance, when I was far from suppos-
> ing myself preferred by you, I studied your character. I felt
> for you, and I often felt with you. You were, as I conceived,
> in a desolate position, surrounded by admirers who could
> not value you, and by friends to whom you were not dear.
> You were either flattered or persecuted. How often have I
> wished that the State of Society would have allowed me to
> offer you my sentiments without restraint.[81]

With its oblique and frustrated demand to be heard this might
anticipate the great climax of *Persuasion*, but Annabella was no
more an Anne Elliot than Byron was Captain Wentworth. From
her earliest youth she had dramatised herself as the self-sacrificing
heroine of her historical daydreams, and the girl who had stood
by Howard in her fantasies now abandoned herself to the role
of Byron's redeemer, uniting herself with him in an imaginary
communion of souls that transcended time, place or vulgar self-
interest. 'Surely the Heaven-born genius without Heavenly grace

must make a Christian clasp the blessing with greater reverence & love, mingled with a sorrow as a Christian that it is not shared', she wrote to her old confidante Lady Gosford in her most ecstatic vein,

> Should it ever happen that he & I ever offer up a heartfelt worship together – I mean in a sacred spot – *my* worship will then be most worthy of the spirit to whom it ascends. It will glow with all the devout and grateful joy which mortal breast can contain. It is a thought too dear to be indulged – not dear for *his* sake, but for the sake of *man*, my brother man, whomever he be – & for any poor, unknown tenant of this earth I believe I should feel the same. It is not the poet – it is the immortal soul lost or saved.[82]

In one of her 'Auto-descriptions,' Annabella confessed this inability to distinguish fiction from fact, but what had been harmless enough in the child was profoundly dangerous in the adult. In the early days of their acquaintance she had self-consciously distanced herself from the 'Byromania' of London, but as she realised with something like panic how much she had lost in turning him down, she set about desperately trying to recreate Byron in an image she could square with her conscience, blindly moving with every exchange of letters towards marriage with a man she scarcely knew. 'I entreat you then to observe the more consistent principles of unwearied benevolence', she wrote to Byron in the language of a tabloid astrologer,

> No longer suffer yourself to be the slave of the moment, nor trust your noble impulses to the chances of Life. Have an object that will permanently occupy your feelings & exercise your reason. Do good. Your powers peculiarly qualify you for performing those duties with success, and may you experience the sacred pleasure of having them dwell in your heart![83]

It is clear from Byron's reply that Annabella's tone had startled him, but if he had to sacrifice Augusta, it hardly seemed to matter

whom he married. 'To the part of your letter regarding myself',
he wrote back, having first assured her that she was the only
person with whom he had ever contemplated marriage,

> I could say much – but I must be brief – if you hear ill of
> me it is probably not untrue though perhaps exaggerated
> – on any point in which you may honour me with an interest
> I shall be glad to satisfy you – to confess the truth or refute
> the calumny. – I must be candid with you on the score of
> Friendship – it is a feeling towards you with which I cannot
> trust myself – I doubt whether I could help loving you –[84]

There was not a scrap of hypocrisy about Byron, but what was
almost as hazardous as he renewed his interest in Lady Melbourne's niece, was the artist's ability to conjure imagined feeling
out of the depths of genuine experience. He would have found
it impossible to preserve his illusions about a future with Annabella had he seen anything of her, but in the safety of letters he
could indulge in an emotional transfer that enabled him to create
an idea of her and himself that could sustain him through the
travesty of an epistolary courtship.

If it was a serious error of judgement on Annabella's part to
imagine she could reform Byron, it was a more culpable misjudge-
ment on his to think that he would ever allow it. It is unlikely
that with Augusta so compulsively in his mind anyone could have
filled her place, but as he edged inexorably towards a second
proposal, it was Annabella's fate to be almost diagrammatically
the wrong person at the wrong time – a poor woman's Dorothea
Brooke, capable of change but not growth, of ardour but not
compassion, sensibility but no real sympathy.

It is possible still that Byron could have forgiven Annabella for
what she *was*, and yet he must have known, as he finally steeled
himself to propose, that he could never forgive her for *not* being
Augusta. In the early days of their courtship her virtues had been
thrown into relief by the extravagances of Caroline Lamb, but
seen now through the distorting prism of his 'perverse passion'[85]
everything about her would inevitably come to seem different, her
goodness primness, her certainties dogmatism, and her learning

pedantry – the five foot three incarnation of all the cultural and moral littleness he despised.

Byron's courtship of Annabella through the late summer of 1814 seems so reckless, so wantonly obtuse in the refusal to recognise the warning signals, that no conventional explanation of his actions seems quite sufficient. In his journals and letters he might describe her as his last hope of salvation, and yet if at some superficial level he managed to convince himself of that, his choice betrays a deeper compulsion to make her the *causa belli* of a rift with the world she embodied that had been threatening since the first success of *Childe Harold*.

It is this secret, unconscious, destructive agenda that gives such an air of inescapable misery to the story that unfolds with his second proposal to Annabella. On 9 September, having prevaricated as long as he could, he wrote to her from Newstead, sealing and despatching the letter 'with the greatest haste', according to Tom Moore, before he could have second thoughts[86]. On the same day that she received it at Seaham, Annabella wrote back, a letter of touching and honest simplicity. 'I have your second letter', she told him,

> and am almost too agitated to write – but you will understand. It would be absurd to suppress anything – I am and have long been pledged to myself to make your happiness my first object in life. If I *can* make you happy, I have no other consideration. I will *trust* to you for all I should look up to – all I can love. The fear of not realizing your expectations is the only one I now feel. Convince me – it is all I wish – that my affection may supply what is wanting in my character to form your happiness.[87]

As Byron opened the letter, Augusta at his side, he turned so pale that she thought he might faint. It never rains but it pours, was his only comment. Even so, he probably did not understand the forces he had set in motion. Nor did a fraught, uncomfortable week at Seaham at the beginning of November, that left him and Annabella as ignorant as ever of each other's character, open his eyes.

On 24 December 1814, after further delays over the marriage settlement, he once more set off for the north, accompanied by his old travelling companion, Hobhouse, and stopped near Newmarket to spend a last Christmas with Augusta. On the 26th the two men continued their reluctant journey towards Seaham. 'Never was lover less in haste'[88], recorded Hobhouse in his journal, and he was right. As the wedding day approached, the air of foreboding spread. In later life Annabella would speak of the sense of inexplicable dread that seized her. At the Leighs' house at Six Mile Bottom, near Newmarket, on the morning of 2 January, at the exact time she knew that the marriage service had begun, Augusta later said that she felt as the sea must do when an earthquake moves it. The panic, the fear, the emotional turmoil were justified. She knew, as Byron had told Lady Melbourne, that her own security and reputation were wrapped up with the success or failure of the marriage. It was, though, already too late.

Almost forty years after that journey north, on the same morning that Annabella Byron and Frederick Robertson boarded the Reigate train at Brighton station, a woman in her late sixties, dressed in mourning and walking with a slow, shuffling step, made her painful way up the first-class staircase of London Bridge's new terminus, and onto the narrow platform of the Brighton line.

It is unlikely that anyone who had ever known Augusta as a young girl, or seen the drawing that Sir George Hayter had done of her in her late twenties, would have recognised her. She might never have been in any conventional sense a beauty, but there had been a charm and elasticity about her that had long since gone, the woman Hayter so wonderfully captured worn away to the faded creature for whom every anxious step seemed an act of atonement to the world around her.

There was even something in the way she carried herself, her long, black shawl pulled tight around her as though she might disappear into it, that suggested the same air of surrender. For most of her lifetime she had struggled with whatever resources she could muster to keep a hostile world at bay, but just two months past her sixty-eighth birthday, and with 'death in her face'[89], the Hon. Mrs Augusta Leigh had at last nothing more to give or ask than to die in peace.

She had only travelled once before on the railway, but even for someone less nervous and sick, the prospect from her window would have been a bewildering one. As the train swung southwards and left the Greenwich line and the teeming slums of Bermondsey behind, the soaring glass house of the Great Exhibition visible in the distance, it began to cross a city that was changing by the week and almost by the day, spreading and growing with the railways that were transforming it, sprouting new villas and settlements, degrading suburbs into slums and villages into suburbs in a thrusting dialectic of population, railway and building that had left any world Augusta had known far behind.

It was a new age that Augusta instinctively and rightly feared, but as the train gathered speed and finally escaped the tentacular spread of London, moving through a landscape still relatively unchanged from her youth, it was this older world that threatened most danger. For more than twenty years she had looked forward to this journey with all the optimism and placatory desire to accommodate that had characterised her youth, but as the train slowed across the common land and farms near Reigate, coming to a standstill at the heart of what one contemporary guide called England's 'forgotten Eden', this older, less resilient Augusta must have known that for the last representative of a 'serpent race'[90] there was little mercy to be expected.

If there had been any doubts about that, the letter she had received, sent from Brighton on 11 February, would have ended them. 'Since the cessation of our personal intercourse', she had read in a neat, firm hand she had not seen in two decades,

> you have more than once asked me to see you. If you still
> feel that wish, I will comply with it. We may not long have
> it in our power, Augusta, to meet again in this life, and
> to do so might be the means of leaving to both of us a
> remembrance of deep though sad thankfulness. But this
> could not be the effect unless every worldly interest were
> absolutely excluded from our conversation, and there were

the most entire and mutual truthfulness. *No other expectations* must be entertained by you for a moment. On any other terms I cannot see you again, unless summoned to your Death-bed.[91]

She had, too, her instructions. A fly would be waiting at the station to take her to the White Hart. When the train stopped she remained sitting where she was, a dowdily dressed figure from a previous age, waiting like some sacrificial victim at the altar of Victorian self-justification and moral rectitude to which she had been brought. After a short while a servant in drab livery carrying a visiting card appeared at her window. On the card was a name: Lady Byron.

II

THE MEETING

Tuesday, 8 April, 1851. The White Hart, Reigate. A large
room decorated in an oppressive clutter of different periods
and styles, an amalgam of the Georgian coaching age and Victorian, the walls sombre maroon relieved only by the glint of
frames, the woodwork dark, the scattered chairs covered in
chintzes. A door, ajar, opens into the left wall, against which is a
long, black, horse-hair sofa. On the opposite side of the room a
wood fire burns low in an open grate. Under a glass dome on
the mantel is an elaborate ivory-faced clock, its pendulum swing-
ing with an insistent, audible ticking. Above, a mirror; on either
side, open bookcases. In the left foreground a heavy square legged
mahogany serving table, with a cut glass vase of dried flowers,
papers scattered across it, a small travelling case with its lid open,
outdoor bonnet, gloves etc. Back right, a window opens onto the
garden beyond, which drops away and rises again to a skyline of
still bare beech trees, and a cold, grey sky. Back left a large corner
cupboard, and between them a regency pier table, with a gilded,
finialled bird cage. Above it, incongruously flanked on either side
by sporting prints, hangs a large framed print of Manfred on the
Jungfrau, the face of Manfred contorted by suffering, his fist raised
in one last gesture of defiance.

In front of the picture, a woman in her late fifties, in a lavender
coloured dress stands staring silently up, her arms folded across
her chest, the fists clenching and unclenching in a compulsive
gesture. She can be no more than a little over five feet in height,
with an unusually high forehead, the habitual pallor of her face

slightly flushed with agitation, hard blue eyes, sharp features, pursed mouth, silver hair under a widow's cap of transparent material.

At the table, papers in his hand, a man stands looking anxiously at her. He is a tall and impressive figure in his early thirties, brown hair just receding at the temples, a broad forehead, deep set eyes, a strong, straight nose, wide, thin mouth, cleft chin, and side whiskers, his whole manner an uneasy mix of deference and authority.

I

ROBERTSON   (*Hesitantly*)
If you would prefer another room, I'm sure –

LADY BYRON   (*Without answering, slowly turns from the picture, and walks to the window. She stands there, looking out to the bare trees, her back to Robertson*)
Was that the fly?

ROBERTSON   (*He takes a watch from his waist-coat pocket, and glances up at the clock*)
She should have been here by now –

LADY BYRON   (*Almost to herself*)
Oh, she will be here soon enough, she'll be here.

ROBERTSON   If she has never taken the railways –
(*He breaks off as a sudden spasm of pain seems to run through the slight figure standing with her back to him*)
Lady Byron?

LADY BYRON   (*Her body relaxes, she waves away his concern with a slight gesture, turns slowly away from the window, and returns to the picture*)
She will be here.

ROBERTSON   I do wish you would let me bring you something –

LADY BYRON   And the papers? Is everything there?

ROBERTSON   Yes, yes I think you have everything that we went through, though I really can't see that you will need them –

LADY BYRON   (*Interrupting, her voice quiet, her eyes still on the picture.*)
But then you have not met Mrs Leigh.
(*She makes a slow circuit of the room, pausing again momentarily in front of the same picture. Her voice is measured*)
I have long since had to learn, that with a certain –
(*She pauses, letting the words hang between*)
with a certain kind of forgetfulness, it is as well to be prepared.
(*She moves on, the subject dismissed*)
And the child's letters, are they with the others?

ROBERTSON   (*Watching her, his voice registering a note of defeat*)
Yes, – yes, I think they are all here.

LADY BYRON   Then if you won't stay, I'll only trouble you for some water –

ROBERTSON   Yes, of course –
(*Takes a jug up from the table, begins to pour a glass, and pauses hesitantly*)
And you know that in any other circumstances I would gladly, but the poor creature is surely going to be more at ease –

LADY BYRON   (*Dryly*)
I thought it was Mrs Leigh's soul that we were concerned with, Mr Robertson, and not her ease.

ROBERTSON   (*Defensively*)
Yes indeed, but in common charity –

LADY BYRON   (*Her tone as measured as ever.*)

I would not have imagined that I had given you
much cause to doubt my charity.

ROBERTSON   (*He takes up his hat from the table, and stands with it
in hand, looking down, his voice almost inaudible*)
No, no. Certainly. But – but when Mrs Leigh has
made her wishes so plain, I can't in all conscience
see how I can simply ignore them –
(*His voice peters away, as he looks at the figure at the
table, seemingly absorbed in pushing papers about as if
he was not there*)
But we have been over all this, so if you will excuse
me –
(*He places the glass of water down on the table, moves
towards the door, and opens it*)
And I will be in the next room if you need me.

LADY BYRON   (*She pauses beside the table, adjusting the papers on it
without any obvious purpose, her voice ironic*)
Ah. Need.
(*She moves away from the table, and towards the fire,
her back to Robertson*)
Why are people so keen to bring up my needs
when they are most bent on thwarting them?

ROBERTSON   (*Pauses at the door*)
That hardly seems fair –

LADY BYRON   (*Underneath the control, her voice has a nervous edge
to it*)
I sometimes think, too, that you imagine that I
enjoy this. There is nothing I could wish more
than to take your view of things, but there are
duties – a duty to truth –
(*Her voice becomes more composed, as if the phrase has
a soothing, almost mantric familiarity*)
a duty to Mrs Leigh herself, Mr Robertson,
(*She turns and looks fixedly at him*)

that as she and I stand on the brink of eternity I
will not shirk.

ROBERTSON   (*Inaudible almost*)
No, indeed.

LADY BYRON   (*Turning away from him, and moving to the window*)
You will tell a servant, that if Mrs Leigh has arrived
she is to be shown in.

ROBERTSON   Of course.

LADY BYRON   And say that we are not to be disturbed.

ROBERTSON   No, indeed.
(*With a final defeated stare at the woman standing with
her back to him, Robertson leaves, shutting the door
behind him. As she resumes her pacing, she takes out a
folded slip of paper tucked into her cuff, begins to unfold
it and tucks it back unread into her sleeve. She stops
again under the Manfred. As she stands in silence looking up at it, her fists clench and unclench in another
spasm of pain. Behind her, unnoticed, the door opens,
and a woman in her late sixties, slightly taller and fuller
in figure, dressed in heavy but shabby mourning, the
black crepe bodice mottled with damp stains, the hem of
her dress spattered with mud, her movements slow, her
air uncertain, appears. She stands by the door a moment
looking across at Lady Byron*)

AUGUSTA   (*Her voice softly attractive, affectionate*)
Annabella.
(*Without waiting for a reply, she moves tentatively for-
ward, her two hands stretched out in greeting*)
Dearest Annabella!
(*Half way across the room she stops as the figure of
Lady Byron remains with her back to her, the only recog-
nition a tensing of her whole body. Slowly Augusta's
hands drop back to her side*)

LADY BYRON   (*Quietly. Without turning*)
              Augusta.
              (*Without looking at her she moves away from the picture
              to the window, only her hands betraying her agitation.
              When she speaks again there is a note of strained control
              in her voice*)
              You found Bridges, then?

AUGUSTA   Yes, yes, or at least he found me.

LADY BYRON   And your journey? Easy I trust?

AUGUSTA   (*Uncertain at her reception.*)
              Thank you, yes

LADY BYRON   (*Staring out of the window, her tone wandering and
              inconsequential*)
              I find the railways so much better – the roads can
              be so disagreeable at this time of the year. Did
              you come alone?

AUGUSTA   Yes. Yes, I had thought to ask Emily, but –

LADY BYRON   (*Her voice remote*)
              Ah, of course, Emily. The child, is she well?

AUGUSTA   Thank you, yes. It has been hard on her since her
              father's death, but –

LADY BYRON   And yourself?

AUGUSTA   (*Her tone almost apologetic*)
              Perhaps now with the warmer days –

LADY BYRON   (*Breaking in, dryly impatient of weakness*)
              I find with age I have less and less time for illness,
              what with my schools – and –
              (*She seems to lose the thread of what she is saying*)
              And other duties . . .
              (*There is a slight pause as she looks out of the window,
              her thoughts elsewhere*)
              I ought in fact to be in Ealing now, but this

was the only day that Mr Robertson could join me.

AUGUSTA   Yes, you wrote.

LADY BYRON   Perhaps you noticed him as you came in? He has been very useful to me over these last years, and he would have wished to have stayed –
(*She turns away from the window, her manner and voice firm again*)
But as you made it clear that you would rather we were alone, I have asked him to wait for us –

AUGUSTA   (*Quietly*)
Thank you.

LADY BYRON   You ought to know, too, that he was against this meeting at all, but though he has only my welfare at heart –
(*Each phrase is carefully weighed*)
I find – I find that I have been thinking of you more and more since Colonel Leigh's death, and while I can accuse myself of no injustice, I have not been easy at the thought that we might never meet again – uneasy –
(*She pauses for a moment in front of the bird in the cage, looking at it with a remote detachment*)
that certain things should remain unsaid between us.

AUGUSTA   (*Softly*)
I am glad.

LADY BYRON   (*She resumes her circuit, with an almost imperceptible movement motioning Augusta to sit down in a chair at the centre of the room.*)
Is there anything I can have them bring you?

AUGUSTA   (*Dropping into the chair, removing her black gloves, and placing them on a small table beside her*)

Thank you, no.

LADY BYRON Some wine after your journey?

AUGUSTA No, nothing.

LADY BYRON (*Indifferent*)
Probably wise, .
(*She pauses at the side table, and runs a finger along a surface, examining it for dust, before casting a slow, look around the cluttered room.*)
Though I begin to find myself oddly at ease in places of this sort – something to do with the restlessness of age I dare say – or merely the price perhaps of having nowhere that one is tempted to think of as home.

(*She stops again in front of the picture, studying it with distaste. Still looking at it, she continues*)
Do you know that when I was a child, I thought Seaham would be my home forever. I used to visit our cottagers with my father, and I would have my own purse to give out pennies and I believed – believed that so long as I could be there nothing could ever harm me, that I would always be happy –
(*There is a slight break*)
and now –
(*With a weary sigh*)
But I have not asked you here to speak of Seaham.

AUGUSTA (*Almost to herself, as if in a private reverie*)
Seaham. I don't know when I last heard that name.
(*There is a slight pause*)
It seems a world away – a lifetime ago –

LADY BYRON (*Slowly and without even seeming to hear*)
Thirty-six years.

(*There is a pause*)
Thirty-six years years, three months –
(*Another pause*)

and six days. The second of January eighteen hundred and fifteen. I often think how blindly we live our lives, of all those childhood years before that date – all those Januaries that I watched that day glide past unnoticed, unconscious of what that anniversary would come to mean to me – the beginning –
(*Her voice has an ominous and measured flatness to it*)
and the end of my life crushed into a single moment. From Spring to Winter
(*She moves out of the window, the panes spattered now with rain, to the bare trees*)
and nothing in between.

AUGUSTA   (*Softly*)
Please.

LADY BYRON   (*With a forced lightness*)
Oh I know how he used to like to mock me, think me dull – and what was his name for me among you all,
(*She glances round momentarily*)
with Moore and Hobhouse and the rest of you? – the Princess of the Parallelograms was it? But there is a kind of poetry in figures too. Each year as that anniversary approaches, I can say to myself, 'On this day
(*She resumes her pacing*)
'On this day one year ago – on this day ten years ago – on this day –

AUGUSTA   (*She is looking at the ground, her voice low and pained*)
Annabella.

LADY BYRON   'On this day twenty years ago my life ended'. And
              I can still recall that day that finished it as if it were
              yesterday, still see the room – the two kneelers side
              by side on the carpet – and the cushions –
              (*She glances at Augusta for corroboration*)
              – and how like him, don't you think, even on his
              wedding day to make a fuss over a cushion! – and
              Mama at the window – Mrs Clermont –

AUGUSTA   (*Quietly*)
              Annabella.

LADY BYRON   (*Entirely caught up in her memory*)
              I never looked at him, you know, the whole time.
              I remember as I walked in on Papa's arm I saw
              Hobhouse, and I can see his face still, long and
              severe, those staring eyes of his on me as if he was
              watching me walk to my execution –
              (*There is a slight mirthless laugh*)
              And perhaps it had been better that it was, rather
              than live to –

AUGUSTA   (*Gently*)
              Please.

LADY BYRON   (*She collects herself with a weary sigh*)
              Did I tell you I was at Leamington last year? There
              was a man at the table behind me, and I could
              hear him talking, telling whoever it was he was
              with that he had seen the hotel register, and that
              Lady Byron was staying, and that you only had to
              look at her – oh, and he was very humorous about
              it, had passed my carriage in Piccadilly years ago,
              he claimed – that you only needed to see her once
              to understand why Byron fled the country.
              (*There is a pause*)
              Something about the primness of the mouth, it
              seems. And the eyes.
              The eyes. As if they had not once been different.

As if they had always been an old woman's eyes,
as if –
(*She breaks off and turns suddenly to face Augusta,
looking at her intently, as if seeing her for the first time.
When she continues, there is a reluctant fascination in
her voice*)
As if they had not once been as young as yours.
And yours! How right the child was – the same
still as ever – the same look to them – the same
– soft –

AUGUSTA   (*So quiet as to be almost inaudible*)
You're very kind.

LADY BYRON   (*With a slight laugh, as she turns away*)
Ah, kind!
(*She walks towards the window, and stands at it, look-
ing out, brooding.*)
Kind. 'Be kind to Augusta' –
(*She turns again, her voice less controlled*)
Do you know that's the only thing your brother
ever left me, the only message? – 'Be kind', he
wrote from Italy, 'Be kind to Augusta, and her
children.'

AUGUSTA   (*Warily, uncertain*)
And you were.

LADY BYRON   (*Dismissively*)
Oh I know you don't think so, but I have always
done what was right.

AUGUSTA   And do you think I have ever forgotten it?

LADY BYRON   (*Slightly querulous*)
And as if he had ever needed to ask! Do you know
from the first time I met you – no even before
that, when I had no more than heard of you from
him – I used to pray that if I could get close to
you – if I could only get you to love me as I was

ready to love you –
(*She clasps and unclasps her hands*)
then perhaps I could make him love me too.
Augusta will know, I used to tell myself –
(*Her tone becomes more agitated*)
Augusta can teach me. Augusta will know how to
humour him, Augusta can quieten him, Augusta
understands him – and that's what he used to say,
you know – 'Augusta would understand,' he'd say,
only Augusta – why couldn't I understand him in
the way Augusta did? Why could I not be more
like Augusta? How did I think that he could ever
have loved someone like me when –

AUGUSTA   (*Pleading*)
Annabella!

LADY BYRON   (*More collected again*)
I was so young too when we married. You can't
think what it is to have spent your life loved and
cosseted on all sides, to be the centre of your own
universe – and oh I was spoiled enough, I know!
– knew it then I suppose – and then – suddenly
– to find yourself hated in the way that he hated
me. To wake at night and discover your husband
standing over your bed, knife in hand –
(*She turns*)
Do you know the first words he spoke, as we drove
away from Seaham after the wedding? Before we
had even left the park? The first words of our
married life?
(*She gives a short laugh*)
'It must come to a separation,' he said. He
couldn't even look at me as he spoke – couldn't
bear even the sight of me. It must come to a
separation. 'It is enough' – he said – 'it is enough
that you are my wife for me to hate you' –
(*She turns back to the window, and stands there seeming*

to see nothing, her voice without emotion)
I thought that journey would never end. Hobhouse
had given me a set of Byron's poems as a wedding
present, and there they lay – between us –
(*She glances round at Augusta, an ironic smile*)
the man I had loved bound in his yellow morocco,
the man I had married as far from me as he could
get.
(*She turns back to the bare landscape*)
It was so cold too. My pelisse so thin. I remember
huddling in the corner of the carriage, staring out
of the window, desperate for something I could
recognise – anything – and finding nothing –
nothing I knew – only snow – an endless white
waste, stretching ahead as far as I could see –

(*She moves from the window and walks over to the fire*)
Did he ever tell you that they rang the bells for
us as we drove though Durham? 'Ringing for our
happiness, I suppose', he said. And then began
to sing. I wondered if he had gone mad – he told
me all the Gordons were mad – half hoped even
that he was, but it wasn't madness –
(*She picks up the poker and jabs at the fire*)
Not madness. Hate. I could hear it in his voice,
in the dark of the carriage. 'I'll be even with you',
he kept murmuring. 'I'll be even with you – I'll
be even –'

AUGUSTA (*Breaking in agitated*)
And do you think I hadn't tried to stop him,
hadn't tried to keep him –

LADY BYRON (*Softly*)
I'll be even with you.

AUGUSTA I tried all I could to save you –

LADY BYRON (*With a slow heavy irony, staring at Augusta*)
Oh yes, you tried, I can still see how you tried to save me. Have you forgotten the first time we met, your brother with his new bride? And how I was sent packing as if I was a servant – how he stood at the fire with you on the rug at his feet, and told me that I was to take myself to bed, that he wanted to talk to his sister – that there was no place for me there. Now I have her, he said, you'll see I have no use more for you. Oh yes, I know how you tried.
(*There is a silence. Lady Byron turns away and walks back to the window. Augusta is motionless. After a pause, Lady Byron goes on, her voice flat*)
It's raining.
(*There is another pause. When she resumes each sentence is deliberate, unemotional*)
It was raining that first night at Newmarket. I don't know how long I lay listening to it on the roof, waiting for the sound of his footsteps, my eyes straining the dark for a crack of light at the door. I don't know how long I lay there. Heaven knows when I fell asleep. Only that when I woke he was there,

(*She moves across to the picture, and stands looking up at it*)
standing at the bed, his face lit by the candle, with that look, muttering. 'Why did you not say yes when I first asked, when we might have been happy, when there might still have been time!'
(*She pauses, wrapped up in the scene. Augusta bends forward in her chair, her face buried in her hands*)
He didn't even know I was awake. Why? he kept saying. Why? Why? When we might yet have been happy; why –

AUGUSTA   (*With sudden passion, rising from the seat, half-sob, half anger in her voice*)

And why couldn't you, when all London was throwing itself at his feet and only you – you

(*Her outburst brings on a fit of coughing, and she steadies herself against the chair before dropping back into it. When she continues all the passion is gone.*)

Could you be so kind as to pour me some water?

(*Without answering, Lady Byron goes over to a table, pours water into a glass from the jug, and carries it to Augusta. She takes it in silence, drinks from it, and hands back the glass.*)

Thank you.

LADY BYRON I could never understand what he meant. I used to think at first that it was his pride I had hurt, and that only pique had driven him to persist – that he only ever wanted what he could not have – only married to revenge himself against me for having said no. But then – sometimes – just sometimes during those first weeks in Piccadilly before you came with Georgey – when for a moment we were happy together – he would look at me, and a pain would cross his face –

(*She turns to Augusta, as if for understanding, and then her eyes move back to the picture*)

a pain like I have never seen on any other face – like a lost soul and – I would have died to spare him that pain if I could. I didn't know it was possible to feel so alone or helpless as in those months. I don't know, either, which I feared more, his pity or his anger. I used to hear him pacing his study late at night, his voice raised as if he had someone – or something – in there with him, – struggling and arguing – but if I ever asked him – Ever tried to get near to him – help him – all he would say was 'Ask Augusta'. Ask Augusta.

(*She stops in front of Augusta, facing her, confronting their shared past. With a quiet hostility*)

Ask Augusta.

AUGUSTA   (*There is a silence. When she speaks she does so without looking at her antagonist, her tone suddenly weary*)
What is there to say that was not said long ago?
(*She pulls herself heavily to her feet*)
Why now? What good can it do either of us?
(*She moves slowly towards the picture, her head shaking in a kind of wondering puzzlement. She glances around at Lady Byron before returning her attention to the picture*)
Or him. What more now can you want?

LADY BYRON   Want? Do you imagine I am here for myself?

AUGUSTA   Do you know I could have wept when I first saw your letter, when I saw again after twenty years my name written in your hand. You cannot think how often in that time I have wanted to write, to beg you that just once more before I die I could hear your voice again, to hear you say as you once used to "Dearest Augusta" – and now –
(*She breaks off and moves towards the bird, staring into its cage. When she speaks again it is with a quiet fatalism*)
But that is not what you want me for. In my heart, too, I think I knew. Knew that you would not have changed. Knew that I could never do penance enough to satisfy you –

LADY BYRON   (*Coldly*)
Do you think it is to me that you'll have to answer?

AUGUSTA   (*She puts a finger through the cage bars, absorbed*)
Has there ever been anyone else? All these years?
(*She lets her hand drop from the cage*)
Poor thing.
(*She moves away from the bird cage, and walks slowly to the other end of the room, the table between them, as*

far away from Lady Byron as is possible. When she speaks it is with the slightly detached voice of a deposition)

I don't know either that I could ever make you understand.
(She takes a stem from the vase of dried flowers and stands examining it as she speaks.)
What it was like for him. For me. What it is to be born a Byron. Do you know that when my mother died and my father married again, my grandmother took me in –
(She puts the stem back in to the vase, and moves slowly towards the fire)

and I don't know how it was, but I knew even then that I should never mention the name – that I should never ask after my father – never ask when I might see him again. When he might come for me. When he might take me home.

LADY BYRON I don't see –

AUGUSTA I remember once – I can't have been more than six or seven – it was at her house in Hertford Street – standing at an open door and hearing the name 'Byron', and shrinking back –
(She pauses at the mirror, and looks at the faded figure reflected back in its clouded surface)
'There's nothing of the Byron in her', my grandmother was saying – and I remember running upstairs to look at myself in a glass – trying to recall what he looked like –and sitting there in front of it dreaming up schemes for us both – romantic fantasies – not knowing what he was really like – knowing nothing about him.
(She turns from the mirror, and begins slowly to pace the room)
I am not even sure when I first knew that he had

given me a brother. I suppose it must have been
when my cousin was killed, and he became heir – he
can only have been six I suppose, but I remember
picturing him, wondering if he was like our father
– like I'd imagined him anyway – and, ah! –

(*She breaks off with a slight laugh*)
You would never dream how little like it he was
when we met – a thirteen-year-old boy – fat – and
awkward – and almost as shy as I was –
(*Her voice is quieter, ruminative*)
I don't know why I had never been allowed to see
him before. I think there had been some ill-
feeling with my grandmother, but his mother
wrote to me when she died – and –
(*The pressure of memories momentarily banishes the
reserve between them*)
do you know for the first time in my life when I
met him I felt needed. Everyone had always been
kind but no one had ever needed me. I was not
an heiress. I was not clever. I was not even very
pretty. He used to write to me, though – dull,
serious, boy's letters to a sister four years older
than himself – letters full of his friends – of Clare
and Long – letters inviting me to Harrow – messages to Colonel Leigh on my engagement –
(*She looks across at her*)
the letters of a child, Annabella, who had no one
else to love, no family but a wretched mother who
shamed him with every word she spoke –

(*There is a slight pause*)
Letters to an imagined sister he had hardly ever
seen. He would write to remind me of some purse
I had promised him, and then in the same breath
of what we would do when he came of age – how
his home – the Byron home –
(*Her face clouds over*)

how Newstead would always be my refuge so long
as ever it was his.
(*There is a silence until she seems to shrug off the
memory, and walks over to the window*)

A refuge! You can't think how remote a dream that
had become when we at last met again. I was twenty-
nine with three children and a husband who –
(*There is a slight hesitation*)
But then I need hardly tell you of Colonel Leigh.
(*She allows her words to hang in the air for a moment,
their meaning unspoken. When she eventually goes on,
her voice gradually strengthens, and becomes more
animated*)
It was at Lady Harrowby's that I saw him again,
the year after his return from the east. He was
talking at the far end of the room as I came in,
and as I stood in the doorway, he suddenly looked
up, and as he walked towards me with that quick
sliding gait of his, his arms outstretched – it was
as if for the first time I was –
(*The voice trails away, the words too elusive. After a
pause, musing*)
He always used to say himself that I was his other
half, that apart we were nothing. And he was
always such an egotist too, such a child when he
was in his 'Wertherish' moods –

(*She smiles with a warmth that robs it of any malice*)
that I think that in loving me he found something
to love in himself – something to be kind to –
that he did not have to hate. It even pleased his
vanity that I looked like him – my form, my features – lineaments – eyes – hair –
(*Her voice takes on a soft incantatory note*)

' – all to the very tone
Even of her voice, they said were like to mine –

(*There is a pause. Lady Byron stares at her. When Augusta speaks it is to herself*)
'But softened all and tempered into beauty.' And ah!
(*She seems suddenly aware of Lady Byron*)
If ever he needed a friend it was that season when he had the whole of London at his feet! He would always rage against the bitterness and humiliation he had known as a child, but success – success and fame! – I think he found them harder still –
(*She turns to Lady Byron*)
Did he ever tell you of the day that he learned our uncle had died? That the title was his?

(*Lady Byron says nothing*)
A lame boy, without a father, at his grammar school in Aberdeen. He burst into tears when he had to answer to his new name at roll call. Dominus de Byron. He was sent for by the master later, and offered wine and cake –
(*She walks slowly away from the window*)
a lesson in deference he never forgot. Oh I know how conscious he was of rank and position, but it made him despise too what others valued – distrusted whatever it was in himself that the world wanted – despise the fame that was his.
(*There is a silence*)
I don't think any man was lonelier than he was that summer when he could call the world his own.

LADY BYRON   (*With a quiet resentment*)
And do you think you were the only one who could see that?

AUGUSTA   (*In a lighter tone suddenly, seeming not to hear the interruption*)
And I could make him laugh as well.

Dynastic alliances and cultural certainties:
The Milbanke and Melbourne families.

Metamorphosis:
From Annabella Milbanke to
Lady Byron: 'I have seen
her of an evening in the
most amiable, cordial and
sunny humour, full of interest and sympathy, and I have
seen her the next morning
come down as if she had lain
all night not on a feather-
bed, but on a glacier –
frozen as it were to the very
soul . . .'

Augusta Leigh:
'Her eyes,
Her hair, her features, all, to the very tone
Even of her voice, they said were like to mine;
But soften'd all, and temper'd into beauty'.

Newstead:
'Hail to the pile!
  More honour'd in the fall
Than modern mansions in
  their pillar'd state;
Proudly majestic frowns the
  vaulted hall,
Scowling defiance on the
  blasts of fate'.

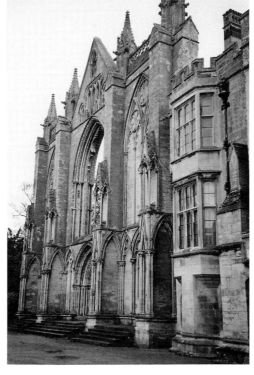

Too dangerous to look at.
The image of Byron that was kept from his daughter
until her marriage.

Manfred on the Jungfrau.
The rawest of all Byron's confessional verse.

Lady Melbourne: 'the best, the kindest
and ablest female I have ever known,
old or young'.

Above Lady Oxford, the
'grande horizontale' of
Whig London. 'She
recalled a landscape
by Claude Lorraine
with a setting sun, her
beauties enhanced by
the knowledge that
they were shedding
their last dying beams.'

Left Lady Caroline
Lamb: 'Correct your
vanity', Byron told her,
'which is ridiculous;
exert your absurd
caprices upon others;
and leave me in peace'.

(She turns with a bright look to Lady Byron, impervious to her cold stare).

No one else could in the way I did. At my ignorance – my nonsense – my 'damn'd crinkumcrankum'. From the day that we met again it was as if we had known each other all our lives. We sometimes used to dream of an imaginary childhood we had shared – make up things that no one but us could know – memories of a father neither of us had known – signs when we wrote – *(The voice trails away, and she turns away from Lady Byron, walks to the fire, staring absent-mindedly into it. When she speaks, her voice is again serious and low)*

I could comfort him too. When he was afraid – of himself – what he might do – who he was. He did really believe that we Byrons were all cursed. Wasn't he himself – wasn't his crooked foot proof of that, proof of his damnation, proof that we belonged to none but our own sort? He would see the whole line in his dreams, standing over him and beckoning, waiting to claim him for their own, their sins loaded on his head, – threatening him –
(She stares into the fire as a log catches and bursts into life)
challenging him. He used to say that he would never marry – that no Byron ever should – that the name should die with us – that only with me could he be safe.
(A pause stretches out into a prolonged silence, each woman locked in her own thoughts. When Augusta finally speaks, almost inaudibly, she is still staring into the fire, her back to Lady Byron)
But even there he knew he wasn't.
(There is a pause. She goes on slowly, picking her way through each sentence)

There above all.

(*She turns away, her eyes still averted*)
I remember the winter – the January of '14 it
would have been – the year before you married –
when we were snowed in at Newstead. I don't
think I have ever been more happy in my life.
The lake frozen. The roads blocked. The world
shut out. No one but the two of us.
(*She turns to look at Lady Byron*)
But even then, though, he lived with its ghosts –
there was no sin that the Byrons had not committed, he'd say, no crime that hadn't taken place
inside those walls, nowhere on earth we could go
to escape our curse –
(*She turns again to look at the picture of Manfred*)
And the misery of it is that it was true too – true
in ways he never even dreamed –

(*She breaks off. When she resumes it seems as though it
is on a different tack*)
As a child I used to have a portrait of my mother
in my room. It was strange, but I don't think I
ever felt anything for her – had never known her
– but I used to love to look at it, and try to see
her as my father had seen her – dream that if I
could grow up to look like her I could somehow
bring him back. But I was wrong – because it was
never her he loved – not his wife – not my mother
– not anyone, I think, but his own sister –

LADY BYRON   Are you mad?

AUGUSTA   (*Ignoring the interruption*)
             Frances. My Aunt. My husband's mother.

LADY BYRON   Dear God, are you all insane?

AUGUSTA   I never knew at the time. Not till much later.
             Never knew how far he was from everything I had
             pictured – everything I had wanted.

(*She walks slowly from the fire, her eyes turned away from Lady Byron*)

We used to visit her sometimes in her old age, and in all those years that she never spoke of him, never mentioned his name even, she had his letters by her – love letters – no, not love letters – fiercer, harsher, more possessive than that – a packet of them, tied in a ribbon, and just waiting for her death for me to see them.

(*She pauses by the bird in the cage*)

And all those times I was with her, and she would sit there, almost motionless, watching, she must have known it. Known that I would see them. Wanted me to have them. Not George. Me. Wanted me to know. Wanted me to know what they had done. That it was in my blood. That there had never been a choice.

LADY BYRON   No choice? –

AUGUSTA   (*Her voice is low*)
And she was right too. Because that first time I saw Byron again, walking across towards me – a stranger and familiar all at once – the figure I had cherished in my imagination all my life – I knew from that moment that there was nothing I would not have done for him.

LADY BYRON   (*Her voice harder than ever*)
Have you no shame?

AUGUSTA   (*She runs a finger across the wires of the cage.*)
It seemed so inevitable, too. That first summer in London he was never away from my side, at the theatre – dance – felt the most natural thing in the world too that a brother and sister should be together, and by the time –
(*She pauses*)

By the time it became more it was too late. When
I tried to leave for Newmarket he followed me.
We were each others' fate, he would say, there
was no escape if we wanted, no way out but
exposure and disgrace. The idea of it tortured
him too, filled him – and
(*There is a baffled incomprehension in her voice*)
this is what I could never understand –
(*Quieter*)
what I still can't – filled him with a sort of reckless
despair – made him loathe himself all the more,
made him hate himself – me – for being what
we were even as he plunged us towards ruin. He
wanted us to leave England together. The East.
Italy. There was nowhere we could have gone,
though,
(*She looks up to the picture of Manfred*)
he could not flee himself. His horror at what he
had done and would do again. I sometimes feared
that winter before your marriage that it would
destroy him, dreaded what he might do – what
would happen if ever –
(*The voice trails away. When she speaks again it is
without emotion, prosaic but firm*)
I would have sacrificed anything to save him.

LADY BYRON   (*With a quiet anger*)
Including me?

AUGUSTA   (*Without rancour*)
Including myself.
(*She moves over to the window*)
I don't think you have ever had any idea what I
gave up for you. You said that all you could see
that day was a white desert –
(*She glances around and then turns back to the cold,
bleak view*)
How do you think I felt that morning of your

marriage? Watching the hand of the clock move towards eleven. Imagining him. You. And poor Charlotte screaming – and screaming. And then suddenly I heard the clock strike and began to shake – tremble – until –
(*She breaks off*)
Do you think it was nothing to let him go? Do you think, too, I couldn't have held him,
(*She turns with the first resentment*)
if I hadn't wanted his safety – his happiness – more than anything else on earth? I had to make myself love you, make myself hope and pray that you could be happy, that he could love you – make myself smile and laugh with him when he said that you would redeem him – that you had goodness enough for the two of you.

LADY BYRON (*Breaking in bitterly*)
Oh yes, I can hear the two of you –

AUGUSTA And can you have forgotten so much – forgotten those months in Piccadilly when there was nothing I would not have done or undone to shield you from him – forgotten how I would argue with him – defy him – plead with him in his drink until you and I became one in his eyes – a single enemy who had trapped him into marriage – betrayed him –

LADY BYRON You can talk of betrayal? Do you know what he told me when we were married, when I had been prised away from everything I loved? –
(*She grips at the chair to steady herself*)
when he had me safely in his power? He told me that he had wagered my own aunt that he could win me over – that he would have my money and my love – have me as mad for him as every other fool-woman in town –

(*She moves swiftly to the window, close to Augusta, her voice a harsh whisper*)

Oh yes, I can hear all of you. I can still hear, when I shut my eyes, the sound of your steps on the stairs with his, the sound of your voices, your laughter. And what was I to you? Cover, was that it? – A screen for the two of you? Never anything more? Not even my money he wanted? Not even his pride I'd hurt?

AUGUSTA   I tried to stop him hurting you.

LADY BYRON   (*Not hearing*)
And you won me over – made me silence every jealousy – made me love you – made me trust you and confide in you. I remember when we first married, pressing him to invite you, even when he insulted me in front of you, even when he gave me every cause to be jealous, longing for you as I would for my own sister if I had ever had one, thinking – praying – that with you, with us it would be all right – smothering my fears – my jealousies – telling myself they were foolish – punishing myself –
(*With a laugh she breaks away from the window, her step and voice agitated, her fingers twisting compulsively on the slip of paper tucked into her sleeve*)

And all those months of his hatred, of his insults and drunkenness, you let me appeal to you, let me write to you, let me ask what it was that I had done. What it was that had come between us. I would write, begging you to help me, begging – begging! – you to intercede for me, and you would smile and weep with me, console me – talk to him for me – and all the time –
(*There is a break in her voice*)
And all the time, all those months I wondered

what I had done –
(*She looks at Augusta as though betrayed*)
My only crime was that I was not you.

AUGUSTA (*Almost inaudibly*)
God knows, I never meant you harm.

LADY BYRON (*With renewed energy*)
What a child I was! Right to the end! When I think
how you let me think him insane, made me think
his taunts and boasts the ravings of a madman!
(*She closes on Augusta*)
So scared were you of what he might say – frightened that he would drag you down with him –
scared that duty and love –

AUGUSTA (*Turning away from her, and looking round the room
slightly distractedly*)
Is that what it was?
(*She moves from the window across to a side table, and
rings a small hand bell. Muttering*)
Come on –
(*She rings the bell again*)
Is that what you gave him? God knows, you wanted
to own him,
(*She rings the bell*)
wanted to possess him – save him –
(*She stops, facing Lady Byron*)
But do you think you know what it is, to love him
– love anyone –
(*She rings again, more agitatedly*)

LADY BYRON (*With a menacing control*)
I have told them that we are not to be disturbed –
(*She turns away from Augusta, as if the sight of her
carries some contagion*)
(*Sotto*)
And how dare you with your criminal passions,
your unnatural lusts, –

(*She rounds on her again with sudden venom*)
How could you know what I went through, those
nine long months that I carried his child, praying
and hoping against hope that it would win him back
to me – protecting him and lying for him – writing
to my parents of our happiness – of his kindness –
bearing up through his insults – silencing my suspicions of you as unworthy of any woman –
(*She breaks off, determined to control herself. When she
speaks again her tone is more prosaic, flat*)

I would have died if it could have made him love
me as I loved him. During those last days before
Ada was born, I would sometimes hear his step pause
outside the door and – God forgive me! – I would
pray that I could die there and then, knowing that
for the moment at least I was in his thoughts.
(*She pauses, reviewing the memory in her own mind.*)
And sometimes I thought if he would just let me
speak to him, or just see me, but he never would.
Not even at the end. Only a note, after Ada's birth.
'Madame', he wrote – I have the words by heart – 'as
I am to leave the country and have no plans to return
pray make arrangements to return with our child to
your parents. My carriage is at your disposal.'
(*She gives a half-laugh*)
My carriage is at your disposal. Can you imagine
what it is to be sent back by your husband,
(*There is an odd detachment in her voice, as if she was
speaking of someone else*)
to be woken by servants in the freezing early
hours, and to crawl with your child out of your
own home, weak and sick in the dark, like a fugi-
tive – and still
(*Her voice breaks as the reality of it intrudes*)

Still love the man who has done it to you? Do you
know that I had to stop myself, as I passed his

room, from lying down on the mat for his dog at his door? Had to stop myself.

(*There is a silence. She stares out of the window, her back to Augusta*)

So do not say, madam, that I did not know what –

AUGUSTA   (*Passionately, ringing the bell again vigorously*)
Then why, why would you not take him back.
(*In her agitation she begins to pace the room again*)

Why when he wanted you – pleaded with you, when he was half-mad with debts and brandy – when he had hardly known what he was doing – why in the name of all that's merciful, if you loved him, would you not forgive him? Why if you loved him did you set out to see him destroyed? Destroyed by the lawyers you set on him. Destroyed by your silence.

LADY BYRON   (*She speaks as if to herself, almost as though she was unaware of Augusta's presence*)
But wasn't that all he ever wanted? All that he was born for? To be destroyed? An outcast? He knew that I could bear with his actresses and his drunkenness, but that wasn't enough for him –
(*She looks at Augusta*)
wasn't enough for him even to have you but he had to fling you in my face until I could blind myself no longer – had to drag you out before his public – His Astarte! – Goddess of Love
(*With a bitter emphasis*)
'of all earthly things that lived, the only thing he seem'd to love'
(*There is a pause while the words echo between them. When she resumes it is with a cold and inflexible sense of righteousness*)
I have never, in all my life, done anything but my duty as I saw it. When I first accepted Byron I swore that I would do all I could to save him from

himself, to rescue what was fine and noble in him
and – and when I left him it was only for a higher
duty –
(*There is stiff primness to the formulation*)
a duty to truth, to my child, to womanhood.

AUGUSTA   (*Quietly*)
Ah, duty?
(*She turns to Lady Byron, her tone wondering in its
disbelief*))
And has anyone ever enjoyed her duty as you
enjoyed yours? I remember when Hobhouse
brought the news –

LADY BYRON   How dare you throw that creature in my face –

AUGUSTA   Remember when it was you he blamed, telling
him that you could never have sanctioned the
whispers – that no wife could ever turn on her
husband like that, but – ah
(*She moves towards Lady Byron, who is still at the
window looking out, and stands close behind her*)
I should have known – should have known that
first time I saw you again in London –
(*Her voice registers her bewilderment at the intensity of
the vision*)
in Mivart's – after the separation – so thin and
pale you seemed more a ghost than flesh and
blood – with nothing left to hold you to anyone
– nothing left of what you had been except the
will to avenge yourself –

LADY BYRON   (*Almost inaudibly*)
And who made me that?

AUGUSTA   (*She turns away*)
I should have seen too just how well you played
your part – the silent wife while your lawyers did
your work for you. Duty?

(*She moves round again to get a better view of Lady Byron's face as she talks*)

How does it feel, Annabella, to enjoy all the pleasures of revenge and call it duty? To watch your husband pilloried and humiliated – severed from his child – branded with every nameless crime and yet remain blameless?

LADY BYRON   (*Without meeting Augusta's look, her voice hard and prim*)

I stood by you when a word could have destroyed you forever.

AUGUSTA   (*Turning away, and moving across the room, until she stands behind the chair. She rings the bell again, but when she speaks her tone is oddly mild*)

Oh yes, you stood by me! And what a price you exacted! I remember how you stood by me during those long months after he had gone abroad, how you bound me to you, held me fast by the fear of your displeasure – the fear of exposure. How you broke me. Made me betray myself. Made me betray him. Oh yes Annabella,

(*She moves away from the chair, pacing the room, her tone more agitated*)

I remember how you stood by me while everyone could say how kind you were to Mrs Leigh, how you used the unspoken threat of the world's hatred – held it over me – wallowed in my penitence, how you enjoyed your duty. Let us save Augusta! Save her from her own weakness. Let us teach her to suffer – remind her every day of what she is. How could I forget how you stood by me or what you made me become? When Byron had no one to turn to, you kept me from him. When he wrote to me you would make me bring his letters to show you. When I answered them you would be there, standing over me, watching, silently guiding and – may God forgive me –

(*She covers her face with her hands*)
when you were sure enough of me – when I had
become what you wanted – you would hand his
letters to me without comment – 'leave me to my
own conscience' – leave me to betray him, certain
that I was too much the coward to resist.
(*There is a pause. She is more collected when she continues*)
Too frightened of the world. And you were right.
I never had his strength. You knew that, knew that
even if he could escape your malice, so long as
you still had me, so long – in the name of duty –
that you could control the one person who wanted
nothing from him – then you could enjoy all the
satisfaction of virtuous revenge.
(*She looks round, all energy exhausted. Her tone is prosaic*)
I have put my gloves somewhere.

LADY BYRON   (*Without looking around. Her voice equally flat*)
You have never understood me, have you?

AUGUSTA   (*She moves over to a table, and picks up her gloves.
There is a sense almost of release in her reply*)
Oh yes, I understand you, Annabella, understand
you at last. I know now, too, why you wanted me
here. You were afraid weren't you, afraid that after
all these years that I was no longer yours – afraid
that I might have slipped beyond the reach of
your 'kindness' –

LADY BYRON   (*Her voice hard with resentment*)
Still the same!

AUGUSTA   (*In control*)
No, not quite. I have never had the strength to
resist you, but I see now that I have always had
something you could never touch – that nothing

you could do or make me do – could threaten – something through these weary years to place me beyond even your resentment – that love, Annabella, that you demanded of him and was always mine.

LADY BYRON   (*Her voice frigid with anger*)
And you believe that, do you?
(*Moving swiftly to the table, and fumbling for a letter among her papers. With a bitter laugh*)
Believe you can defy every decency and imagine there is no reckoning? – Are you so bereft of sense or shame – so much the moral idiot to believe the world will just forget what you are? That your own family will forget?
(*Fumbles at the letter, she begins to read, rapidly, triumphantly*)
'My Dearest Pip' – And you know that's what he called me – I taught her to call me it too – Pip, her dearest Pip – 'I have this instant met my Mother. She was crossing the square' –
(*She looks up*)
and did you know your child was watching you? see – see –
(*She moves to Augusta, brandishing the letter in her face*)
do you recognise the hand, your daughter's – see what she says of you, of her own mother

AUGUSTA   Stop it!

LADY BYRON   (*Reading on over her*)
'She was crossing the square coming from York Street as the carriage drove up to the door. I instantly recognised her – she is unchanged in face ... Her large eyes are ever & indeed unchanged – she shuffles along as if she tried to carry the ground she walks on with her & looks WICKED.'

AUGUSTA   Stop it!

LADY BYRON   (*Continues reading, inexorably*)
'Oh, were there a thing I had hoped to be spared
it was this ... This has shocked me, pained me,
but it is over. I have drunk quantities of wine
since, & now there is nothing left for me to suffer
that I dread. Oh how dearly fondly I loved her,
and had she only stifled the existence her sin gave
me'

AUGUSTA   (*Her voice a cry of pain as she collapses back into the
chair*)
Stop it, stop it!
(*Broken*)
Stop it –

LADY BYRON   (*Her voice hard with triumph as she reads on*)
'– but God is there & I will do my best to bear as
I have ever done – God forgive her. Oh how horrible she looked – so wicked – so hyena-like. That
I could have loved her so! Bear in mind one feeling the sight of her has given me yet more strongly
– for my good – intimidate her – she will grovel
on the ground, fawn, lick the dust – all – all that
is despicable and bad.'
(*As she is reading, the door behind her opens, and
Robertson appears, stands there aghast as he hears these
last words. Without being aware of him Lady Byron,
lowers the letter and looks down in victory on the sobbing
figure of Augusta. She speaks with a slow emphasis*)
'All that is despicable and bad.' Even my own
daughter was called after you, the child I bore
Byron in misery and hope, called after his sister
– Augusta Ada. Well.

(*It is pronounced like a sentence*)
A child for a child, Augusta, a daughter for a
daughter –

ROBERTSON   (*Moving quickly forward towards the weeping figure of
                   Augusta, and speaking with scarcely restrained anger*)
                   Lady Byron, for pity's sake!

LADY BYRON   (*Turns and for a moment holds Robertson's gaze before
                   she continues, ignoring him*)
                   Did you think you could be allowed to keep the
                   child, Augusta –

ROBERTSON   (*Bending over Augusta, stretching for the water glass
                   as he props her up*)
                   For God's sake, Lady Byron, can't you see what
                   you are doing – can't you –
                   (*He looks around for the bell*)
                   And where in Heaven's name are the servants in
                   this place! –
                   (*He calls out loudly*)
                   Boy!

LADY BYRON   (*Turning away from them, and speaking with cold cer-
                   tainty*)
                   I don't think Mrs Leigh would thank you for
                   bringing the servants here.

ROBERTSON   (*Continuing to fuss over Augusta*)
                   Can't you see the poor creature is ill?

AUGUSTA   (*Trying to get up*)
                   Please. You're very kind, but if you could just ask
                   them to fetch a fly –

ROBERTSON   You are in no fit state to travel –

LADY BYRON   (*Remorseless*)
                   No fit state to exist. Did you imagine, Augusta,
                   she could be allowed to grow up ignorant of what
                   you are? Not know what you had done to her?
                   And who all these years did you think it was who
                   told her, Augusta, saved her from you? Who told
                   Medora who she was? What she was. The child of
                   incest. Byron's ape.

II

(*Augusta stands at the window looking out, her back to the seated Lady Byron. When she speaks it is quietly, baffled*)

AUGUSTA   You cannot bear anyone to show me kindness, can you? No one – except you.

LADY BYRON   (*Grimly*)
Why should I watch while another man falls for your wiles.

AUGUSTA   Nobody. Not even my daughter. Why did you have to tell her?
(*There is no answer. Lady Byron watches her back with a cold and still concentration. After a moment Augusta turns, searching the other woman's face for an answer to her unanswered question.*)
Wasn't Byron enough? Wasn't it enough to take him from me, that you had to take Medora too, make her hate her own mother –

LADY BYRON   (*Bitterly breaking in*)
And she should love you, I suppose?

AUGUSTA   (*She seems scarcely aware to whom she is speaking, her eyes no longer on Lady Byron, her whole being caught up in the memories.*)
All these years and I never dreamed that it could have been you –
(*Almost to herself*)
that any woman with a child of her own – anyone who had ever once loved Byron could do that – take from her –

LADY BYRON   (*Sullenly*)
Take what from her? A mother who abandoned her to sin – a father whose vices coursed through her veins?

AUGUSTA   Take from her the only thing the poor creature had left to her – the memory of her childhood happiness.
(*She turns from the window, walks slowly to the table, picks up the letter that lies on it*)
And turn her into that. She was so beautiful too. So alive. Do you remember her, then – remember how like him she was – not –
(*She breaks off with an involuntary smile*)
Not so much in her face, but the way she carried her head, the sudden petulance – the charm –
(*Her voice trails away as she is absorbed by one memory. When she speaks again it is slowly, abstracted*)
I don't think I ever knew how much it meant to have her with me until that week they brought his poor body home. Do you know sometimes at night I walk my rooms at Flag Court, and I can still see Hobhouse when he brought the news that the Florida had docked, standing there in the open door, the tears running down his face – and I remember – I could take in nothing that he was telling me – but I remember him saying that he'd thought he had no more grief left in him until he saw Byron's dogs playing on the deck. He'd sat on his coffin, and Lion had settled at his feet. Only then he knew what it meant to lose him. He couldn't bring himself to look at the corpse, he said, but he came with me to George Street, and –

(*Each sentence is like a studied act of memory*)
I have never seen such crowds. The length of the street. They had hung the room in black. And there was a hatchment daubed with our arms. And the coffin lay on a bier – with candles – and a wreath – quite withered – and his face – his poor, battered face –

(*She turns to Lady Byron who looks suddenly older, shrunken, cut off from memories in which she can have no part*)

but you never saw him, did you? It was so cold, Annabella – inanimate – so altered – the hair gone white – I could hardly believe it was him.

(*She turns her gaze from Lady Byron*)

I don't even know what I'd thought I should see. The Byron I'd parted from eight years before, I suppose. But he was gone. Dead. And I'd done my bit, along with all the rest of you, to kill him. That's what I couldn't bear. What I still can't bear.

(*She goes back to the window and stares out. Her voice low*)

I thought that week would never end. The day of the funeral, I remember sitting in the dark – the shutters drawn – hardly able to breathe – listening as the Abbey bell drifted across to St James's – waiting for each toll – following the cortege in my mind – measuring with every peal the distance they were taking him from me when I heard the child's laughter – from another room I heard it, and it was him, it was Byron, Annabella, and I knew then I had not lost him, knew they could not take him away from me so long as I had her –

LADY BYRON   And was I to live on nothing?

AUGUSTA   (*Ignoring her*)
She can have been no more than ten, but she was so different from her sisters too,

(*She turns and moves across the room, animated by the memory*)

so much quicker, more alert than they had ever been. Even when she was scarcely more than a baby, she could make them do whatever she wanted, would have them running after her – ready to do whatever she demanded. I used to

fear sometimes that poor Georgey would grow to resent her, but I don't think she ever did –
(*Her voice is quiet, ruminative*)
Feared her maybe – wary of her as something she could not understand – or resist – but was as much under her spell as I was myself.

LADY BYRON (*Her voice quiet too, anger dissolved in the shared memory*)
And do you think I was not? – Do you think I could look at her and not see him? Hear her and not hear him – do you think I couldn't feel his coils tighten round me with every look that child gave me?

(*She crosses the room, and begins mechanically shifting papers around on the table*)
I can still see, too, the first time that I ever saw him with her. Only weeks after our marriage. I remember him taking her up on his knee, and the expression on his face – a look I'd never seen there before – and I remember telling him that I'd like to have him painted with just such an expression as he had at that moment –
(*There is a slight pause before she goes on again*)
Do you know I prayed that when Ada was born she might bring him back to me. But he could never have loved her, because she was too like me to love, too like me –
(*She gives a cold, humourless laugh*)
even for me to love.
(*She turns from the table, her voice weary*)
He'd hoped she would be born dead, you know. He'd come into my room during those last weeks, and stand by the bed, brandy on his breath, staring down at me. 'It's already dead', he would say. 'And if you could die with it then –

AUGUSTA Dear God, can you think he meant half of what he said – even knew what he was saying –

LADY BYRON   (*On her own single-minded track*)
He was ready enough to use her against me if he
could – exploit her – but I don't think he could
ever see anything else in her but me. I remember
only days after she was born, resting with the door
half open, and hearing him speaking to Mrs Clermont. He was looking at the child. 'Let me see
its legs,' he said. And then – I can hear the bitterness in his voice – 'What a sweet temper it will
have. There is no Byron there.'

AUGUSTA   (*Almost with pity*)
How can you have known him so little – or your
own daughter?

LADY BYRON   And the misery of it is, that he was right too. When
she was still a child crowds would gather outside
hotels if the word got out, fighting to catch a
glimpse of Byron's daughter as if she were some
fair-ground show– and I used to look at her – such
a plain thing – and wonder what they hoped to
see in her – compare her to Medora and . . . But
what a fool I was! – ever to have wondered why
she seemed so much more a Byron than his own
daughter did, why – God help me! – I found
myself drawn to her in a way I wasn't to my own
child,
(*There is a slight pause as she brings herself under
control. She takes a long slow breath*)
Drawn to her as I had been to you.

AUGUSTA   (*Quietly, to herself, as she stands looking intently up at
the Manfred picture*)
Ah, but if you'd had to watch her grow up, too –
watch her as I had to. You can't imagine what it
is to love and fear your child at the same time, to
hope and dread that others will see in her what
you can see – to watch as every day she becomes

more and more like him – more reckless and wayward – more demanding – more wilful – to hold
your breath and wait for it to start all over again
– the rumours – the scandal –
(*She breaks away from the picture, and walks across to
the caged bird, putting a finger through the bars*)
That was why I was so relieved when her sister
could get away – so – so grateful almost to Trevanion when he asked for Georgey's hand. The
poor child had always been so much under Medora's shadow at home, was so timid – so –
(*She glances round at Lady Byron*)
so like me at her age, that I hoped at last that she
could grow –

LADY BYRON   Then why in Heavens let the child live with them?

AUGUSTA   (*Turning back to the bird. Wearily*)
Let her? Whenever did anyone say no to Medora?
Even at fourteen. You know as well as I how she
could make us all do what she wanted, but
Georgey –
(*She again puts a finger through the bars*)
Poor, soft Georgiana was wax in her hands.
(*For a moment she seems more engaged with the bird
than Lady Byron*)
It was Georgey, you know, who wrote begging that
she should live with them.

LADY BYRON   I don't believe you.

AUGUSTA   (*Still intent on the bird*)
Which only shows how little you ever understood
of Georgey – of what a child she was still – even
at seventeen – so clinging – so afraid of leaving
behind everything she knew –
(*She glances around*)
And God knows there was little enough joy for
her at home but at least there –

(*She turns back to the bird with a sigh*)
At least in her family there was no more to fear
than her father's temper. I think perhaps that was
what attracted her to Trevanion, too, the fact that
he was her cousin, someone she could almost
believe she had known all her life.
(*She moves away from the bird, pausing in front of one
of the sporting prints*)

And then I remember the morning of her marriage – the poor child's face – the look on it when
she realised that Leigh was not even there – I
don't think she had ever really loved him – she'd
always been too afraid of him for that – but I don't
think until that moment – until she saw that she
had no one with her but Medora and me – did
she realise the step she was taking –

LADY BYRON (*Menacingly*)
Ah, but you knew well enough –

AUGUSTA (*Ignoring her*)
I think after the marriage, too, it only made it
worse when you lent them Bifrons. We had all
hoped his father could find them something
closer, but alone with him in that great barrack –
(*She looks round at Lady Byron*)
Without even the face of a maid she could recognise – with no one to speak with – no one to turn
to – no one at all from morning till night except
a man she was only just learning to know –

LADY BYRON And who had kept her ignorant –

AUGUSTA (*She turns back to the print*)
I think I was even glad, too, when she wrote to
ask for Medora. Glad for both of them by that
time. Because you can't think what it became
those months after Georgey was gone –

LADY BYRON   I don't recall that I was ever allowed to forget.

AUGUSTA   (*Wearily*)
Ah, you won't understand, will you – won't ever
hear what you don't want to. Now any more than
then. How hopeless it was. How completely hopeless. And lonely.

LADY BYRON   You had a husband, didn't you?

AUGUSTA   (*With a slight laugh and an ironic gesture towards the
print*)
Ah yes, I had a husband! For the first time in my life
I had a husband! Do you know that I hardly ever
saw him when he could afford to be anywhere else,
but one of the great blessings of poverty was that I
found that after all I did have a husband – a husband who never left his rooms except to rage at me
for defying him over Georgey – a husband to blame
me for everything that had gone wrong for him, for
every horse that had ever gone lame, every jockey
who had cheated him, for every imagined slight,
every sound the children made – Oh yes,
(*Her tone is more ironic than bitter*)
I had a husband.

LADY BYRON   Which was more than you ever left to me.

AUGUSTA   (*As if she had not heard. Her voice softer*)
Not that I could ever blame him for being what
he was. Then or now. Byron could never understand how I had ever borne with such a helpless
creature, but he was not a bad man – just –
(*She looks at Lady Byron*)
just never made to be poor – to hold up under
the debts – the failures – the indignities – the
rejections at court –
(*She breaks off*)
until the only revenge on life left to him was to

take it out on me – turn my sons against me –
cut Georgey off from me – terrorise even poor,
helpless Charlotte into her fits and tantrums until
I could no longer even hold on to her –
(*She pauses at the window, lost in her own thought,
tracing a rivulet of rain with her finger across the glass
pane.*)
And that was the only time, I think, that I ever
grew close to hating him. Charlotte was so
defenceless. So easily hurt. Even as a little child
she could never bear to see anything in pain, and
he knew that – and would rage at me in front of
her until she could stand it no longer – would
throw herself on the ground – harm herself –
scratch at her face – tear at her hair
(*She turns back to Lady Byron*)

Oh yes, I was glad to have Medora escape. If it
had not been for Emily I think I would have done
so myself. If I could have ever found the strength.
But there were times –
(*She turns away, her voice weary*)
times I thought I should lose my mind. Times I
think when I did –

LADY BYRON And is that all you can think of? What it did to
you?

AUGUSTA (*Her voice leaden*)
It's all I can bear to think of. But do you imagine
there's a thing you can say that I haven't said to
myself, a day that's passed when I haven't gone
over it again in my mind – wondered what I could
have done – what if I'd only known –

LADY BYRON And how could you alone have not known –

AUGUSTA (*Bitterly*)
Ah, but I never had your spies, did I? – nor even

the friends who might have helped – you had
made only too sure of that –

(*The bitterness goes*)

And Georgey would never have breathed a word
of it to me. Would have sooner died. I don't think
her sister had been with them a month, though,
when she discovered it was Medora he had
wanted, but by that time Georgey was so – I've
never understood what it was – not quite fear but
something worse –

(*She struggles to make sense of it*)

so completely in his power – so completely under
the influence of the two of them – that she would
have done anything they wanted – borne any
humiliation – said anything – hidden anything –

LADY BYRON (*Moves menacingly forward*)

Only what was there for the wretched child to
hide from you? What could she have told you that
you had not always known? Hadn't planned?

(*She closes on Augusta, standing behind her*)

And to think how I once pitied you for what Byron
had brought you to, made excuses for your weakness, blamed him when –

(*She moves around so she can see Augusta's face, only
inches from her own*)

when there's never been anything you won't do
– when there is no one who is safe – not your
brother – not even your daughter's husband –

AUGUSTA Good God! What are you saying?

LADY BYRON (*Her voice filled with hatred*)

When you'd sacrifice your own children to your
lusts – as you once sacrificed me.

(*She turns away in disgust, pacing the room, her hands
clenching and unclenching*)

And to think I was weak enough to give you the money for Georgey to marry him! – fool enough to be your dupe a second time –
(*She whips round on Augusta*)
And what did you have to promise Trevanion – a wretch half your age – what did you have to give him to have him for yourself? Was it just Georgey or was it both daughters from the start?

AUGUSTA   (*Crumpling into a chair. Almost inaudible*)
How could even you –

LADY BYRON   (*An unbalanced edge to her voice*)
I should have known that there was no depravity to which you wouldn't sink – nothing you wouldn't do to cling on to what you wanted. Do you think all those years ago, I didn't see the way you'd let Byron look at Georgey –

AUGUSTA   (*In horror*)
Are you mad?

LADY BYRON   (*To herself*)
As if he couldn't wait to corrupt his niece as he corrupted everything he touched.
(*She stops in front of Augusta and stares down at her.*)
It's in your blood, isn't it? Your whole serpent race. Byrons. Trevanions.
(*She leans down, her hands resting on the arms of the chair, her voice low*)
How could I have thought that you could ever change? And did you imagine I didn't know? Do you think Trevanion didn't boast of it? Of his hold over you? Do you imagine, too, that I have not seen your letters? Love letters to your daughter's husband?

AUGUSTA   (*Pushing her way out of the chair. Fiercely*)
No, no!

LADY BYRON   Promising him your love – whatever he did to
             Medora –

AUGUSTA   (*More pitifully*)
             No. Yes, no, no – I loved him – but loved him as
             a son –

LADY BYRON   Yes, as you had loved Byron as a brother –
             (*Continuing to pace the room*)
             and just as you once gave Byron your blessing to
             have me, you stood by and watched Trevanion
             seduce your child – his wife's own sister – stood by in
             silence while she was smuggled out of the country –
             a fifteen-year-old girl in a foreign country –

AUGUSTA   No!

LADY BYRON   Hid his crimes from the world – rid yourselves of
             the baby – lied to your husband for him – prosti-
             tuted your own daughters

AUGUSTA   (*Almost unable to speak*)
             No, no – how in Heaven can you think I ever
             knew – ever knew any of it – ever guessed what I
             was sending them to – what kind of man Trev-
             anion was?

LADY BYRON   Your husband did.

AUGUSTA   (*With sudden anger*)
             Oh no, no he didn't. Oh he was against the mar-
             riage true enough, but don't think that was for
             any reason but money – if Trevanion had only
             been rich enough –
             (*There is bitterness in her voice*)
             Colonel Leigh would willingly have given him all
             his daughters.

LADY BYRON   And were you any different? Wasn't it to be Emily
             next – as soon as she was old enough? Isn't that
             what you promised him?

AUGUSTA   (*Exhausted, her voice and movement sluggish as she turns away*)
What can I say now if you can believe that of me?

LADY BYRON   And what else should I believe?

AUGUSTA   (*Beyond caring if she is believed or not*)
Believe? Oh, you'll believe what you want. You always have. But if you had ever known Trevanion, listened to him, seen him –
(*She glances round*)
and there was a time when you were not so immune to the Byron charm –
(*She looks round again, staring into the fire*)
and he was like him too – or so, at least, I thought then. When he first appeared. When, God knows, I needed someone's kindness. Someone who wouldn't look at me as if I were a pariah. I was already learning to live, too, with the knowledge that my own sons were going the way of their father –
(*She picks up a poker and prods weakly at the fire, as if physically punctuating the words*)
arrogant – thoughtless –
(*She turns to look at Lady Byron*)

and Trevanion had seemed so much the son I had wanted, that when he at last confessed about Medora – begged my help – then – yes –
(*Her tone suddenly bitter, challenging*)
But whom would you have blamed, Annabella, with all you know – all you believe? A man who could appear everything a mother could have hoped for – or a 'child of sin' – a Byron 'Ape'?
(*She breaks off and turns back to the fire, jabbing feebly at it. The bitterness has gone when she continues*)
And even then I had no idea what he was doing to those girls. It was not only Georgey, either, who

was too frightened to breathe a word against him. I could never have dreamed that anything could cow Medora, but by the time she found out what he was like – discovered that she could not master him as she had everyone else in her life – she was too far under his control to escape even when she had the chance.

LADY BYRON   (*With a slow, righteous anger*)
And yet you let her back to him. Even when you knew she was carrying his child again – encouraged them to elope –

AUGUSTA   (*Dully*)
And what else was there to be done? Do you think I could have stopped Leigh killing him had he found out – and God knows he hated him enough to do it! – hated him as he'd hated Byron – as he hated anything he couldn't understand –

LADY BYRON   And after what they had done to him, he should have embraced them both I suppose?

AUGUSTA   (*Ignoring her. Obstinate*)
I did what I had to

LADY BYRON   Oh yes, you did that – you did that well enough,
(*She moves towards her*)
Even as far as trying to force her to destroy the thing –

AUGUSTA   (*Her voice flat*)
Is that what she told you?

LADY BYRON   And I'm to suppose she was lying –

AUGUSTA   (*Quietly, without rancour*)
When did you ever hear Medora do anything else?
(*She turns away from Lady Byron, walks to the table, picks up one of the letters, and drops it without looking at it*)

(*Almost to herself*)

When did anybody? I don't think the poor creature could even help it. She had been so open
when she was a child, too –

LADY BYRON　She was a child!

AUGUSTA　But once Trevanion had got hold of her, twisted
her – I think she would have said anything he told
her and believed it –
(*She breaks off*)
Even after she had ruined herself for him she
found out that he no more loved her – not for
herself – than he had done Georgey –.
(*She moves over to the window, and stares out into the
rain*)
Or any of us. I remember when he first came up
from Caerhays, the passion with which he would
always talk of Byron,
(*She glances around*)
and he was the only one, you know – the only one
from our whole family – to have been there at his
funeral –
(*She turns back to the rain*)
But it was something more than passion – more
than loyalty – more as if he wanted to possess him
– to possess everything that had ever been his –
sister – niece – child – and – above all – the thing
that only that child could give him.
(*She moves away from the window*)
I don't think I have ever seen a man take anything
so hard as when her infant died. I don't think he
ever gave a thought to poor Georgey's children,
but it was as though he could not let go of Medora
until she had given him the living child he craved
– until he had linked his blood with Byron's own
– possessed him in her and her child –

LADY BYRON   And when she'd served her use – did you think
of her then? – when he'd ruined and abandoned
her – barely more than a child herself still – eaten
by a shame that should have been yours –

AUGUSTA   (*Her voice scarcely audible*)
Can you have so little mercy?

LADY BYRON   (*The words are almost hissed*)
And did you have mercy on her?
(*She seizes Augusta's wrist, forcing her to look at her*)
You talk of her lies. Did you ever confess what she
owed to you – warn her of what she was – a creature doomed to madness from her birth, polluted
by the blood that ran in her veins, corrupted by
her mother's and father's sin?
(*She drops her wrist in disgust and moves away, turning
again from the other end of the room her voice clear and
hard*)
And do you ever wonder what state I found her
in – when I learned of it and tracked her down
to her French garret – brought her home with
her infant child,

AUGUSTA   Stop it.

LADY BYRON   Do you ever hear in your dreams her racking
cough, and see the blood on her pillow? – Do
you ever see her so thin and worn that her own
relations could not recognise her? So beside herself with misery that she scarce even knew herself?

AUGUSTA   (*Almost unable to breathe*)
Stop it, stop it!
(*Then with a sudden burst of energy, her question half
a challenge, half plea*)
And what could I have done? Do you think there
was no one else? Who do you think had to look after
Georgey, and her children? Who had to scrape

together every penny to support them? Her husband? Her father? His family? Do you think, too, I
didn't send her what I could – to keep her alive –
to keep her safe – for her sake to keep her away –

LADY BYRON   (*With contempt*)
For her sake, was it? – her disgrace you feared,
(*She closes on Augusta again, her tone insidious*)
Or your own Augusta? Did you hear the whispers
starting once more? The world closing in on you,
only now without me to stand between you and
its hate –

AUGUSTA   (*Weary*)
And what, anyway, could I do
(*More heavily still*) –
What had I ever been able to do? Do you think
that Medora would have listened to anything I
said? – Do you think that if she did not care what
happened to herself – to her sister – to her family
– do you think I could have said or done anything
to reach her? There was nothing –
(*Her voice quavering*)
Nothing I could do – no way I could see – nothing
ahead but ruin if any of it should come out – ruin
if she ever came back to England –
(*She suddenly breaks down, each word punctuated by
sobs*)
the ruin I had dreaded every day for twenty years.

LADY BYRON   (*As Augusta is convulsed with sobs, Lady Byron watches
her, rigid and implacable*)
Ever the coward.
(*There is no answer*)
Afraid, as always, for yourself.

AUGUSTA   (*Quieter now, wiping at her eyes, her voice low and dull,
she walks to the window where she stands, her back to
Lady Byron.*)

What would you know of fear? You don't know what it is to walk into a room and be cut on all sides – to have friends turn from you – to hear the whispers behind your back – to feel the rumours spreading – have your letters returned unopened – your gifts for a child's birthday sent back unwanted –

(*She stops and turns to face her*)

Oh yes, I was afraid, afraid of the world, of you all. Afraid for myself. Afraid for Medora. Afraid that you would tear her apart as you did Byron –

LADY BYRON (*A break in her voice*)

I would have loved her if she had let me, saved her –.

AUGUSTA (*Wearily*)

As you had tried to save him, to break and control him and only made him hate you? Did you think that when you saw him in her, that it would be any easier to tame her? Did you imagine she would end by hating you less? You could turn her against her mother, as you once turned me from him, but when she had rounded on her own kind, Annabella – when you had taught her to hate her very self, did you think that she would love you for it? –

LADY BYRON (*Coldly*)

It was not her love I asked for.

AUGUSTA No, only her submission.

LADY BYRON (*Self-justifying*)

And was that so wrong?

(*She gains in power as she speaks*)

So criminal to want to save her from herself? When I found her she was on the point of death, but I dragged her back from illness and despair –

watched over her as she strengthened – watched the
colour come back into her pinched face – watched
the life come back into her eyes – taught her to know
herself, to fear and hate that sickness that was at the
core of her being – like a disease of the blood – the
blight and curse of her birth. I prayed then when I
found her and brought her back to England –
(*There is an evangelical fervour to her*)
united her as a sister with my own child, – spared
you adding the guilt of her death to that of her
birth – I prayed that God would give me the
strength to watch over her, uproot the evil that
was in her being – to triumph –
(*The evangelical fervour dies away, her voice quiet*)
to triumph where I had failed her father.
(*She moves across to the Manfred, and stares up at it*)
And oh, she was beautiful like him too. When she
was strong enough she had her likeness taken for
me – had it inscribed to her 'Dearest Pip'. She
asked me if she might call me 'Mama', told me
she had no one else to love but me –
(*Her voice is unsteady*)
And – do you know – I let her – let her call me
Pip as he had done – let her nurse me when I was
ill – believed her – believed her as I believed that
he could love me – believed once that you might –
(*Her voice is scarcely audible*)
Believed that so much grace and beauty could not
be bad.
(*She pauses. When she continues her voice has a harder,
ironic edge.*)
What a slow learner I have been! Do you know
that as a girl when I first saw Byron –

(*She checks herself*)
No, no before that, before ever I had seen him
even, I could not believe – could not believe of

the man who could have written such things as
he had done –
(*She looks across at Augusta as if the sight of her is still
baffling*)
that the beauty and the sin were not separable –
could not see that with you all they are one – your
evil only the more dangerous and insidious for its
beauty, more sickening in its hypocrisy – the same
hypocrisy that was your child's birthright.
(*She breaks off, and paces the room nervously. She stops
at the table and picks up a paper and puts it down
without looking at it. Her voice is querulous, bitter.*)

There was nothing I would not have done for that
child. I had never been able to reach Ada, but
with Medora I prayed –
(*She falters*)
I gave her everything she could want. I gave her
my roof to live under. I showed her goodness and
she chose sin, gave her freedom and she chose
servitude – lied to me – traduced me – took and
took and took from me and then went back to
the life of vice from which I had saved her.
(*She controls herself, the dominant note sadness*)
Gave her my love –
(*She looks across at Augusta*)
as I once gave it to you, to have it thrown back in
my face.
(*Softly, musing, looking at the ring on her hand*)
Dear God, when I think what a dupe I have been!
I often tell Robertson that I will have my own
signet made, with a gull upon it – a gull impaled
upon the Byron arms. – Crede Byron – believe in
Byron!
(*Incredulously*)
My God how I have paid for doing that!
(*She looks at Augusta*)

How the three of you have made me pay for loving you.

AUGUSTA   (*Quietly*)
And haven't we paid too?
(*Lady Byron turns away without answering*)
Haven't we suffered enough to satisfy even you?

LADY BYRON   (*Her back to Augusta, her voice low but clear*)
Do you think any of you can suffer enough for what you have done? For what you have made me become?

AUGUSTA   (*With a soft surprise*)
Ah, how you do hate us!

LADY BYRON   (*Her back to Augusta still, her tone detached*)
Do you know those were my mother's words, after I fled Byron – How Augusta must hate you, she warned me, how she must hate you for everything you are!

AUGUSTA   (*A tired recognition in her voice, as she stands at the table, a hand on Lady Byron's open travelling case*)
Hate you?
(*She half pulls a letter out from the case and drops it back*)
Hate you, Annabella, when all these years now I have belonged to you? When I have never entered a room without wondering who you had shared your secrets with –
(*She draws out another letter and looks at the envelope*)
When everything I have ever said or done – every letter I have ever written – every friend I have had is here – neatly filed away – ready to be used – ready to be held over me should I ever try to escape you.
(*She puts the letter carefully back in its place, closes the lid, and looks vaguely around the room for something, as if about to leave*)

Hate you? How could I ever hate you, Annabella,
when everything I am and have is yours to dispose
of as you like – my name – reputation –
(*Her voice drops*)
Even my child.

LADY BYRON (*Turns away in disgust*)
Your child! Ah! She's that again now, is she – now
she's past harming you – now you think yourself
safe again –

AUGUSTA (*Her hand stretches out to a chair for support, her eyes
on Lady Byron's back, her voice almost inaudible*)
What?

LADY BYRON (*Contemptuously*)
Your child! And ah, how she loathed you! If you
could only have heard her – if you could have
seen her face at the mention of your name! Do
you know she told me how she used to pick flowers
for you, how every year she'd search until she'd
found your favourite violets for your birthday –
and that how after everything you'd done to her
– how every extra year of your life sickened her –
how the mere thought of you out there, shuffling
on with your secrets – growing older – wickeder
– more ugly by the day filled her with horror! –
Horror. And fear.
(*She swings round on Augusta*)
Your child! When you had no place for her when
she was alive – when you had kept the money that
was hers from her – when you'd abandoned her
to her lovers – with no one but her own daughter –
(*There is an edge of hysteria in her voice*)
And what would Byron have made of her, do you
think, his Medora's bastard a nun – his prayers
for the extinction of your serpent race answered
within the walls of a French convent –

AUGUSTA   (*Her eyes on Lady Byron, but hearing nothing, her voice soft*)
Medora. Dear God –

LADY BYRON   (*Savagely picking up on the last word*)
God? Do you think God will hear you – think you can ever undo what you have done

AUGUSTA   Medora.

LADY BYRON   (*Remorseless*)
And do you think you can wash away your crimes with your tears now? When she died cursing you – cursing you for everything you'd done to her?

AUGUSTA   (*Looks at her, the tears flowing down her face, the voice mild*)
Tears? No, no tears – none that is
(*She shuts her eyes in a half-smile of release, her hand closing over a small closed locket at her throat*)
None but relief – gratitude – that it's at last over – because, because you see Annabella
(*She looks at her with a slow shake of the head*)
I didn't know – didn't know she was gone

LADY BYRON   (*She is stopped in her tracks, an old woman suddenly, her voice shrivelled with horror*)
What?

AUGUSTA   (*She moves to the window, and as she stands there looking out, the sun comes out bathing her in light.*)
Didn't know she was beyond your reach at last –

LADY BYRON   (*Slumping heavily into a chair, her voice small*)
Dear God.

AUGUSTA   Safe from you all.
(*She opens the locket at her neck, looks down at a double miniature, addresses it with a note almost of surprise in her voice*)
But dead? Is it possible, child – and I not know?

LADY BYRON (*Collapsed in the chair, in the shadow that cuts the room into two, her face hidden in her hands, her body shaking with the attempt to control herself*)
Didn't know? Didn't know? Dear God, what have I become – what have I done –

AUGUSTA (*To herself*)
Together, and without me?

LADY BYRON What have I become.

AUGUSTA (*Still looking at the miniature, oblivious to Lady Byron's presence*)
I remember when they wrote from the asylum, to say that poor Charlotte had died. The release. The thankfulness that she was out of pain. That nothing could touch her again. Touch any of you now –

LADY BYRON What have I done –

AUGUSTA (*She glances round, as if only just aware of her, her voice strangely serene*)
Done? God knows how often over the years I've wondered if you would ever ask yourself that, whether you'd ever understand what it might feel like to have your child taken from you – not even to know where she was – to weep over letters and have nowhere to send them – to glimpse the back of a stranger turning a corner and wonder if she is your daughter – to know that changed and bruised beyond all recognition she is out there still – somewhere –
(*She looks across at Lady Byron, Augusta outlined against the bright sunlight*)
Do you know last night I couldn't sleep, and I got up, and went into the room she had when she was a child – and I looked at her bed – and her things still there – her ribbons – a drawing she had done for me – and I could hardly bring myself

to think of her – to think what you would know
of her – what you would tell me – but now, now –
(*She snaps the locket shut*)
Now you have given her back to me – given them
both back.
(*She moves from the window towards the table, and
picks up her gloves as a cloud covers the sun, darkening
the room*)

LADY BYRON   (*Without looking up*)
How could I have known?

AUGUSTA   (*Putting her gloves on, her voice calm and low*)
Known? No. When did the child die?

LADY BYRON   (*Low*)
The winter.

AUGUSTA   (*After a pause*)
In pain?

LADY BYRON   (*Her face still turned away*)
How could I have known you had not been told –

AUGUSTA   (*She moves towards the door, and pauses, speaking without looking back*)
And was there any word?

LADY BYRON   (*Pulls herself to her feet, and walks slowly towards the
other end of the room, beneath the Manfred print. Her
voice is leaden*)
No. Only – only that she forgave those that had
harmed her.

AUGUSTA   (*Her voice unnaturally quiet*)
Ah!
(*She pulls on her second glove.*)
Mr Robertson will have my fly.

LADY BYRON   (*Without looking round*)
All I have ever wanted of you – of any of you –
all I still want –

AUGUSTA   (*Quiet but unbending*)
I will be late for my train.
(*She half opens the door, and pauses, looking across the room without rancour or feeling*).
There was a moment even today when I might still have been yours, but no more. When I think of all these years I have struggled to appease your hatred, afraid of you – afraid of my own weakness – afraid that one day I would have to face Byron with the knowledge that I had let you take that child from me –
(*She lets the door half-close again*)
But not now, not when you can no longer touch her – no longer avenge yourself on him through either of us –
(*She stares intently at Lady Byron, as if to fix her face in her memory for one last time*)
Because you were right, Annabella – you did not need to say anything, but I could see it in your look when I walked in – I am dying. It's over between us. Over. We will not meet again.

LADY BYRON   (*Her tone flat and dull*)
We will not meet again. Those were his last words to me, too. 'We will not meet again,' he wrote, 'in this world –

(*She pauses for effect*)
or the next.'

AUGUSTA   (*With a kind of sober bravery as she confronts what is being said*)
No.

LADY BYRON   (*Looks at her*)
And have you no fear?

AUGUSTA   (*She smiles slightly*)
Of death?

LADY BYRON   Of your Maker?

AUGUSTA   (*Her voice calm*)
Why should I fear Him when I no longer fear you?

LADY BYRON   (*Wearily, without hostility, she turns away from the picture and moves to the window, her back to the room, as the rain blows against the glass. Her voice is slow and lifeless*)
And do you think that can be the end of it? That the world will leave you alone? Any of you? Him. You. Medora.
(*As she is talking, Augusta opens the door, pauses for a moment to take in the room in all its cluttered gloom for one last time, looks over to Lady Byron and, silently and unnoticed, leaves. Lady Byron goes on, in the same flat voice, to an empty room*)
You're all the same. He always believed he could do as he liked with the world's love – take it and despise it at the same time – despise the very beings he had quickened into life.
(*She looks fixedly out through the window*)
Do you have any idea what it means to be taught to feel and then be abandoned? To be left with nothing but your own self? Your littleness? And do you imagine I don't know what I am? That I have never looked in the glass? Seen myself? Heard myself? Do you think, though, there was ever any choice? Any choice but to destroy you – or be destroyed?
(*Her voice takes on a grimmer note*)
And do you think it's for you now to say that it's over? When you have shadowed my whole life? When before I even knew you, you were there, between us. When there has not been a day in all these years when I have not tried to think of him and seen only you? Do you think now that I will

let you go? Or the world will be any kinder? When
it knows you as I do? Knows how it has been
duped? When it sees everything it has admired is
corrupt – listens to everything it has loved and
hears only the lies – do you think when your own
child grew to hate you for what you'd made her,
that the grave –
(*She turns, to find Augusta gone, and Robertson standing in the open doorway, watching her*)
will protect Byron's Astarte?
(*For a long moment she holds Robertson's shocked look,
and then turns away, and walks over to Manfred. Her
voice when she speaks is without emotion*)
I didn't hear you come in.

ROBERTSON (*Awkward*)
I'm sorry, but I heard Mrs Leigh leave, and wondered if there was anything I could do –

LADY BYRON (*Without turning*)
No, nothing.

ROBERTSON Then perhaps –

LADY BYRON (*She raises a hand to silence him*)
Nothing.
(*There is a pause*)
She is gone then?

ROBERTSON (*Apologetic*)
Yes.

LADY BYRON (*To herself, a note of quiet bitterness that makes a mock-
ery of the words*)
Then 'Fare thee well – and if for ever – still forever
fare thee well' –
(*She moves into the middle of the room, her movements
automatic. She stands at the table, staring into space,
compulsively twisting her wedding ring round and
round on her finger*)

(*Her voice is defensive.*)
I know what you are thinking –

ROBERTSON   I would never dream, dear lady –

LADY BYRON   I know what you are thinking. You've no idea, though, what she is. Even now, on the edge of the grave.
(*She stares down at the wedding ring on her small, delicate hand*)
It has never fitted. I had to tie it with a black ribbon, the first day I wore it. He said it was an omen. He would have come back to me though. If it had not been for her. He would have come to see it. That I was his only true friend. The only one who could ever have protected him against himself. The only one who –
(*She turns away, her hands clenching and unclenching*)

ROBERTSON   (*He moves anxiously forward*)
Lady Byron?

LADY BYRON   (*She holds up a hand, her back to him, her voice remote*)
It would be a kindness if you would collect up these papers for me, and send for my carriage –

ROBERTSON   Yes, of course.

LADY BYRON   And Mr Robertson – one more thing.

ROBERTSON   (*About to go out*)
Lady Byron?

LADY BYRON   (*Without looking at him*)
I shall need pen and ink before we leave – I do not want there to be any – misapprehensions – about today. Lies.
(*There is a slight pause. Her voice is firm again, unyielding*)
And I shall be wanting, too, your signature.

ROBERTSON   *(For a moment he stands in the door, looking across at the figure standing rigid and isolated, her back to him, staring up at the Manfred. His voice carries a note of defeat)*
Yes, yes of course.
(Lady Byron is left standing alone. Outside the rain beats against the window panes)

A SENSE OF FAILURE

> Look! The beautiful Daughter of Albion sits naked upon her Stone,
> Her panting Victim beside her; her heart is drunk with blood,
> Tho' her brain is not drunk with wine; she goes forth from Albion
> In pride of beauty, in cruelty of holiness, in the brightness
> Of her tabernacle, and her arc and secret place . . .
> O beautiful Daughter of Albion, cruelty is thy delight!
>
> *Blake* Jerusalem[1]

O n the north wall of the chancel of St Peter's, Croft, a few miles south of Darlington, a royal coat of arms proclaims the indivisible union of Shelley's hated trinity of 'God and King and Law'. There is nothing about the painted board that could not be found in a hundred other parish churches, but the inscription at the bottom of it gives it a peculiar interest here. 'Given to this church by Sir Mark Milbanke' it reads, '1702.'*

A world of theological and social difference lay between the idiosyncratic faith of Annabella Byron and the early Milbankes of Halnaby, and yet there is a feeling that as she parted from Augusta for the last time, she had returned to her Milbanke roots. For the best part of a lifetime Annabella had flirted with the dangers of

---

* The church is particularly worth seeing for the Milbankes' monuments and family pew, a grotesque red curtained and canopied celebration of position and power. It is possible that Byron sat in it with Annabella on their honeymoon, and if so throws an interesting sidelight on the apocrypha that surrounds his wedding night. 'Good God', he is supposed to have recorded in his memoirs, as he woke to see candles flickering through the red of his bed curtains, 'I am surely in hell.' Far more likely in the pew.

Byronic romanticism in one incarnation or another, but never again after the misery of Reigate would she risk her moral or emotional wellbeing outside the safety of Lawrence's 'walled city'.

'Crede Byron' – Believe a Byron – was the family motto and the bitterness Annabella felt was in direct proportion to the passion with which she had embraced that faith. From Trelawny to George Eliot, the history of the nineteenth century is littered with men and women who could never forgive Byron for 'failing' their expectations or needs, but in Annabella's case it was not just Byron himself, but sister and child who had rescued her only to throw her back to drown in the shallows of her own emotional inadequacy.

It is impossible to believe that anything that Augusta could have said at Reigate would have appeased Annabella, but it was the finality of this last disappointment that was so bitter. For almost forty years she had fought to save the Byrons from themselves, and as she felt Augusta slipping through her fingers – 'impenitent' to the last as she told Robertson – she knew that the crusade that had begun in the summer of 1812 had ended in failure. 'Feeling broke loose', she recorded her frustrations after Augusta had left, in a 'Memorandum of my Interview with Mrs Leigh at Reigate' that runs to six and a half angry sides,

> & I said something about it all having been in vain – I felt utterly hopeless – and asked to be left alone to comfort myself.[2]

It was not only the frustration of failure that Annabella felt, however, but the heavier knowledge that with this meeting she had lost all chance of a peace she had been craving since she had first heard the news of Byron's death. Twenty seven years earlier she had pleaded with his servant Fletcher to recall any message Byron might have left her on his deathbed, and more than anything else she had wanted a confession from Augusta that it was she who had prevented his return. 'Elizb [Medora] – how. where – my line of conduct', she had scribbled in an almost illegible hand on the tiny scrap of paper that she had carried with her to the meeting, and then –

3. Question – *you* kept up hatred – you put things in a false
&[?] point of view.[3]

Against all evidence and probability, she had managed to convince
herself that Augusta had withheld – and even forged – letters to
keep Byron from her, and it was an accusation she had repeated
at the meeting. 'I told her I had become convinced that it was
not in human nature for any one to keep up such animosity as
Lord Byron had shown to me', she noted, sounding a theme that
had grown over the years since his death into an obsession,

> unless it had been *fed* – that for *his* sake, that he might not
> be blamed more than he deserved, I sought to know the
> truth about this ... A L could not have been fair, or he
> could not have continued to feel bitterly so long.[4]

The irony of it was that if there was one charge against which
Augusta could comfortably defend herself it was this, as it had
been as much a matter of self-interest as affection to bring about
a reconciliation between Annabella and Byron. She denied that
she had ever said anything to alienate him from his wife, and when
Annabella – convinced of 'her smooth way of making mischief'[5] –
retorted that 'there was a difference between exasperating and
not softening', Augusta appealed to Hobhouse's testimony. 'She
said that she had recollected a proof that she had acted justly to
me', Annabella continued, outraged that the name of one of
Byron's hated 'Piccadilly crew' should be dragged in as a witness
against her,

> for Sir J. Hobhouse had said to her, in speaking of what
> she had said of me to Lord Byron: 'You risked his affection
> by doing so.'
>   At such a testimony I started up, and all but uttered an
> ironical answer – but she had *trusted me unconditionally,* and
> I replied: 'I don't understand it.' From that moment there
> was a mingling of indignation with the intense pity I had
> before felt – and I was afraid of myself. I said, I believe,
> that I should always wish her the blessing I could not give
> her, or something kind if my tears did not prevent me

uttering it – but the strongest desire to be out of her presence took possession of me, lest I should be tempted beyond my strength.[6]

It was the paradox of her attitude, however, that even while she believed that Augusta had withheld and forged letters to keep Byron away, she could never quite obliterate an image so closely involved with all the aspiration of her youth. 'I thought Mrs Leigh my friend', she had told Robertson only months before Reigate, 'I loved her – I love her still! I cannot help it.'[7]

If that was no more than the truth, in the bitter aftermath of the meeting it only served to fuel her sense of betrayal. On her return to Brighton she dictated a brief note announcing her safe arrival, but when at the end of April, Augusta attempted one last defence of herself the letter was returned unopened. 'I had not, and never implied that I had anything to reveal to you with which *you* were not previously acquainted', Augusta had written – a final and moving plea for justice that, even when she sent it back again, with a covering letter to Robertson asking to see him, Annabella refused to look at.

> Nor can I at all express to you the regret I have felt since those words escaped you, showing that you imagined I had encouraged a bitterness of feeling in Lord Byron towards you. I can as solemnly declare as if I were on my death-bed that I never did so in any one instance but that I invariably did the contrary.[8]

'Madam,' Frederick Robertson wrote back on Annabella's behalf to Augusta at her apartments at St James's, on 21 May 1851 – the last communication, bar two words, the women would ever share,

> I regret to say that I feel it impossible to accede to the proposal that you have made, viz. to favour me with an interview in which you might substantiate your assertion made to Lady Byron.
>
> In the meeting at Reigate Lady Byron expressed a conviction that your influence on Lord Byron's mind had been unfavourable to his coming to just conclusions respecting himself.

This you denied strongly and distinctly; and you quoted a speech of Sir John Hobhouse, one sentence of which appeared to shock and startle Lady Byron exceedingly.

No-one but myself was witness of this conversation. I am a stranger to you, and my opinion can be of no importance. I need scarcely say that the topics of that interview are sacred, and that they will never pass my lips. The proofs which you desire to give me could only be given in Lady Byron's presence, and she will never consent to another meeting. The last was final ... If your own conscience is free and clear, and Lady Byron is no way injured by you, the sense of innocence in God's sight will make the opinion of any human being a matter of small importance. If on the contrary there was anything for the sorrowful acknowledgement of which that meeting was the last and final opportunity which you can ever have in this world, then, of course, no opinion of Sir John Hobhouse, written or expressed, nor of Lord Byron to himself, can reverse the solemn judgement upon the whole matter, which must be heard very, very soon, when you meet God face to face.

I remain, Madam, your obedient servant,

Fred. W. Robertson

P. S. – I ought, perhaps, to add that I did not transmit your letter to Lady Byron and therefore return it. She is resolved that the communication was ended with the last letter she wrote; and, indeed, the result of that interview has been a dangerous illness.

I trust you will not look upon the plain words I have spoken as expressing harshness of feeling. I would gladly, now or hereafter, as a minister of Christ, do what might be in my power to alleviate sadness, but I am quite sure that it is not my duty to receive any evidence of the nature you propose.[9]

If it would have come as a surprise to Frederick Robertson's congregation to know that he would go down in history for his uneasy role in the Augusta affair, the tone of this letter perhaps suggests why. To many contemporaries who had heard Arnold and Newman preach, Frederick Robertson was simply the greatest orator of his day, and yet if he is remembered at all now it is as one of those emasculated Victorians whom women of the stamp of Annabella or Florence Nightingale could reduce to the hopeless bondage of the superior 'bagman'.

Were it not a *donné* of the whole Byron story that Byron has 'devoted friends' and Annabella 'hangers-on', Robertson might yet enjoy a better press than he has, but he is too firmly established now as a Brighton *Slope* to make rehabilitation much worth trying. Annabella and Robertson had first met when her restless, wandering life took her to a house near the Pavilion at Brighton in 1848, and within a year she had begun to confide her history to him, graduating over their meetings and letters from theological discussions of Byron's childhood Calvinism to the full revelations of his incest with Augusta.

There were twenty-five years between them, and Robertson was a married man, but it was still a relationship of supreme importance to both. For most of her middle age Annabella's closest friendships had been with women, but with the charismatic and theologically maverick Robertson she rediscovered a capacity for spiritual and emotional ardour that she had not known since her courtship of Byron. 'I must thank you for the greatest gift that a human being can make to his fellow', she wrote to her cousin, Robert Noel, in 1848 after he had introduced them, 'the means of intercourse with a great soul – Robertson's.'[10] 'Between the widow of the greatest poet of his age and the fervid young priest', wrote Frederick Arnold,

> there had gradually grown up an intense and famous friendship worthy of comparison with the renowned friendships of antiquity.[11]

For Frederick Robertson, brought up like all his generation on Byron, there was an obvious excitement in the revelations, and yet nothing else we know of him suggests a man easily seduced by the frisson of scandal. There was invariably an element of patronage in Annabella's friendships, but if it was never entirely absent from her dealings with Robertson, it should at least make one pause that a man of his instinctive independence and generos-

ity could have found in her character and history so compelling
a cause for sympathy.

Even when that is said, however, it seems there was a gap
between what Robertson felt and what Annabella demanded that
can be accurately measured by the fact that when he copied that
letter out for her he carefully omitted his postscript. There was
a quixotic streak in him that would always be vulnerable to a
woman like Augusta, but no one who had ever dealt with Annabella for any length of time could have had any illusions that
impartiality was an option.

The hand that wrote that final letter to Augusta may be
Robertson's, but the presence looming behind it with all the force
and sanction of the Victorian age, is unmistakably Annabella's.
For the best part of a lifetime she had been justifying herself in
terms of moral and religious 'duties', and in the implacable and
ruthless certainty of rejection, in its demonstration of a will strong
enough to bend a man of Robertson's generosity to the unforgiving dogmatisms of Evangelical righteousness, we come face to
face with the Annabella Byron of old age.

It is one thing, however, simply to register the fact, but it is
quite another to understand what could have turned the Regency
Magdalene Hayter painted in 1812 into the woman capable of
dictating that letter to Augusta. With anyone but Annabella a life
of rejection and disappointment might seem answer enough, but
if one reads that letter again or looks into the face – sexless and
joyless as an old Boer trekker's – that stares out of photographs
of her in old age, it is clear that whatever else might be said of
her, she was *not* the natural stuff of victims.

It cannot simply be the operations of revenge or jealousy,
either, that explain a lifetime's self-laceration in the cause of a
family she never ceased to love. After all she had suffered at the
Byrons' hands it would have been extraordinary if such feelings
had not played their part, but as one contemplates the emotional
wasteland of her life, something more complex and elusive –
more *tragic* in the fullest sense of the word – is needed to explain
what could have driven a woman of her intelligence and aspirations to consume her health, energies and ultimately humanity

in a campaign of self-justification and moral tyranny that ended only with her death.

It is that question that is explored here, and while Annabella would never have recognised the terms in which it is couched, she would have acknowledged the emptiness it describes. Until the end of her life she was always able to restock her immediate circle with new acolytes and admirers, but with that brief, vivid exception of Brighton and Robertson nothing in her whole life began to fill the void that opened before her when her marriage to Byron failed.

And wherever eventually they might lead, every question ever asked of Annabella – or any question she asked of herself – always begins with Byron and marriage. She once described herself as 'embalmed by a name'[12], and if to the outward eye the only thing that connected the wealthy philanthropist of old age to her younger self was that name, no one knew better than Annabella that the only 'life' that had ever mattered was the one that had opened and as suddenly closed when she swapped the name of Milbanke for that of Byron almost forty years before.

MARRIAGE

There is possibly no marriage about which we know so much as that of Byron and Annabella, but still after the best part of two centuries of partisan controversy the mystery at its heart remains as elusive as ever. From the day it collapsed in rumours of cruelty, sodomy, rape and incest there has not been a single moment unexplored, and yet the paradox is that it is the very weight of surviving evidence that exposes those areas of emotional and sexual truth and human vulnerability at which we can do no more than guess.

The same could be said, of course, of any relationship that can only be viewed from the outside, but it is the nature of the accounts that we have in this case that makes any 'truth' much harder to find. In the weeks after the separation servants, doctors, family and friends all left a mass of testimony, but it is almost exclusively on the word of a wife determined not just to fight her public cause but also to mask the truth from *herself* that we still have to rely for any sense of the texture of their married year.*

Even when every caution is taken, however, and the obvious embellishments of subsequent years discounted, the profound misery of those twelve months still has a power to shock that no repetition can blunt. There is such a deceptive and lulling air of normality about the wedding itself too, that the sudden descent from the comforting mundanity of a world defined by such details as family, gloves, pelisse and kneeling cushions to the secret and

---

* Byron also left his own memoir – one that Annabella refused to look at when he offered it to her – but that went up in flames in John Murray's offices and the different fragments the various incendiaries 'remembered' need to be treated with extreme caution.

sudden misery of an enclosed carriage has a Gothic quality about it that cannot merely be the product of Annabella's imagination.

'At the altar she did not know that she was a sacrifice', Harriet Martineau wrote of Annabella's wedding day, 'but before sunset on that winter day she knew it.'[13] 'As soon as we got into the carriage his countenance changed to gloom and defiance', Annabella remembered in one of her many versions of events,

> He began singing in a wild manner as he usually does when angry and scarcely spoke to me till we came near Durham, when he said amongst other things calculated to excite mistrust, 'You had better have married —, he would have made you a better husband.' On hearing the Joy-bells of Durham ringing for us, he appeared to be struck with horror, and said something very bitter about 'our happiness' . . . He called me to account for having so long withheld my consent to marry him, signifying I should suffer for it, and had better not have married him at all.
>
> At the Inn at Rushford he turned to me with a bitter look & said, 'I wonder how much longer I shall be able to keep up *the part I have been* playing' – or some equivalent expression, decidedly expressing that he had worn a mask which he now intended to throw aside.[14]

It is impossible to know whether or not that first wedding journey had the nightmare air it later assumed in her imagination, but the butler's memory of Annabella's face as he handed her from the carriage, 'agonised and listless with horror and despair'[15], suggests that she was not exaggerating Byron's antipathy. It is clear from his own admissions that Byron thought that he had suffered some kind of nervous attack in these first days of marriage, and if Annabella's memories of the journey demonstrably changed with time there is evidence enough of Byron's capacity for the kind of mental cruelty she charged him with to believe the substance of her account.

It was not Byron's anger that crushed her, though – the well-rehearsed details of those first days at Halnaby, the ravings, the loaded pistols, the daggers, the oblique confessions, have a curiously 'stagey' quality about them – but the hopeless realisation of the desert that lay ahead. In the whole period that Byron had courted Annabella they can have spent no more than a week in each other's company, but now with no one but servants in the house, she found herself cut off by the dreary, ice bound landscape of the West Riding, immured with a man beyond her reach – two people mutually ignorant of each other, divided by temperament, expectations, history, faith and, above all, that invisible 'third' who from the first day of their marriage had always been with them.

There had been a letter to Byron from Augusta, addressed to the 'Dearest, first and best of human beings'[16], on the first day of their 'treaclemoon', and his constant lament was that she was the only person who could ever love or understand him. In later accounts Annabella dated her first 'blasting' suspicions of 'something most dreadful between him and his sister'[17] to these weeks at Halnaby, and if that is true, there can be no more eloquent testimony to her loneliness, than the fact that within three days of marriage she had turned to Augusta herself for help.

The two women had seen each other – without meeting – across the crowded rooms of a London season in 1813, and although they had exchanged properly affectionate letters after the engagement, it was from these first weeks of marriage that their lifetime's intimacy dates. From the first day that she re-entered Byron's life Augusta had been able to laugh him out of his *Wertherish* moods in a way that no-one else could, and with a generosity tempered by self-interest she did her best now to advise his new wife, forging between them in the process a kind of solidarity that had Byron at its heart – a wayward, consuming, demanding presence that was simultaneously the rationale and fatal flaw of their improbable sisterhood.

Even by the time that Annabella received Augusta's first letter, however, pledging as Annabella had begged of her, to be her 'ONLY friend'[18], Byron's mood had begun to lift. In a later confession to Hobhouse he admitted to a 'melancholy' that had descended on his wedding night, and while 'attack' was the only way in life or art Byron ever knew of assuaging guilt or anger, he was too instinctively generous to remain unmoved by Annabella's desolation.

It was, in fact, his 'unrelenting pity'[19] rather than any histrionics that had brought Annabella's misery home to her, but gradually a sort of exhausted calm seems to have settled over Halnaby. 'You would think we had been married these fifty years,' he wrote to Lady Melbourne,

> Bell is fast asleep on a corner of the Sopha, and I am keeping myself awake with this epistle – she desires her love – and mine you have had ever since we were acquainted.[20]

'Bell and I go on extremely well', he reported to her again, and as they settled into a domestic rhythm, with Byron working while Annabella transcribed his Hebrew Melodies, the first stirrings of hope appear that the mutual horror of the opening days was behind them. 'I don't dislike this place', he wrote on 7 January –

> it is just the spot for a Moon . . . I have great hopes that this match will turn out well – I have found nothing yet I could wish changed for the better –[21]

It was an optimism that survived even a return to Seaham, where in spite of Byron's reluctance, they went on 21 January. For the next month Byron found himself at the centre of a domestic world of which he had no real experience, and if familiarity made him no fonder of his mother-in-law, he endured the boredom of Sir Ralph's interminable prosing with a decent good humour. 'My spouse and I agree to – and in – admiration', he wrote to Tom Moore after ten days of Seaham,

> Swift says 'no *wise* man ever married;' but, for a fool, I think it the most ambrosial of all future states. I still think one ought to marry upon *lease;* but am very sure I should renew mine at the expiration, though next term were for ninety and nine years . . .
>
> My Papa, Sir Ralph, hath recently made a speech at a Durham tax-meeting; and not only at Durham, but here, several times since, after dinner. He is now, I believe, speak-

ing it to himself (I left him in the middle) over various
decanters, which can neither interrupt him nor fall asleep,
– as might have been the case with some of his audience.

Ever thine,
B.

I must go to tea – damn tea. I wish it was Kinnaird's brandy,
and with you to lecture me about it.[22]

And after the claustrophobic weeks at Halnaby, incarcerated in a
featureless landscape, the sight of the sea lifted his spirits as it
always did. During the breaks in the rain and family games Byron
and Annabella would scramble over the rocks she had known
since childhood, his sensitivity to his lameness eased by her kindness and tact – the Childe, as Annabella contentedly reported to
Augusta, a wild and boisterous boy again.

And yet even at their happiest together it was significantly images
of freedom and escape – of Biscay and Aegean squalls – that the
desolate north-eastern shoreline stirred in Byron and there was
scarcely a day when Annabella was not left in tears by some cruelty.
More than twenty years later her old servant Mrs Clermont
recalled her anxieties at this time, and if there seemed to her
some fear running through the whole Milbanke household that
stopped anyone naming their apprehensions even Sir Ralph was
not blind to the danger. 'Her father during their stay saw what
he did not like', Dr Bence Jones recorded Mrs Clermont telling
him,

& one day said to Mrs. C., He persecuted her to marry him
& I believe he only married her to persecute her – if it is
so he shall have my dying curse.[23]

If Byron had had any hopes that marriage might bury his obsessive
need for Augusta, he already knew that it had failed. On the day
after they reached Seaham he had written to allay his new 'tante's'

anxieties, but ten days later he was writing again, as he had done so often in the year before the marriage, to confess his helplessness. 'I suppose your 'C- noir is +', he wrote to Lady Melbourne – his 'Corbeau blanc' – on 2 February, employing his habitual '+' symbol for Augusta,

> but if + were a raven or a griffin I must still take my omens
> from her flight – I can't help *loving* her though –[24]

With negotiations for the sale of Newstead underway, Byron had wanted to leave Annabella at Seaham while he found a house for them in London, but when finally they left on 9 March for Augusta's home near Newmarket she insisted on accompanying him.

It was the second time in just over two months that Annabella had to give up the security and sympathy of family life to be alone with Byron. In many ways – emotionally and physically – Seaham had been a greater success than either of them could have hoped, but from the moment she stepped into the carriage she might have been on her way to Halnaby again, with Byron railing bitterly against her parents or flinging her own physical helplessness in her face.

On their second night south they stopped at Wandsford, and as Byron's mood briefly lifted, Annabella enjoyed probably the last unalloyed moment of happiness of her married life. In the early evening his behaviour had seemed as capricious as ever, but later, Annabella recalled, 'he said to me the kindest words I could ever wish to have heard.

> 'You married me to make me happy, didn't you' – I
> answered with some expression of attachment – 'Well then,
> you *do* make me happy!' – with passionate affection, I fan-
> cied. I was silent, and he saw not, but felt the tears of joy
> which rose from my heart.[25]

There is something so pathetic in Annabella's gratitude here – so humiliating in the poverty of her expectations – that it brings home her misery in a way that no story of Byronic violence does. It is difficult to read the self-justifying accounts she later wrote with much sympathy, but whatever Annabella eventually *became* should not disguise the courage and genuine goodness she brought as a young bride to these first weeks of married life.

The tragedy of Annabella Milbanke is of wasted humanity, and the selflessness of her behaviour during these beleaguered months makes one wonder what kindness and love might have made of her. The passionate affection she showed Augusta during the first days of her separation from Byron underline a capacity for loyalty for which she has had little credit, but if she had learned anything in two months of married life it was that there was nothing she could do – and no-one she could be – that could avert the fate Byron had *willed* for her.

In many of her accounts she dated her first suspicions about Byron and Augusta to the honeymoon, but it was the fortnight at the Leighs' house at Six Mile Bottom that left little room for doubt. From the first evening Byron seemed determined to force the knowledge of it on her, packing her off to bed early while he stayed up alone with Augusta, only finally appearing in a black rage in Annabella's room, to make his loathing for her clear.

Evening after evening the same pattern repeated itself, but, as Annabella herself saw, Byron was equally bent on making his sister's life a misery. During the last weeks at Seaham Augusta had written as often as ever to the new couple, but for all her friendliness there had been an ambivalence of tone that Byron could not have missed, a sort of tactical – even occasionally ironical – withdrawal from intimacy that opened up for him a prospect of loss that he could neither accept nor forgive.

For the only time in his life his treatment of Augusta seemed to be actuated more by an urge for power and ownership than by love. It is impossible to know if he had ever fully envisaged the consequences of marriage on his relations with her, but as they were now brought home by Augusta's reluctance to resume their old intimacy, she seems to have become as much an object of his hatred and revenge as his unwitting wife. He would sit between the pair of them, comparing their kisses, and talk in front of Annabella of Augusta's underwear. 'His delight was', Annabella later wrote,

to work us both well. (he kept her in a state of misery beyond
mine I thought) – that she was in his power from some
cause I could not often doubt – with all my endeavours to
do so – and that he made the most cruel use of that power.
I pitied her from my heart if Guilt had brought her thus
low, and would not have aggravated her oppression of mind
by a single look.[26]

It never seems to have occurred to Byron, however, that his
attempt to play one woman off against the other would simply
drive them into an alliance of their own. During her long courtship Annabella had seen herself in the role of Byron's redeemer,
but as she began to realise that he was beyond her control, her
emotional commitment shifted to the thing closest to him,
embracing Augusta with the same romanticising and possessive
ardour that she had expended on him.

It is one of the bizarre paradoxes of this fortnight that while
it signalled the death of her marriage, it sealed Annabella's compact with the Byrons for good. At the centre of the strange *ménage
à trois* still towered the figure of Byron of course, but as Annabella
and Augusta grew closer together, other emotional currents and
connections developed from which he was inevitably excluded.

Augusta might obediently wear the brooch, complete with his
lock of hair and coded '+'s, that Byron had ordered from London,
but it seemed more a badge of emotional slavery than love. Whenever the weather permitted, the two women would walk in the
garden and talk, and if the great issue that lay between them
remained unspoken, its mere existence brought them closer
together, binding them into that dangerous and unstable inter-
dependence that would only end with their lives.

As their carriage pulled away from Augusta's home, however,
and Byron turned on Annabella to demand what she had thought
of *her*, there seemed nothing in front of them but the blank misery
of marriage. During their stay at Six Mile Bottom Annabella had
shown the first signs of 'Symptoms which look a little gestatory'[27],
but even the prospect of an heir apparently filled Byron with no
pleasure. 'It is a subject upon which I am not particularly anxious',
he told Moore,

Except that I think it would please her uncle, Lord Wentworth, and her father and mother. The former (Lord W)
is now in town, and in very indifferent health. You perhaps
know that his property, amounting to seven or eight thousand a year, will eventually devolve upon Bell. But the old
gentleman has been so very kind to her and me, that I
hardly know how to wish him in heaven, if he can be
comfortable on earth.[28]

Not for the first time in his letters as a married man, Byron strikes
here a note of financial anxiety that was to be the constant background to all their troubles. Through the early months of 1815
negotiations over the sale of Newstead dragged on in their usual
frustrating fashion, and the house that Lady Melbourne had rented
on their behalf from the Duchess of Devonshire only exacerbated
problems that not even Lord Wentworth's death could avert.

If anything, in fact, it made their position even worse, because
as the news that Annabella was now an heiress spread, Byron's
creditors closed in. Sir Ralph's own difficulties had meant that
Byron had seen nothing of the money owed him under the
marriage settlement, and as settlement of the Wentworth will
was delayed by litigation, Byron found himself facing the real
possibility of the bailiffs and the compulsory sale of his posses-
sions.

In the letters and recollections of contemporaries, there is an
occasional glimpse of a happier and more stable life at 13 Piccadilly, or of a benign and solicitous husband hovering over Annabella's chair at the theatre, but a little has been made to go a
long way. For Byron there was a literary and public life beyond
the straitening confines of his home to divert him, and yet there
seems something oddly unsettled even in his letters from this year,
something in the patching of old quarrels or frenetic activities at
the theatre or the drinking bouts with old friends that carries a
faint valedictory flavour.

After a relative calm of ten days, Augusta was with them again,
in London to prepare for her new duties as lady-in-waiting to
Queen Charlotte. An apartment in St James's Palace went with
the position, but Annabella had written echoing Byron's invitation

to stay with them in Piccadilly, and on 30 March an uncertain
Augusta wrote back to accept. 'Dearest Sis', she replied,

> . . . You will perhaps be a better judge bye & bye whether
> I shall not be a plague – & you must tell me *truly* if I am
> likely to be so – you know I should not be 'affronted' . . .[29]

Almost immediately on Augusta's arrival with her eldest daughter,
Georgey, it was as if they were all again at Six Mile Bottom, though
to add to the humiliations, Annabella was in her own home and
in the first stages of pregnancy. In her defence Augusta seems to
have done whatever she could to shield her from the worst
excesses, but with Byron's mood swings getting ever wilder his
sister's mere presence seemed goad enough.

'You were a fool to let her come', he told Annabella the first
night that the three of them were reunited, 'You will find it will
make a good deal of difference to you *in all ways*'[30] and he was
as good as his word. During the next two months Annabella again
found herself driven upstairs in the evenings, forced to listen to
their voices below, waiting in a frenzy of misery for the sound of
their footsteps, learning by bitter experience to read into the
weight and speed of his tread his mood and intentions as he came
to her room.

There is a genuine horror to her descriptions of these vigils,
an unconscious echo of Macbeth's vision of murder approaching with 'Tarquin's ravishing stride', that more than anything
catches the psychological and sexual violence that filled the
household at 13 Piccadilly.* She never seems to have felt herself in any physical danger from Byron at this point, but for a
woman who had committed herself to him with such hope and
belief only months earlier, the brutal alternations of conjugal
demands and physical abhorrence were in their way even more
degrading.

---

* It is fascinating to catch literary echoes in Annabella's writing because it shows
how her mind worked as she set about shaping experience into dramatic form. It
has often been pointed out how her descriptions of the honeymoon have the
flavour of a gothic novel, and among her papers from 1812 survives a lengthy
analysis of Mrs Siddons's views on Macbeth that eventually seems to have provided
the language to understand and articulate her own loneliness.

Even the one consolation of the fortnight at Six Mile Bottom, the friendship of Augusta, seemed polluted. 'I must not (having so far spoken of myself as to imply that I preserved, generally, self-possession and forbearance)', she confessed many years later,

> omit to state that my feelings were once – in London – so worked up by the continual excitement of horrible ideas ... that in a moment when one of them became to my imagination a *fact* – I turned round to use a deadly weapon lying by – not against him, but against one whose treachery seemed at that instant revealed ... There are moments of one's past life before which one stands in awe.[31]

And yet it was only now, alone in face of what seemed a double betrayal by brother and sister, that Annabella showed the extraordinary strength – part courage, part absolute inner certainty – that was to characterise her behaviour through the rest of her life. It would be possible to read her letters from this period and gain no sense of misery at all, but if that has been held up as proof of later exaggerations it more likely stems from a pride that made her determined to see that family or strangers should never guess the truth. 'She is pretty, not beautiful', the American George Ticknor described her after visiting Piccadilly in June,

> has a large fortune, is rich in intellectual endowments, is a mathematician, possesses common accomplishments in an uncommon degree, and adds to all this a sweet temper.[32]

'She did not seem to me as pretty as she did the other day', he wrote again after a second visit,

> but what she may have lost in regular beauty she made up in variety and expression of countenance during the conversation. She is diffident, – she is very young, not more, I think, than nineteen, – but is obviously possessed of talent, and did not talk at all for display. For the quarter of an hour during which I was with her, she talked upon a considerable variety of subjects – America, of which she seemed to know considerable; of France, and Greece, with something of her husband's visit there, – and spoke of all with a justness and a light good-humour.[33]

Annabella was not only determined to maintain appearances, but to fight her corner too, and in the middle of June, after almost two months vacillating between thoughts of murder and spasms of guilt, she asked Augusta to leave. In a poignant comment on her feelings Annabella later described the way that she had sublimated revenge into a cult of 'romantic forgiveness'[34], and yet if that tells part of the truth it conceals a subtle shift in the balance of power between the two women that is perfectly caught in all the loaded connotations of that word 'forgiveness'.

It is only in retrospect that one can see it, perhaps, but that request for Augusta to go also signalled the first step in an emotional withdrawal from Byron that would only end with their separation. In their letters Annabella and Augusta had talked of 'Baby' Byron as though they were dealing with some errant child, but for the first time since her marriage Annabella now seemed secure enough in her own judgement to regard her husband with the eye of the Seaham moralist as well as the wife. 'My head is better,' she told Augusta,

> And I wish to make a few observations respecting the nature of my greatest fears for B. – and I think I daily understand the case better. His misfortune is an habitual *passion for Excitement*, which is always found in ardent temperaments, where the pursuits are not in some degree organised. It is the ennui of a monotonous existence that drives the best hearted people of this description to the most dangerous paths, and makes them often seem to act from bad motives, when in fact they are only flying from internal suffering by any external stimulus. The love of tormenting rises chiefly from this source. Drinking, Gaming &c are all of the same origin. How far it may depend on body or mind it is difficult to ascertain. I am inclined to think that a vitiated stomach, particularly if it arises from habits of excess, is a chief cause of the sensations of Ennui; and that change of scene, air, & exercise are more efficient to its removal than any efforts of Reason.[35]

In a curious way marriage had both matured and arrested Annabella, forcing her to grow up, and yet confirming her in all the

rigidity of her old beliefs. For a few brief months she had succumbed to the temptations of Byronism, but under the provo-
cation of his hate she had been forced to fall back on herself and
assert in the face of his abuse and contempt the dull verities of
her stable, moral world.

With their finances in ever deepening crisis, and Byron unable
to do anything about it, and too proud to accept money for his
verse, he had also failed her in the simplest terms that he had
spoken of when he first proposed. It was to her great credit that
she never resented for herself the financial anxieties he had
brought on her, but with Annabella protectiveness and patronage
were never far apart, and it is possible that Byron saw his own
sense of impotence reflected back in her eyes.

More important than anything, however, even for so un-
maternal a woman as Annabella, was the simple fact that as she
moved into the last stages of her pregnancy other duties and
imperatives asserted themselves. In its first weeks she had hoped
that a child would bring Byron closer again, but long before the
birth both instinctively saw that it was an end not a beginning,
the flash point that would bring those fundamental divisions on
which their marriage had foundered – divisions between orthodoxy and rebellion, continuity and change, licence and control,
convention and originality, between the natural outsider and that
deep 'human compact by which we all live together'[36] – to open
war.

With bailiffs now in the house, his books for sale, and Byron
drinking more and more, the weeks before the birth saw him at
his savage worst. He talked constantly of separation or escape, or
of his hopes that Annabella and her baby might die. At the end
of October, too, he took a mistress in a joyless revenge on both
Annabella and Augusta, now equally to blame in his eyes for the
hell in which he was trapped. 'He leaves the house, telling me
he will at once abandon himself to every desperation', Annabella
wrote to Augusta,

> speaks to me only to upbraid me with having married him
> when he wished not, and says he is therefore acquitted of

all principle towards me, and I must consider myself, *only* to be answerable for the vicious courses to which his despair will drive him. The going out of the house & the drinking are the most fatal. He was really quite frantic yesterday – said he did not care for any consequences to me, and it seemed impossible to tell if his feelings towards you or me were the most completely reversed; for as I have told you, he loves or hates us together.[37]

On 15 November, at Annabella's own desperate request, Augusta returned to Piccadilly for the approaching confinement, to find Byron smashing furniture and letting off his pistols beneath his wife's room. Within the household there were now genuine fears for her safety and even for Augusta there could be no other issue but the protection of mother and child. Under her improbable leadership the forces of normality and retribution began to mass, closing ranks against the outsider in the classic rhythms of tragedy. To the Milbankes' old servant, Mrs Clermont, invited to help by Augusta, was added the figure of Captain George Byron, Byron's impeccably ordinary cousin and heir. In the middle of November Annabella's mother – Lady Noel as she now was by the terms of her brother's will – arrived in town, and on 9 December, the first of those professionals who would eventually preside over Byron's ruin, Sergeant Heywood, was consulted on the advisability of removing Annabella from Byron's reach.

It was decided, however, that it was safer that she should stay at Piccadilly, and the following day, Sunday 10 December, a girl was born and named Augusta Ada – Ada in a piece of Byronic family flummery, Augusta after the sister expected to be the child's godmother. A 'horrid story' reached an appalled Hobhouse that Byron had demanded to know whether the child was dead while Annabella was still in labour, but whether that is true or not another comment recorded by an old family friend of the Milbankes, captures the air of gothic nightmare that had enveloped the household. 'When her lovely little child was born', Lady Anne Barnard wrote, and it was laid beside its mother on the bed, and he was informed 'he might see his daughter', after gazing at it with an exulting smile, this was the ejaculation that broke from him, 'Oh! What an instrument of torture I have acquired in you!'[38]

For two people who had driven each other to such a pitch of mutual despair, however, neither Annabella nor Byron seemed fully conscious that with the birth of Ada they had crossed some invisible line. Throughout the whole period of his marriage it would seem that Byron was in fact only ever half aware of what he was doing, as if the man who sat on the Drury Lane committee and helped fellow writers like Coleridge, Godwin or Maturin with such tact and grace had nothing to do with the tyrant and drunk he had become at home.

With the deepest part of his personality, though, with that part of him that found both its relief and profoundest expression in his poetry, Byron had *willed* the rupture that Ada's birth made inevitable. The sufferings of Annabella during their year together have rightly dominated judgements of their marriage, and yet if they constitute no excuse for him, Byron's own miseries were just as acute, his sense of suffocation and impotence driving him to the brink of what he himself called madness.

The only two major poems of this period, *Parisina* with its theme of incest and death, and *The Siege of Corinth*, a tale of banishment and revenge, underline too just how constant was the call to exile. From his earliest childhood there had been something oppressive in English life to Byron, but marriage and Piccadilly had intensified dislike into a claustrophobia that had a physical urgency to it, lending a Wildean poignancy to the images of escape and freedom that haunted his imagination. 'This is but a dull scrawl, and I am but a dull fellow', he wrote plaintively to Moore after the birth of Ada,

> I am absorbed in 500 contradictory contemplations, though with but one object in view – which will probably end in nothing, as most things we wish do. But never mind – as somebody says, 'for the blue sky bends over all'. I only could

be glad, if it bent over me where it is a little bluer, like the 'skyish top of blue Olympus', which, by the way, looked very white when I last saw it.[39]

Byron was wrong, though, if he thought that life in Piccadilly would simply drift, because whether or not he knew it, the marriage was now beyond redemption. While there was no one else but herself to think of, Annabella had been able to sustain herself with images of self-sacrifice, but with anxieties for her child – the fear above all that Byron might remove her abroad with him – there was no longer room for the luxury of romantic delusions.

The birth had done nothing to calm Byron's rages either, and as he fed himself on de Sade's writings, it seemed for the first time that Caroline Lamb's 'mad, bad and dangerous to know' might be no more than the truth. There is nothing in his letters from these weeks to suggest the slightest trace of mental instability, and yet under the influence of drink he seemed increasingly incapable of controlling himself, driven by some compulsive *necessity* to the destructive outbursts that mark the last phase of his marriage. 'The principal insane ideas are – that he *must* be wicked', Annabella noted for Doctor Baillie, who was consulted on Byron's possible insanity,

> Undoubtedly I am more than anyone the subject of his irritation, because he deems himself (as he has said) a villain for marrying me on account of former circumstances – adding that the more I love him, & the better I am, the more accursed is he.[40]

With Byron littering his rages and remorse with hints of some unforgivable sin, the attractions of insanity to Augusta are obvious, but it had no less profound an appeal for Annabella. There was a clear tactical advantage to such a diagnosis if it ever came to a struggle over Ada, but more importantly it enabled her to cling to the last vestiges of self-respect, allowing her not only to blind herself to Augusta's role in her misery but to the raw intensity of Byron's hatred.

By the time that Annabella turned to Dr Baillie, however, it was too late for any medical advice to save the marriage. On

6 January – almost exactly a year after her wedding – she was handed a note by Augusta from Byron. 'When you are disposed to leave London', he had written,

> it would be convenient that a date should be fixed – & (if possible) not a very remote one for that purpose. Of my opinion upon that subject you are sufficiently in possession – & of the circumstances which have led to it – as also to my plans – or rather intentions – for the future. When in the country I will write to you more fully. As Lady Noel has asked you to Kirkby, there you can be for the present – unless you prefer Seaham.
>
> As the dismissal of the present establishment is of importance to me, the sooner you can fix on the date the better – though of course your convenience & inclination shall be first consulted.
>
> The child will of course accompany you – there is a more easy and safer carriage than the chariot (unless you prefer it) which I mentioned before – on that you can do as you please.[41]

It was Byron's last written communication to her of their married life together. For another week Annabella held on at Piccadilly, taking soundings on his mental health, but one last burst of rage decided her. Early on the morning of 15 January 1816, she got up with the five-week-old Ada, and without saying goodbye, walked past Byron's room and out to the waiting carriage. She confessed later that she had to steel her will against throwing herself down at his door on the mat on which his Newfoundland used to lie.

The temptation lasted only a second, and was gone. That night was spent at Woburn, and the following day she was with her parents at Kirkby. She had seen Byron for the last time.

SLEEPING WITH THE VAMPIRE

If anyone had asked the ageing Annabella to flesh out this skeletal account of her married life, it is unlikely that after all the years of introspection she could have done so with any honesty even if she had wanted to. At the height of the separation battle that followed her departure Byron had generously declared that she was 'truth itself', and yet as her life had spiralled out of her control and the most intimate details of her marriage became the lawyers' and the public's property, truth soon became a luxury she could less and less afford.

The process began almost from that day in the middle of January 1816, when thin, ill and exhausted from her journey, she arrived with Ada at her family home at Kirkby. For twelve months of married life she had somehow succeeded in disguising from herself the ambiguities of her relationship with Byron and Augusta, but confronted suddenly by her parents' indignant interrogation she felt, as she told Augusta, as if she 'were going to receive sentence from the Judge with his black cap on'[42].

Even after all that she had gone through, she confessed, there were times when she would have forgotten self, child and principles to devote herself to the 'being who cast me off', and there can be little doubt that she had no idea of leaving Byron when she first arrived at Kirkby. 'Dearest Duck', she wrote to him the following day, the second of two loving letters that would come back to haunt her over the weeks and years ahead, undermining all she said of Byron's unmitigated brutality to her through their marriage,

> We got here quite well last night, and were ushered into
> the kitchen instead of the drawing-room, by a mistake that

might have been agreeable enough to hungry people. Of this and other incidents Dad wants to write you a jocose account, & both he & Mam long to have the family party completed ... If I were not always looking about for B., I should be a great deal better already for country air. *Miss* finds her provisions increased, & fattens thereon. It is a good thing she can't understand all the flattery bestowed upon her, 'Little Angel.' Love to the good Goose [Augusta], & everybody's love to you both from hence.

Ever thy most loving
Pippin ... Pip ... Pip[43]

In the weeks ahead it became Byron's bitter conviction that Annabella's family had turned her against him, and if that was not true in the way he imagined it, it was in another and more important sense. In the last days of her marriage Annabella had clutched at every excuse from madness to drink to explain away Byron's loathing, but as one by one the revelations were prised out of her, as suspicions of incest were added to accusations of cruelty, unspecified suggestions of sexual deviance to legal charges of adultery and insanity discounted by the doctors, it became a matter of absolute self-preservation to distance herself as far as possible from the Piccadilly menage and the 'Pip' who had written that letter.

The harrowing irony of her position, too, was that it was still at Piccadilly that she felt at home, because in a curious anticipation of the Stockholm syndrome, it was with her tormentors and not her rescuers that she most closely identified. In the eyes of her parents there could be no room for compromise or forgiveness of Byron's conduct to their daughter, but if Annabella had learned anything from her marriage it was that life was more complex than Milbanke morality would allow. 'Independent of Malady', she wrote to Augusta, still at Piccadilly and sending off daily bulletins on Byron's behaviour to her 'sis' at Kirkby,

I do not think of the past with any spirit of resentment & scarcely with sense of injury – God bless him.[44]

These were emotions, too, that she could share only with Augusta. 'Dearest A,' she addressed her again from her parents' home, writing almost as if from an enemy camp, guarded by supporters she refers to as 'them', her mind 'overstrained and my body weak in compassion',

> Do not wish anything *for me*, except that I may fulfil my duties whilst I am amongst them – and render me more thankful in performing them, by the comfort of being dear to one who feels for me as you do . . . You can not know the feelings with which I receive every mark of your affection . . . No, if all the world had told me you were doing me an injury, I *ought not* to have believed it.[45]

Whatever Annabella's feelings under her parents' roof, however, the conduct and progress of the separation had slipped for the time being out of her hands. On 20th January her outraged mother had set off for London to consult a lawyer, and armed with the advice of Sir Samuel Romilly and a statement from Annabella detailing Byron's 'dismissal' and his 'settled aversion' to marriage, the Milbankes made their first overtures to him for a quiet and amicable separation.

At this early stage in the process, the charges against Byron were of so unspecified a nature that in his reply to Annabella's father he was able to hide behind a blanket of mystification. In his long and evasive answer to Sir Ralph, Byron conceded 'a morbid irritability of temper'[46] over the last year, but while he was prepared to admit that Annabella had sometimes seen him gloomy or violent under the pressure of illness and financial worries, he insisted that they had parted in such 'apparent harmony'[47], that he could not believe Sir Ralph was acting with her sanction.

A letter from Annabella to Augusta, followed by a second dogged letter to Byron himself, left little room for doubt of that, and not even a stream of appeals from Byron at his most contrite or insinuating could reach her. It was Byron's and Augusta's belief that if he could only have *seen* her they could have made it up, but from the opening manoeuvres it had been a deliberate part of the Milbanke strategy to keep her out of his way, and with every day that distanced Annabella from her old self and Piccadilly, his hold on her weakened.

There can never be any doubt, though, that the tragedy which now began to unfold was of Byron's making, or one that he could have escaped, but to do that would have been to renege on those very instincts that had pushed him into the marriage in the first place. By the middle of February even his most loyal friends had recognised that a separation was inevitable, and yet with a self-destructive recklessness that is either the most baffling mystery or the key to the whole business, Byron refused to grasp the chance while the stakes were still relatively low.

The moment, however, that the issue is posed in such a way, 'mystery' or 'key' cease to be viable alternatives, for when in the whole of Byron's life were the stakes anything but high? From the first day of his married life he had seen Annabella as the incarnation of a world of which he wanted no part, and the brutal truth is that he had not married the most unsuitable woman in England to let her quietly escape him now on the grounds of mental cruelty or mutual incompatibility.

There is, in fact, for all its apparent contradictions – his attempts at reconciliation, the gestures of penitence, the legal stalling – a terrible and remorseless logic to Byron's behaviour that links it directly back to those months before his proposal to Annabella Milbanke. In his journals and letters at that time he had tried to convince himself that marriage was a last hope of 'salvation', but if at some superficial level he did manage to delude himself, his choice of anyone so supremely unfit as Annabella betrayed a deeper compulsion to make it the pretext for the battle that now finally beckoned.

In Lawrence's vision there is always this suicidal element in the fall of the aristocrat, but it is important to remember too that for Byron social destruction and creative survival were one and the same thing. In the supreme masterpieces of his exile he would show what he could do when freed from the stifling restrictions of English life, and in his blind determination to turn the separation from a private into a public issue, from a matter of domestic difference into the great test of principles that it became, he was simply obeying imperatives that he could no more resist than he could have become Bob Southey.

And if it was a battle that he wanted, a tactical error from the Byron camp made sure that the Milbankes were more than ready to oblige. Through the last days of January Annabella had continued to receive almost daily reports from Augusta on the state of Byron's physical and mental state, and on the 30th his cousin, George, brought another lengthy letter from her to Kirkby. 'I shall tell George in a few words what I wish which is nearly as I expressed myself yesterday', Augusta had written, desperate to avert the separation for her own sake as well as Byron's and Annabella's,

> That you would *pause* a few days, consider the *probable* and *possible* consequences of this letter from ye effects on B – for they *must* affect *you & your child.* I am very strongly of opinion *revenge* will be uppermost & this from my late observations. What revenge could he take so effectual as depriving you of the child! & *who* could prevent him. Can *we* all say that a man who is not deranged *sufficiently* to admit of being *controuled* is unfit to have the care of his own child! & what would be the consequences to that child & your own feelings![48]

If Augusta imagined that she could frighten Annabella into compromise with this threat, she had fatally miscalculated. By her own admission there was scarcely a maternal bone in Annabella's whole body, but the mere thought of losing Ada was enough to trigger off among the Milbankes all those paranoid social anxieties Byron had been born to provoke.

The threat was also enough to bring Annabella more directly into the drama, and on 22 February, leaving Ada behind, she joined her father in London and for the first time told her lawyer, Stephen Lushington, of her suspicions of incest. Lushington had hoped before this first meeting that he might bring about a reconciliation, but with such an accusation in the air he knew that this was impossible, and over the next weeks Annabella composed under his direction the series of statements that collectively form the historical case against Byron and Augusta.

The separation drama had now taken on an independent life of its own, and if Augusta had any lingering hopes that she might still have some influence, those were destroyed when on 5 March the two 'sisters' finally met for the first time since Annabella's departure. Annabella was '*perfectly determined* NEVER to return to him, happen what might', a shocked Augusta reported to Byron's friend Hodgson the same day, in a letter that tells us more about Annabella than all the legal documents of the separation put together,

> that if *her own* friends even *knelt* to her to do so she felt herself bound by every moral and religious duty to refuse ... I never can describe Lady Bs appearance to you – but by comparing it to what I should imagine that of a Being of another world. She is positively reduced to a Skeleton – pale as *ashes* – a deep hollow tone of voice & a *calm* in her manner quite supernatural. She received *me* kindly, but that really appeared the only SURVIVING *feeling* – all else was *death like* calm. *I* never can forget it – never![49]

It was not just Byron's fate Augusta should have read into that icy calm, but her own too. In the weeks before this meeting Augusta had clung to her faith in the strength of Annabella's affection, but with the pressures from Lushington mounting and rumours of incest common currency now even among Eton schoolboys, she had become as necessary a casualty as Byron of Annabella's overwhelming need for respectability.

Through the rest of the month the two women continued to meet occasionally, but unknown to Augusta, Annabella had already begun that exquisite campaign of innuendo and muted half-confidences that she was to sustain for the next forty years. At the end of February she received a letter from an old friend of Augusta's begging her to scotch the rumours circulating London, but in the gap between what Mrs Villiers asked and what

Annabella was prepared to say, Augusta stood as exposed as if she had been openly denounced. 'I deeply regret the reports which have been circulated relative to the causes of Separation between Lord Byron & myself', she wrote back,

> and none can occasion me more sorrow than that which you mention as reflecting on Augusta's character – but as I can *positively* assert that not one of the many reports now current, have been sanctioned or encouraged by me, my family, or my friends, I cannot consider myself in any degree responsible for them . . .
>
> In the state of circumstances you must be aware that a publication of the real grounds of difference between Lord B. and myself would be extremely improper – and in conformity with the advice I have received, I *must* abstain from any further disclosure.[50]

It was not in the end, though, the pressures from her lawyers or parents that finally released Annabella from the ties of gratitude and affection, but an intervention of a very different sort. At the end of March Annabella was on the point of returning to Kirkby and Ada, when she received a note from Lady Caroline Lamb, asking to see her in secret for a moment before she left town.

There could scarcely be a more perfect demonstration of Byron's genius for uniting the most disparate elements of English society in a common cause against him than this meeting of polar opposites. In the first days of the separation Caroline had written to offer him her passionate support, but when her letter went unanswered she was determined to make him pay for the confidences and indiscretions that had left him dangerously in her power.

When Annabella met her at George Lamb's house, she found Caroline in a state of apparent agitation at the thought of breaking 'solemn promises'[51], but with the interests of revenge and higher morality in such perfect conjunction the consciences of both were soon comfortably squared. 'Oh I never knew what it was to love before', Caroline reported Byron confessing to her,

> there is a woman I love so passionately – she is with child by me, and if a daughter it shall be called *Medora* –[52]

Judging from Annabella's notes, it was Caroline's subsequent denunciations of Byron's homosexuality, his perversion of his page, Rushton, and his 'unrestricted practice' in the east, that most jolted Annabella at the time, but it was the revelations over Augusta that lodged deepest. Caroline told her that from the time Augusta had arrived at Bennet Street in 1813 Byron had hinted at an illicit passion, and when Caroline had piqued him with the comment that whatever she might believe of him she would not credit it of Mrs Leigh, he had brutally retorted that 'the seduction had not given him much trouble'[53].

It did not matter whether the accusations were true or not, or that the source was so wildly unreliable, the meeting proved the final blow for Augusta, because it allowed Annabella to bend to her lawyer's demands without any apparent sacrifice of principle or consistency. Up until this point she could plausibly argue that so long as there was any doubt as to Augusta's guilt Christian duty dictated kindness, but in the name now of the same morality her obligations were plain.

On leaving Caroline she wrote to Lushington, telling him that her suspicions had now hardened to *absolute* conviction'[54]. Through an intermediary, she broke the news of a change of heart to Augusta, explaining that neither her spirits nor health would allow them to meet again. 'I hope you will approve the purport of the accompanying letter to Mrs Wilmot', she wrote in a prophetic covering note to Robert Wilmot, a cousin of Byron's,

> which is intended to convey to Augusta, with the least poss-
> ible pain, the line of conduct that now appears necessary
> – for whatever a solitary moment of indignation may have
> prompted me to express, my permanent feelings will always
> be to soften, as far as my principles will permit, the misery
> that awaits her –[55]

It was a moment of tragedy for both of them, a moment when under the pressures of social necessity and self-preservation, their respective characters began to mutate into the forms of their later lives. There is no need to sentimentalise Augusta into a sort of wronged

Hermione, but in these weeks either side of the separation, when she had first defied Byron to protect Annabella and then against all advice and self-interest stayed loyally at his side at Piccadilly, the pliancy at the heart of her character acquired a quality that has a kind of grandeur about it. 'When all around grew drear and dark', Byron wrote in a celebration of her almost reckless selflessness,

> And reason half withheld her ray-
> And hope but shed a dying spark
> Which more misled my lonely way;
>
> In that deep midnight of the mind,
> And that internal strife of heart,
> When dreading to be deem'd too kind,
> The weak despair – the cold depart;
> . . .
> Thou stood'st, as stands a lovely tree,
> That still unbroke, though gently bent,
> Still waves with fond fidelity
> Its boughs above a monument.
>
> The winds might rend – the skies might pour,
> But there thou wert – and still wouldst be
> Devoted in the stormiest hour
> To shed thy weeping leaves o'er me.[56]

For someone as innately shy as Augusta, there could have been no crueller proof of the cost of her loyalty than the notorious incident just over a week later when she and Byron were both publicly cut at Lady Jersey's. From the very start of the crisis her courage had been of the private sort that shirks exposure, but as the separation battle entered its last days and Byron prepared to sign the papers and leave England for ever, it became the public contest he had always sought. 'Lady Jersey had a party a few nights ago, at which *he* appeared to the surprise of the company', Annabella reported the incident to her mother with a shallow triumphalism that shows how far she had travelled since the first days of the separation,

Mrs. G Lamb cut both him and Mrs. Leigh – Brougham &
some other Gentlemen, *him.* Lady Jersey has since called
on me. So have many people – Lady Derby three or four
times . . .

   Mrs Ellison, whose kindness has been most zealous, says
that now one has an opportunity of knowing who are bad
& good – that there never was a question which disclosed
morals so decisively.[57]

When every act of Annabella's during these months is scrutinised,
however, every single discrepancy in her different accounts of her
marriage pounced on by Byron partisans, the crucial fact so often
forgotten is that *she* was as much on trial as was Byron. In its
earliest days their courtship might have progressed in the lax
world of the 'spider queen', but if Annabella had been married
off by the rules of the Regency her separation and marriage were
to be judged by a morality that we now think of as 'Victorian'.

   And born of the political and religious convulsions of the sixteenth and seventeenth centuries, nurtured by Addisonian morality, held at bay for another century by the vigour and intelligence
of the Augustan age, 'Victorianism' was a force that only the most
independent mind could have resisted. As the rumours of sexual
deviancy circulated through London, England and the nineteenth
century had found their true voice. To the old and familiar attacks
of the Tory papers was added the snakelike voice of Henry
Brougham; to the Manse-born outrage of Joanna Baillie, the slurs
of the gutter press. Even Lady Melbourne, mercifully only two
years from the grave, felt discretion the better part of valour. In
the middle year of Lord Liverpool's premiership – while Thomas
Bowdler was preparing his notorious edition of Shakespeare and
Shelley and the daughter of Godwin and Mary Wollstonecraft were
going into exile – his 'corbeau blanc' knew there was nowhere a
Byron could hide. 'I was accused of every monstrous vice by public
rumour and private rancour', he later wrote,

   my name, which had been a knightly or a noble one since
   my fathers helped to conquer the kingdom for William the

Norman, was tainted. I felt that, if what was whispered and
muttered was true, I was unfit for England; if false, England
was unfit for me. I withdrew; but this was not enough. In
other countries – in Switzerland, in the shadow of the Alps,
and by the blue depths of the lakes – I was pursued and
breathed upon by the same blight. I crossed the mountains,
but it was the same; so I went a little farther, and settled
myself by the waves of the Adriatic, like a stag at bay, who
betakes him to the waters.[58]

For all the self-dramatisation of this apologia, not to mention a
healthy dollop of equivocation, the hysteria which greeted the
publication of *Don Juan* two years later underlines that Byron was
essentially right. There would be the odd dissenting voice raised
in its praise, but when the radical Thelwall and the apostate
Wordsworth can join forces, William Roberts of the Evangelical,
Tory-supporting *British Review* and the liberal *Edinburgh's* Jeffrey
share the same platform, one is looking at a country fighting for
its moral life. 'You will probably see Gifford, the Editor of the
Quarterly Review', Wordsworth wrote to Crabb Robinson, a man
who would later call Annabella 'the most noble woman'[59] he had
ever known,

Tell him from me, if you think proper, that every true-born
Englishman will regard the pretensions of the Review to
the character of a faithful defender of the institutions of
the country, as *hollow*, while it leaves that infamous publication Don Juan unbranded . . . What avails it to hunt down
Shelley, whom few read, and leave Byron untouched?[60]

But if in a land of 'true-born Englishmen' there was nowhere for
Byron to hide, there was still less chance, on this cusp of the
Georgian and Victorian ages, of a woman escaping her share of
criticism. In his letters and poems Byron had always addressed
Annabella in the classic terms of nineteenth century fiction as
'angel' or 'devil', and as the rumours surrounding her marriage
grew louder she could only be one or the other, the 'pure woman'
enshrined in the fantasies of the coming age or her demonic

'other' – Jane Eyre or Bertha Mason, Amelia Sedley or Becky Sharpe, Mina Murray or Lucy Westenra, the 'Annabella' that Byron had imagined when he first saw her, or another Caroline Lamb, whose rampant sexuality was already degenerating into the madness of her last broken days. 'How could you go on?'[61] Annabella was asked by Lady Ann Barnard, as if somehow the integrity of all womanhood had been compromised by her silence. Why had she not returned to her father's home from Halnaby in the first days of her honeymoon? How could a woman of any purity have remained in that Piccadilly household with her sus- picions, Mrs Stowe needed to know. How could she protect and befriend a woman guilty of Augusta's crimes? How could she have invited Augusta in the first place? Or left her there, with a man she believed deranged, if she suspected the danger? How could she allow any gratitude or scruple of conscience to stand in the way of sterner moral obligations? 'The most degraded of street walkers in the Haymarket was a worthier character' than a woman who could have lived with those suspicions, a Victorian journalist wrote. 'How weak, and worse than weak', another writer con- demned her,

> delicacy should have died, and nature was privileged to show – if such there were – the records of uttermost pol- lution.[62]

In a sense, Annabella had only herself to blame for this crisis, because it was her decision alone to make incest an issue of the separation. The accounts of her first meetings with her lawyer, Lushington, make it plain how wary he was of any such accusa- tions, but from the moment that Augusta became any part of the equation Annabella could either be sullied with the taint of her own sexuality or begin the metamorphosis from wife to 'madonna', and from madonna into that disembodied and sexless spirit from a higher world that became the final, hideous avatar of Victorian femininity.

And only Annabella knew what a long journey that was, how deeply compromised she was by Byronic 'sin', just how vulnerable she was to any question of when she first knew of Byron's and

Augusta's relationship. Over the years she would shunt that
moment backwards or forwards as the varying demands of drama,
morality or legal advantage required, and yet if there is one thing
that no tampering can disguise it is that in her fascination with
the Byrons she had willed herself to an ignorance long past any
time that was humanly possible to sustain.

To any neutral, the misery of her honeymoon, the anxieties of
a bride imprisoned by the snows of Halnaby, or the claustrophobic
misery of Piccadilly would be explanation enough for any equivocation but not to the over scrupulous mind of Annabella. Over
the years in public she might justify her passivity as Christian
charity or the uncertainty of innocence, but in that complex,
morbid conscience of hers she knew that she had allowed herself
to be tangled in a web of deception and self-deception subtler and
more morally dangerous than anything the 'spider' had woven for
her.

These scruples have come to seem in many ways so alien, the
language in which they are invariably couched so unattractive,
that it is easy to forget how seriously they preyed on a young
woman of twenty-four whose conscience had been shaped by early
nineteenth-century evangelicalism. In the last statement she made
about her life with Byron the year before she died, Annabella
described the temptations of the kind of moral relativism that she
had faced in her marriage, and of the sterner imperatives of
religion that had steeled her against them: 'I felt a responsibility
for him as well as myself,' she wrote

> and when my own interpretation of the *natural law* was
> clouded by my feelings, I referred to the *Revealed* will – in
> this sense J. Christ may indeed be said to have been my
> Saviour – I found in his precepts that 'immutable morality'
> which the reason of man is often incapable of discerning.[63]

To anyone who can think like this, it would be no consolation
either that there had been no moment of choice, no incident
that forced her to see the love of Byron and Augusta for what it
was; there had been no balancing of suspicions and probabilities,

but only a gradual slide into acquiescence that was so much easier to bear than the alternatives. In the early days of her marriage when she begged Augusta to be her 'ONLY friend' she can have had little idea of the unholy compact she was forming, but long before that cold January morning when she left Byron's house for the last time she knew that she had crossed some invisible boundary that separated her married self from the Seaham moralist for good.

After the first desperate week of the honeymoon when Byron emerged from the blackness of his wedding day, there had been a period of emotional and sexual happiness that left an even deeper scar on her psyche. From the earliest correspondence of her marriage it is clear that she took an almost coquettish pleasure in her own sexuality, but as she was swept up on the public demand for female 'purity', the playful fears she had confessed to Augusta that she would shock even Byron with her sexual demands were memories that had to be ruthlessly suppressed.

'Were you then *never* happy?[64]' Byron wrote to her in genuine bewilderment after the separation, and Annabella could no more have answered that truthfully to herself than to her lawyers. There is nothing in her correspondence during her marriage that remotely suggests the unremitting misery of later statements, but in her memory even the briefest flash of fulfilment had to be buried under the visceral horror of Byron's footsteps echoing outside her bedroom door at Piccadilly or Six Mile Bottom.

It is interesting, though, that almost alone in the Piccadilly household – Augusta included – Annabella seemed to know that even in Byron's blackest moods she was in no physical danger from him. In the weeks after the birth it is plain from the servants' testimony that he tried to force himself on her, but that poignant cry from Kirkby that she would prefer even the coal hole at Piccadilly to the safety of her parents' home conjures up an image of emotional servitude more complicated, elusive – and ultimately destructive – than physical brutality alone might indicate.

And if in the end there is nothing that lies so completely or properly beyond the reach of biography than another's sexuality, the obsessive denial that began with the separation process suggests the guilt of the disillusioned acolyte rather than the cruder trauma of the victim.* It is notable that in a literary context Byron's bitterest enemies invariably came from the ranks of his former disciples, and when, as in Annabella's case, the Byronic 'contagion' was literal and not figurative – the impregnation physical and not mental – the revulsion was of a different order altogether.

If this must be speculative, there is corroborative evidence of Annabella's disgust and self-disgust in the pattern of physical illnesses that began with her marriage and dogged the rest of her adult life. There has been a lot of savage play made of the 'professional' invalidism that became such a feature of her long widowhood, and yet one hardly needs the tools of psychology to recognise in her history of nervous illness, mimetic pains, and bouts of bulimia, the physical symptoms of those suppressive, hysterical disorders that fill the medical textbooks of her age.

The behavioural patterns of her whole life, too – the self-dramatisation, the emotional lability, the 'sibling' rivalry with Augusta, the violent alternatives of love and hatred – read like case notes on hysteria and whether her illnesses were psychosomatic or not it is revealing that she herself traced her disorders to the womb and the birth of her daughter. 'He is equally positive that all my complaints are dependent upon a disorder of the womb', she passed on a medical opinion to her mother as early as 1819, foreshadowing, perhaps, one reason for the emotional frigidity of her relations with her adult daughter,

> that has existed ever since Ada's birth ... The vessels of that region are in consequence overloaded and will require continual depletion by cupping and leeches.[65]

*   *   *

* In a brave book, written in a very different sexual and legal climate more than forty years ago, G. Wilson Knight was less tentative. In 'Lord Byron's Marriage' he argued that the fear and guilt that drove Annabella was that of consensual sodomy, a conviction he largely based on the Don Leon poems, to which he gives a kind of apostolic authority on the subject of the marriage that derived from Byron himself.

That last sentence is particularly revealing, and at times of emotional crisis throughout her life she regularly cupped or 'depleted' her abdomen, as if to rid herself of the contagion of her own sexuality, to 'drain' herself – as Byron accused her of doing to their daughter – of the Byronic blood that had infected her. 'Yet, though dull hate as duty should be taught', Byron addressed the infant Ada in the third canto of *Childe Harold* with a prescience that would only be finally realised in the family vault at Hucknall,

I know that thou will love me; though my name
Should be shut from thee, as a spell still fraught
With desolation, and a broken claim:
Though the grave closed between us, – 'twere the same,
I know that thou wilt love me; though to drain
My blood from out thy being were an aim
And an attainment, – all would be in vain,
Still thou wouldst love me, still that more than life retain.[66]

Byron's imagery was unerring, because if one incarnation among all the myths of Byronic corruption might define Annabella's trauma in the months after the separation, it is that of the vampire. In the popular fiction of the century a loose association of Byron and vampirism would come to enjoy a harmless vogue, but for the woman who had blindly accepted him in marriage, the identification of Byron with physical and moral pollution that began with Polidori's *The Vampyre* had a complex and erotically charged significance that was at once more disturbing and liberating. 'It happened in the dissipations attendant upon a London winter', *The Vampyre* opens with a macabre reprise of that *annus mirabilis* of 1812 – the year of *Childe Harold*, Caroline Lamb and Annabella Milbanke's first sight of Byron,

> there appeared at the various parties, a nobleman more remarkable for his singularities, than his rank. He gazed upon the mirth around him, as if he could not participate therein. Apparently, the light laughter of the fair only attracted his attention, that he might by a look quell it and throw fear into those breasts where thoughtlessness reigned . . . His peculiarities caused him to be invited to every house;

all wished to see him, and those who had been accustomed to violent excitement, and now felt the weight of ennui, were pleased at having something in their presence capable of engaging their attention. In spite of the deadly hue of his face, which never gained a warmer tint, either from the blush of modesty, or from the strong emotion of passion, though its form and outline were beautiful, many of the female hunters after notoriety attempted to win his attentions, and gain, at least, some marks of what they might term affection: yet such was the apparent caution with which he spoke to the virtuous wife and innocent daughter, that few knew he ever addressed himself to females. He had, however, the reputation of a winning tongue; and whether it was that it even overcame the dread of his singular character, or that they were moved by his apparent hatred of vice, he was as often among those females who form the boast of their sex from their domestic virtues, as among those who sully it by their vices.[67]*

It is fascinating, in fact, to see the ways in which expressions of Byronic 'evil' that became the stock metaphors of nineteenth century fiction seemed to have an almost *literal* urgency for acolytes who fell under his spell. In the *roman à clef* with which she took her revenge on Byron in 1816, Caroline Lamb likened his impact on England to that of infection, and at the heart of Mary Shelley's *The Last Man*, written in the wake of his death at Missolonghi, lies precisely the same sense of physical contagion that *The Vampyre* and *Glenarvon* both voiced.

There is, of course, nothing new or unusual in the harnessing of 'sin' to disease in this way, but in the mythologising of Byron to which these three fictions contributed there was a slightly differ-

---

* For all its plagiarisms – it was based on an idea of Byron's – and the commercial deceptions with which it was launched, the story has won Polidori, Byron's talented but emotionally unstable doctor, a place in literary history that in one sense at least is deserved. *The Vampyre* is no better or worse than the hundreds of gothic or horror stories that filled nineteenth-century magazines, but with the Byronic figure of Lord Ruthven, Polidori changed the mythology of the vampire for good, rescuing him from his roots in the peasant folklore of eastern Europe, and reinventing him in the guise of the 'aristocratic predator' that in popular western culture he has remained ever since.

ent process at work. From the Black Death to AIDS, disease and illness have been routinely ascribed to moral causes, and yet in the case of Byron cause and effect have always been subtly complicated, the physical and sexual glamour of the living man being first stigmatised as moral threat and then in turn metamorphosed back into images of plague or vampirism that stretch out beyond the grave to endanger the world.

And if three such different, but dependent, personalities as Polidori, Caroline Lamb and Mary Shelley, can have seen Byron in these similar terms, it is unlikely his wife would not also have clutched at the same kind of associations. One of the subtler attractions of the vampire myth for the nineteenth century was that it enabled people to project a sense of inner pollution onto an external enemy, and for Annabella more than anyone, the haunting consciousness of her own submission – the secret fear of her own sexuality – would have given this demonisation of Byron an almost redemptive urgency.[68]

If there was a kind of comfort in the notion of Byron as an *external* threat, however, the fictional rituals of vampirism would come to enshrine a more disturbing aspect of Annabella's predicament as she tried to reinvent the psychological and sexual realities of married life. In the popular mythology of the creature it is always the victim who invites the enemy across the threshold, and the truth that Annabella could never have admitted to herself let alone her lawyers or parents was that it was *she* who had courted Byron – *she* who had renewed their relationship in 1813 – *she* who had surprised him even before their marriage at Seaham with her ardour – *she* who had joked of her sexuality to Augusta – *she* (and her subsequent denial and self-denial were so complete that her descendants could not believe the evidence when they saw it) who had invited Augusta into her household and begged her to stay.

As the separation ground towards its conclusion, more mundane arguments over money and procedures also inevitably took their toll, but the sense of guilt that fuelled Annabella's growing intransigence cannot be ignored. If she could have talked to the one person in a position to understand the moral and emotional confusions of her feelings it might have been different, but cut off as she was from Augusta and surrounded by advisers and sympathisers determined to raise her on a pedestal, Annabella abandoned herself to the myth of pure womanhood her public demanded.

Given the pressures on her, the process was probably inevitable, but during these last weeks of the separation battle Byron's own behaviour certainly made her retreat into martyrdom and denial all the easier. On 18 March he sent Annabella a draft version of the first verses he ever wrote for her, and whatever sympathy they temporarily won for him at large – and schoolgirls in America wept over them – their manipulative dishonesty only hardened her resolve. 'Fare thee well!', the verses begin and end, with every shade of emotional exploitation and half-truth sandwiched in between,

> Fare thee well! and if forever,
> Still for ever, fare thee well:
> Even though unforgiving, never
> 'Gainst thee shall my heart rebel.
> Fare thee well! thus disunited,
> Torn from every nearer tie,
> Sear'd in heart, and lone, and blighted,
> More than this I scarce can die.[69]

'Serenely purest of her sex that live', Byron wrote of her again a fortnight later, 'But wanting one sweet weakness – to forgive'.[70] It was not a sentiment likely to mollify Annabella. It was not even a charge that she had yet earned. It did, though, invert a truth that, in one of those flashes of insight which sometimes illuminate her pages of soul-searching, Annabella herself recognised. He had injured her too badly, she noted, ever to be able to forgive her.

He had, also, hurt her too much for the Milbanke camp to forgive or bend. Right through to the middle of April 1816, three months after Annabella had first left Piccadilly, Byron continued to struggle against the inevitable, contesting detail by detail the terms of the separation, and with every delay making his position worse. There had never been any question of Annabella's lawyers using the charge of incest in court against him, but with the swell of public opinion running strongly in their favour and every week spawning fresh rumours, Lushington knew that they had no need.

With the end only a matter of time, Byron prepared to leave the country. On Sunday 14 April, Byron and Augusta said their final goodbyes, brother and sister both convulsed with grief at the certainty that they would never see each other again. A week later his lawyer Hanson brought the deed of separation to Piccadilly, and with a final curse for Annabella's helpless old confidante, Mrs Clermont, Byron signed it and, two days later, on 23 April – abandoning birds, squirrel and everything else in the house to the bailiffs – set off for Dover and exile.

If there could scarcely be a more symbolic day for the outsider to quit London, or a more defiant way to do it than in his new coach modelled on Napoleon's campaigning carriage, Byron marked his arrival in Dover the next day with a second and less grandiose gesture of identification. The sea was too rough for the Ostend packet to sail, and with Hobhouse and that other exile-in-waiting, Scrope Davies, he made a pilgrimage to the churchyard where Charles Churchill, eighteenth-century satirist and archetypal outcast, lay buried. Byron lay down on Churchill's grave, measuring himself, as it were, for his future role in life. 'I stood beside the grave of him Who blazed the Comet of a season', he recalled in a poem that veers uneasily between pastiche Wordsworth and sober self-questioning,

> And I saw
> The humblest of all sepulchres, and gazed
> With not the less of sorrow and of awe
> On that neglected turf and quiet stone,
> With name no clearer than the names unknown,
> Which lay unread around it.
> And is this all? I thought – and do we rip
> The veil of Immortality, and crave
> I know not what of honour and of light,
> Through unborn ages, to endure this blight,
> So soon, and so successless.[71]

Had Byron left no other hostage to fortune but his fame, he could have afforded his philosophy, but he had fatally done more than that. 'I have just parted from Augusta', he had written bitterly to Annabella the previous week, the same day that he had seen his sister off to Newmarket for the final time,

> Almost the last being you had left me to part with – & the only unshattered tie of my existence – wherever I may go – & I am going far – you & I can never meet again in this world – nor in the next – let this content or atone. – If any accident occurs to me – be kind to *her*. If she is then nothing – to her children ... I say therefor – be kind to her & hers – for never has she acted or spoken otherwise towards you – she has ever been your friend – this may seem valueless to one who has now so many: – be kind to her.[72]

Byron never wrote a more thoughtless letter. Exhausted but triumphant, Annabella had been handed the blue print for her whole future life. 'But first on earth as Vampire sent', Byron had written in a mood of extravagant self-parody in the Giaour,

> Thy corse shall from its tomb be rent:
> Then ghastly haunt thy native place,
> And suck the blood of all thy race;
> There from thy daughter, sister, wife,
> At midnight drain the stream of life;
> Yet loathe the banquet which perforce
> Must feed thy livid living corse:
> Thy victims, ere they yet expire,
> Shall know the demon for their sire,
> As cursing thee, thou cursing them,
> Thy flowers are wither'd on the stem.[73]

It was such a threat that Annabella was coming to see in Byron. 'And shall I take a thing so blind', another apostate Byronist, Tennyson, would demand in a passage that might have been written for her,

> Embrace it as a common good,
> Or crush it like a vice of blood
> On the threshold of the mind.[74]

For Annabella, as for Tennyson, there could in the end be only one answer. She had felt not just the glamour, but the dangerous, liberating, potency of Byronic freedom and would never forgive herself for having almost succumbed. At the age of just twenty-three, reunited after almost two months with Byron's sole legitimate daughter, her course was set. Self-preservation and moral duty pointed her in the same direction. She owed an obligation not just to herself but to Byron. She had failed him but she could save those that he had loved from the pollution of his influence. Her life's crusade, prosecuted with all the unquestioning, melodramatic conviction of the saved, would be to redeem the Giaour's blood-line from the curse of its own inheritance.

THE KINDNESS OF SISTERS

On the same day that Byron sailed from Dover, Annabella left for Kirkby, her job in London complete. For a short time after the publication of 'Fare Thee Well' public support might have wavered, but for a month at least the tide had been running strongly in her favour, the sympathy won by Byron undone by the savage sequel he directed against a defenceless Mrs Clermont. 'Good God', Mrs George Lamb had written after Annabella asked her not to discuss the separation,

> can I sit by and hear him defended when I know him to
> be the greatest Villain on earth, and you the most injured
> and excellent of human beings. I really *cannot*. As to the
> other person, I do not wish to reveal her faults, for I could
> almost pity her, when I think how unhappy she must be
> and I look upon her more as his victim than as his
> accomplice.[75]

As Annabella returned to her family, it was to take possession of the more palpable spoils suggested in a cartoon George Cruikshank drew of Byron's departure from Dover. He stands in a bottle-laden rowing boat taking him out to the Ostend packet, the Drury Lane actress Charlotte Mardyn on one arm, a couple of doxies clinging to a leg apiece, a smirk on his face and his hat doffed in a last gesture of ironic farewell to the receding shore line of England. Out of his mouth, the key words heavily underlined in case the irony was lost on anyone, come those lines from his poem to Annabella,

> All my faults perchance thou knowest –
> All my madness – none can know; –
> Fare thee well! thus disunited –

Torn from every nearer tie,
Seared in heart –. & love – & blighted –
More than this I scarce can die!!!!!

It is not so much the richly comic figure in the rowing boat,
though, that makes this cartoon so relevant here, as the background. On the left is just visible the stern of the vessel that will
take him to freedom. On the right, is a miniature England, church
spire rising from the kind of landscape that had so bored Byron,
the cliffs of Dover lapped still by a pre-Arnoldian sea of certainty.
On the white cliff top, guardian of its morals – half Blakean
figure of innocence, half archangel at the gates of Eden – stands
Annabella, her daughter Ada in her arms.

It is the presence of Ada in this cartoon, as in another entitled
'The Separation', that pinpoints the role that Annabella had
found for herself with the end of her marriage and return to
Kirkby. It is ironic that both cartoons should have made such
insistent capital of a daughter that Annabella had not actually
seen for two months, but in an important sense they were right
because it was on that child and the future she embodied that
Annabella lodged her moral justification to pursue the course
that would consume the rest of her life.

When one is talking about the 'life' of Annabella, though, one
is talking about an inner life that, as with so many men and
women touched by Byron, seems to run parallel with an outer
existence with which it has little obvious connection. If one
charted Annabella's external career in the years after Byron's
exile, one might see a woman gradually freeing herself from the
legacy of marriage, moving with age and recovering self-
confidence from the private to the public sphere, immersing herself in the reforming issues of the day, doing good works, founding
schools and raising a daughter, with seemingly nothing but
chronic ill-health and something akin to the terminal restlessness
of the dying to link her to her secret life that fed off the corpse
of her married self.

In a piece of autobiography she wrote at the age of sixty-seven she spoke vividly of the cold unreality of the outside world to her during these years, and if it is the Annabella of Reigate one is after – the frail and driven figure of old age – then it is in the history of that feverish other world with its inescapable realities of guilt and fear that one has to look.

In the first weeks after Byron's departure, however, it was as if even that was dead. During the last phase of the separation struggle Annabella had lived on the adrenalin of battle, but back with her parents and cut off from the excitement of a controversy, the inevitable physical and emotional reaction set in. 'I feel more weakness now than during my greater exertions', she confessed at the beginning of June, 'Sleepless nights, and head-achy days.'[76]

By the time that Annabella wrote that letter, just six weeks after arriving at Kirkby, she had also clearly had enough of the enforced intimacy of home life, and on 8 June she set off on the cross-country journey with Ada to Lowestoft where she had taken a cottage for the sea air. On their journey westwards the crowds came out in force to stare at Byron's wife and child, and yet judging from the easy tone of Annabella's reports, notoriety held fewer fears for her than the oblivion of Kirkby. 'The people at Ely and Peterborough Stared at us very much', Annabella wrote, as if recording her infant daughter's impressions, 'and Mama said we were "Lionesses"'.[77]

As Benita Eisler has shrewdly underlined, Annabella's months at Lowestoft mark an important phase in her development, because it was there that she made her first contacts with a group of those 'saints' who provided nineteenth-century Evangelicalism with its moral and social leadership. In her early years there had always been an essentially cerebral quality to Annabella's religious convictions, but under the influence now of the rector of Harrow, John Cunningham, whom she met during this Lowestoft summer, Annabella's faith and language began to assume the distinctive tones of her maturity. 'I have talked to Cunningham a great deal about Lord Byron', she reported back to Kirkby on 7 August,

which his Harrow connections with him naturally led to,
and found him very accessible to Truth. I have accompanied the Cunninghams to some of the Cottages of
the Poor, and have very much admired the way in which
they administered the comforts of Christianity ... I have
done as much good as I could amongst the sufferers in this
place, & I fancy there will be a general mourning at my
departure.[78]

If there is any evidence needed of the dangers of Evangelicalism
to a woman of Annabella's temperament it can be found in that
letter. In the immediate days after her flight from Piccadilly there
was an astonishing lack of priggishness or rancour in her memories of Byron, but one only has to look at the complacent certainty of her use of the word 'Truth' to see how far Lowestoft had
taken her towards identifying her own cause and that of public
virtue as one and the same.

For all the contacts with Evangelicalism, however, the Cunninghams' influence was one of tone rather than substance, because
long before Lowestoft she had already begun her campaign of
self-justification. In the final separation agreement the question
of Ada's future had been left undecided, and although there was
never any real prospect that Byron might hand her over to
Augusta's care, the threat of it had been excuse enough for Annabella to resume those contacts with her sister-in law that answered
to some of the deepest but most unattractive needs of her personality.

To be fair to Annabella, however, it had cost her far more to
cut herself off from Augusta in the first place than it ever had
from her husband. In the first days after leaving Piccadilly she
had clearly felt a real anguish at losing Byron, but more startling
is not that she could have still loved him after everything she had
suffered, but the speed and determination with which she was
able to crush her affections.

It was her great fear, she told Lady Ann Barnard, after the
separation, that she would think only too kindly of Byron, but
while she genuinely believed that, she had misunderstood an
important aspect of her attraction to him. From the first day that

she had seen him he had been at least as much a 'cause' as a man for her, whereas with Augusta every feeling was real, forged by the strangest of intimacies, tested among the miseries of New-market and Piccadilly, and rewarded by an affection and kindness that was genuine on both sides.

If Byron and his wife brought out the worst in each other, the oddity of the marriage is that Augusta and Annabella had brought out the best. There were certainly times during that year when Annabella could have 'plunged a dagger'[79] into her rival's heart, but those spasms of jealousy and anger were balanced by months of reciprocal support without which neither of them could have survived a hostility that at times fused them in Byron's mind into a single, composite enemy.

Even during the most antagonistic moments of the separation, too, when the gap between the two women had inevitably widened to an open breach, the most partisan of Annabella's supporters could never forget the protective kindness Augusta had shown her. '[In] regard to Mrs. Leigh', Mrs Clermont had written to Lady Noel, trying to allay those fears that Byron would remove Ada from her mother and put her in Augusta's care,

> you have I think been very unjust, as I am confident, how-ever maliciously he may act, it never has been her wish to take it from A or ever will be, although I feel she must have felt herself much hurt of late by a change of manner on this side. I know she has acted weakly but I do firmly believe her intentions have been good – nor can I ever forget the kindness A experienced from her the latter part of the time she was in Piccadilly; even for her life, I believe we may thank Mrs. Leigh.[80]

Something more than gratitude should have bound Annabella to Augusta, however, because if she needed to free herself of her husband, she could not banish Augusta without – in Falstaff's phrase – banishing the world. There was a concentration and destructive intent to Byron that Annabella rightly feared, but with all the messiness of her circumstances, with her hopeless husband

and ailing children, her endless pregnancies and financial crises, her mixture of kindness and selfishness, of moral laxity, self-sacrifice and stumbling pieties, Augusta was her lifeline to a fuller sense of humanity.

More disturbingly, though, Augusta was also her lifeline to a fuller sense of her own personality, and as with Byron, it was not so much Augusta's faults as the reality of her *fascination* that turned Annabella against a woman to whose sense and kindness she owed so much. In later life she would tell the novelist Harriet Beecher Stowe that there had never been anything physically or mentally attractive about Augusta, but it was actually she who was the 'Byron' Annabella had always wanted, alien but sympathetic, sensuous but unaggressive, fallen but pliant in ways that answered to all her most chronic needs. 'Dearest A.', she had written in the first days of the separation,

> I know you feel for me as I do for you, and perhaps am better understood than I think. You have been, ever since I knew you, my best comforter, and will so remain, unless you grow tired of the office, which may well be.[81]

'In this at least I am "truth itself"', she wrote again, in the same vein,

> when I say that, whatever the situation may be, there is no one whose society is dearer to me, or can contribute more to my happiness. These feelings will not change under any circumstances, and I should be grieved if you did not understand them. Should you hereafter condemn me I shall not love you less . . . I wish you to consider yourself, if you could be wise enough to do that for the first time in your life.*[82]

This profound and passionate attraction was something that Annabella could never admit to her family during the separation, nor increasingly to herself. Throughout most of her future life her closest friendships would be with other women, but if Annabella

---

* When these letters – and they are not the only ones – came to light after Annabella's death, her family was so astonished that they thought them forgeries.

had so much as suspected a sexual dimension to her feelings for Augusta it would have only doubled her resolve to crush her.

The story of her campaign for the 'redemption' of Augusta in the months after Byron's exile forms as ugly an episode as any in the bitter history of the marriage. It is difficult to think of the ghost-like figure at Mivart's Hotel and forget the tragedy that lay behind it, and yet it is harder still to imagine what circumstances could ever justify the campaign of mental cruelty with which Annabella attempted to stamp out the memories of her own complicity in Byronic 'sinfulness'.

'Be kind to Augusta and her children'[83], Byron had asked her in a fit of deluded optimism, and there is something awesome in the ferocity with which she interpreted that injunction. Under the repellent guise of duty there was no refinement of moral tyranny that could not be justified, no letters to and from Byron that should not be censored, no retrospective adjustment of fact, no minute advance or withdrawal of affections – held over her like a prisoner's privileges – that was not warranted by the duty of reducing Augusta to that proper 'spirit of humility and repentance'.[84]

It would have been unpleasant enough if this had been a silent and solitary persecution, but throughout her life Annabella's treatment of Augusta was characterised by a mix of public forbearance and private indiscretions. During the days of the separation her suspicions of incest were confided only to her lawyers and parents, but on the day before she left London for Kirkby, and Byron for the continent, she paid a visit to a friend of Augusta's that marked a significant broadening of her campaign.

That friend was the forty-year-old great-great-great granddaughter of Oliver Cromwell, the Hon. Mrs George Villiers, the former Theresa – or Therese as she preferred to be known – Parker. She had first written to Annabella at the end of February in an attempt to stem the rumours sweeping through London, but from Annabella's first visit she seems to have become a willing convert to her side, united in the pursuit of what she labelled 'the *great* object'[85], and only divided by the tactics that should be used. 'My dear Mrs. Villiers', Annabella wrote to her from Kirkby less than two weeks after their meeting, explaining why she had decided not to confront Augusta directly with incest as her new ally was advocating,

> ...Your argument that the Physician should know the whole of the Malady, would lead me to regret that a natural horror of the subject, and a feeling for her, had kept me so long silent to you – and even when I did speak, the only effect I meant to produce was that of inclining you to forgive whilst you lamented this *impression on my mind*, without at all convincing you of its justice. Nor do I now assert that it is in my power to convince you, though my own opinion is unalterable – but you shall receive any information by which you may be enabled to do her good. My great object, next to the Security of my Child, is, therefore, the restoration of her mind to that state which is religiously desirable. I differ from you in regard to the effects of an unequivocal communication. It is easier for the injured than the guilty to pardon, & I doubt if any woman would forgive to another such an avowal ...
>
> Perhaps no human being can create the spirit of humility and repentance which I pray God to bestow upon her – If you would do her good, you judge most wisely in appearing wholly unsuspicious – Let us not be impatient with a 'mind diseased' – but wait to assist the effects of Time – Absence – and I hope – Solitude – for it is not whilst reflection is excluded by the engagements of Society, that moral principle can be revived ... Whatever may be the intermediate circumstances, it will be in her power to reclaim my friendship whenever it can *really* serve her for more than worldly purposes – to speak seriously as I feel, I regard this as a Christian duty –[86]

If this note of Christian oppression seems repulsive enough, Mrs Villiers was ready to go even further in their bid to rescue Augusta from 'the most infernal plot it had ever entered the heart of man to conceive.' 'Now I cannot but think,' she wrote back on 18 May to a further detailed apologia from Annabella, suggesting in her crusading enthusiasm a way to break Augusta's faith in Byron's loyalty, that if she was told by some proper person, & perhaps no one could do this so properly as Mr. Wilmot, [a cousin of Byron's co-opted to Annabella's cause] how completely he had committed her to you: if she could be told certain facts which could only be known to her thro' him & which perhaps *she* must *feel* to be true – if above all she could be made to believe the fact you mention in your letter of his having betrayed her in writing to two or three women, surely nobody but *Calantha* [the heroine of Caroline Lamb's *Glenarvon*] could remain infatuated after that. With such knowledge absence would essentially save her. Without it I cannot but foresee a probable evil – that from the state of their circumstances he may propose to her to go abroad to him . . . You say she would never forgive you for such an avowal of your knowledge – but who is to suffer for her forgiveness – not you – but her – & this she has sense enough to see after the first *entetement* is over – & her affection for her children will I think prevent her attempting to make any resistance that shd. produce an *eclat* which must terminate in *her* ruin and *theirs*.[87]

There was clearly a real satisfaction for Annabella in these exchanges of confidences, but as she prepared to leave Kirkby for Lowestoft a war by proxy was no substitute for the real thing. Through the rest of May long and detailed letters did the rounds between Annabella, Theresa Villiers and even Wilmot, but it was Augusta herself Annabella was after and on the 23rd she announced her intention of extending a 'limited intercourse'[88] to a woman she could not in truth live without. Her intention was, she told Theresa Villiers,

to make *herself* acquainted with my real opinions & feelings, without binding me to avow them publicly, should she be so desperate in the first impulse – that it will nevertheless suspend this terror over her, to be used as her future dispositions and conduct may render expedient, whilst it leaves her the power of profiting by my forbearance, without compelling the utterly degrading confession of her own guilt.[89]

Alone and vulnerable at Newmarket, physically and emotionally
exhausted by the separation crisis and the birth of her fifth child,
dogged by incessant money worries and dependent for her very
social existence on Annabella's patronage, Augusta was in no
position to resist even the most insulting concession. While Byron
was still in England she had stood by him with a wonderful disregard for her own reputation, but Augusta's courage was not of
the kind to survive in isolation. 'My dear Annabella', she wrote
back on 6 June to the first, chilly offer of friendship, superbly
dignified in defeat, but defeated for all that,

> . . . I cannot say that I am *wholly surprised* at its contents.
> Your silence towards me during so long an interval and
> when all *obvious* necessity for it must have ceased formed
> so decided a contrast to your former kindness to me – and
> to what *my Conscience tells me my conduct towards you deserved
> from you* that it could not but require some explanation . . .
> To general accusations I must answer in general terms –
> and if I were on my death Bed I could affirm as I *now* do
> that I have uniformly considered you and consulted your
> happiness before and above any thing in this world. No
> sister ever could have the claims upon me that *you* had – I
> felt it – & acted up to the feeling to the best of my judge-
> ment. We are all perhaps too much inclined to magnify our
> trials, yet I think I may venture to pronounce my situation to
> *have been & to be still* one of extraordinary difficulty. I have
> been assured that the tide of public opinion has been so
> turned against my Brother that the least appearance of
> coolness on your part towards me would injure me most
> seriously – & I am therefore *for the sake of my children* com-
> pelled to accept from your *compassion* the 'limited inter-
> course' which is all you can grant to one whom you
> pronounce no longer worthy of your esteem or affection.[90]

Even Annabella was impressed by the letter, but it was Augusta's
last throw, the last time she ever appealed to the emotional *truth*
of a relationship that no one but the two of them could have
possibly recognised. For the next three months she would
continue to plead her innocence of any *intent*, but long before

she and Annabella finally met at the beginning of September the hauteur of this first reaction was gone, the '*pride* of innocence'[91] broken to a complete and increasingly masochistic subjection. 'You would pity me did you know what I must *ever* feel', she wrote to the tormentor she called with decreasing irony her 'Guardian Angel'

> either in your absence or presence for having been *the cause* of one moment's unhappiness to you! But rely upon *one* thing. I will never *seek* to see you while it is *your wish* I should not – One ray of comfort & hope suggested itself in the thought that *we may meet again* – that *my future conduct* may conduce to it – Tell me – pray – of anything in that which could by any possibility atone for the past – in pity – tell it me dearest A. that I may have one more chance of happiness –[92]

There could be no more revealing proof of the despondency and fear that Augusta felt at this time than the depths to which she allowed Annabella to drag her. There was of course a sense in which with a husband and position at court she could do nothing but take friendship on any terms that it was offered, but within four months of Byron's exile she had so completely identified with the image of herself as victim that she was sending his letters on to Annabella and answering to her dictation. 'His feelings towards you have varied', Annabella wrote to her on 30 July, from Lowestoft, where alternate bouts of gorging herself and taking out a boat to vomit at sea testify to her own nervous condition,

> & they were very seldom suppressed with me – Sometimes he has spoken of you with compassion – sometimes with bitter scorn – & sometimes with dispositions more reprehensible . . . Till you feel that he has in reality been your worst friend – indeed, *not* your friend – you cannot altogether think rightly – yet I am far from thinking any uncharitable feelings are to follow – forgive him – desire his welfare – but resign the pernicious view of being his friend more nearly . . .
>
> There is another reason too of the greatest weight – For

the sake of your children – both as respects the world's opinion of yourself and still more from the injury young minds must receive in the society of one so unprincipled – I feel most anxious for your children in this respect, & for dear Georgiana particularly, whom, as you must remember he had every disposition to injure –[93]

It was still almost a month before Augusta and Annabella would meet again, and resume something like their old relationship, but in the meantime Augusta was risking nothing. 'I have no idea of his returning', she wrote back on 5 August – just two weeks, that is, after Byron, alone at the Villa Diodati on the shore of Lake Geneva, had celebrated her constancy in his 'Stanzas to Augusta',

> & if I gave way to my own forebodings, they wd incline me to think we should never meet again – but to dwell on such is useless – I assure you most solemnly – most truly – I have *long* felt that he has *not* been my friend – but from my heart I forgive him – & pray to God to forgive him & change his heart – to restore him to peace – & there is nothing I would not do which could be done consistently with my duty to God and to others to contribute to his good – how far & whether I may ever be able to do it is I think impossible to foresee – since *futurity* is veiled from us – I perfectly agree with you my dearest A that the *present* presents no hope of the sort –[94]

To be fair to Augusta, though, with the series of verses that began with 'Stanzas', and climaxed the following summer with Manfred's vision of Astarte, Byron was giving her as much reason to fear as miss him. She had never at any time in their relationship been remotely possessive or selfish in her love, but from the first coded confessions of the *Bride of Abydos* and *Parasina* she had known only too well that there was an egotism to his that was prepared to engulf them both.

If that had been true while he was still in England, it was even more so abroad, where freedom and distance inured him to any of the consequences scandal might have for her. In his early letters to her from Switzerland there is a tenderness and sense of loss that is profoundly moving, but for all his real grief at losing Augusta, his retreat from England had not been exile but *escape*.

Byron had *needed* to get out of England, as he had brutally, egotistically needed to provoke Annabella into confrontation, and anyone who admires him has to accept that along with the charm, grace and kindness that make him so endlessly compelling. In his letters to Augusta and Lady Melbourne from as far back as 1813 he had spoke of his boredom and disgust with everything in English life, but it had needed the emotional and mental restraints of marriage to give the physical and claustrophobic urgency to his dissatisfaction necessary to propel him into action.

'God bless him for a gallant spirit and a kind one'[95], Hobhouse had touchingly written in his journal for 25 April, after waving him farewell, and if that was no more than the truth it was truth in a sense that was only fully revealed in exile. It is only too easy to mistake coincidence for cause and effect, but it is impossible not to feel that Byron's growth as a poet and a man is directly linked to his decision to quit England. The triumphs of the years ahead with such poems as *Beppo* and *Don Juan* are of course essentially matters of prosody and technique, of finding in the *ottava rima* a form that could answer to all parts of his personality, a stanza that in its almost infinite flexibility, its ability to undercut itself, could allow the author of *Childe Harold* and *English Bards* to bed down in the same verse together.

And yet even when that is conceded, prosody can only take one so far in any discussion of Byron, because it is hardly an exaggeration to say – rather as with Churchill on the pivotal importance of El Alamein – that before he left England he never did a thing right and afterwards hardly put a foot wrong. There is nothing that apologists can say to excuse the cruelties of his married life, but with the possible exception of a Venetian interlude that strained even Shelley's tolerance, Byron found on the continent a political, emotional, and artistic maturity that he could never have achieved in the straitjacket of English life.

Above all, it allowed him the licence to *live*, and live in ways that marriage to Annabella, or probably anyone else for that matter, would never have done. In one of her interminable analyses of his character Annabella herself recognised how utterly constrained Byron felt by life in his native country, and it is the supreme paradox of his later poetry – and a sad comment on English culture – that it was only in 'exile' and a foreign verse form that Byron discovered that rich, generous, subversive and inclusive 'Englishness' that makes him one of the greatest comic poets in the language. 'As to Don Juan', he wrote to Douglas Kinnaird in October 1818 – 'Bowdler's Year' – making this point, as almost everything else, better than anyone else could,

> Confess – confess – you dog – and be candid – that it is the sublime of *that there* sort of writing – it may be bawdy – but is it not good English? – it may be profligate – but is it not *life*, is it not the *thing*? – Could any man have written it – who has not lived in the world? – and tooled in a post-chaise? in a hackney coach? in a Gondola? against a wall? in a court carriage? in a vis a vis? – on a table? – and under it? I have written about a hundred stanzas of a third Canto – but it is damned modest – the outcry has frightened me. – I had such projects for the Don – but the *Cant* is so much stronger than *Cunt* – now a days, – that the benefit of experience in a man who had well weighed the worth of both syllables – must be lost to despairing posterity.[96]

The hardship for Augusta was that there was no more room for her in this world than there was for Annabella. In the journal he kept of his Swiss travels he was as desperate as ever that she should share in his experiences, but as he crossed the Alps into Italy and the gravitational pull of English responsibilities weakened, he was ready in his verse to put his passion for Augusta to a more brutal and public use. 'She was like me in lineaments', the tortured but defiant Manfred – the most confessional of all Byron's creations – conjures up Augusta's image in the figure of the dead Astarte, destroyed by his incestuous love,

> Her eyes,
> Her hair, her features, all, to the very tone
> Even of her voice, they said were like to mine;
> But soften'd all, and temper'd into beauty.
>
>   Hear me, hear me –
> Astarte! my beloved! Speak to me:
> I have so much endured – so much endure –
> Look on me! the grave hath not changed thee more
> Than I am changed for thee. Thou lovedst me
> Too much, as I loved thee: we were not made
> To torture thus each other, though it were
> The deadliest sin to love as we have loved . . .
> For I have call'd on thee in the still night,
> Startled the slumbering birds from the hush'd boughs,
> And woke the mountain wolves, and made the caves
> Acquainted with thy vainly echoed name . . .
>   I have outwatch'd the stars,
> And gazed o'er heaven in vain search of thee.
> Speak to me! I have wander'd o'er the earth,
> And never found thy likeness – Speak to me![97]

It was incomprehensible to Augusta's friends and family that Byron should be willing to risk her reputation so callously, but the miseries of Six Mile Bottom and Piccadilly had already taught Augusta the destructiveness that co-existed with the love expressed in his invocation of Astarte. In his verses to her he could speak of that love as something that dissolved the boundaries of personality, and yet if they were united in affection they were united in guilt too, and Byron could no more have freed Augusta from their doom than he could himself. 'No avowal can be more complete', an outraged Mrs Villiers wrote, when she finally read Manfred in the summer of 1817,

> It is too barefaced for her friends to attempt to deny this allusion. All that appeared to me practicable I have done with her own family, who have all spoke to me about it. I have said that I had long been aware that his whole object was to ruin others, and particularly those to whom he owed

the most, and I had long been convinced of his wish to confirm the reports of last year to Augusta's prejudice.[98]

The hysteria seems understandable, but other responses to the drama suggest that Mrs Villiers was over-reacting, and perhaps at least part of the anger that fuelled Manfred was Byron's growing sense that Augusta had uncoupled herself from their common fate. It is impossible to imagine that she could have survived the poem in the immediate aftermath of the separation, but if the lack of public comment in 1817 is anything to go by, her campaign of self-abasement over the previous twelve months had done its job.

And consciously or not, in gaining even the limited recognition that she had from Annabella, Augusta had secured the immunity she craved for herself and her family from Byron's worst revelations. 'And so – Lady B has been "kind to you" you tell me', he had written grumpily to her the previous September, just seven days after the first meeting of Annabella and Augusta had given the final public imprimatur to Augusta's rehabilitation,

'very kind' – umph – it is as well she should be kind to some of us – and I am glad she has the heart & discernment to be still *your* friend – you was ever so to her.[99]

'*A thousand loves* to *you* from *me*' ended another letter from Milan just over a month later, 'which is very generous for I only ask *one* in return'[100]. That '*one*', though, he was not prepared to relinquish without a fight. In the first months of exile he had written to tell her that it would kill him if she ever ceased to love him, but as it gradually dawned on him from her increasingly evasive letters that she had sold out to the Milbanke camp the misery of loss took on a sharper, more critical edge. Remember, he adjured Augusta, what they had done to her brother. 'I curse her from the bottom of my heart' he wrote from Venice the following spring, after discovering that Annabella and her lawyers had instituted a Chancery suit to make Ada a ward of court and deprive him of his paternal rights,

& in the bitterness of my soul – & I only hope she may one day feel what she made me suffer; – they will break my heart or drive me mad one day or the other – but she is a wretch & will end ill – she was born to be my destruction – & has been so – ten thousand curses be upon her and her father and mother's family now & forever.[101]

It seemed, too, that with distance Byron was incapable of seeing the misery to which he had condemned Augusta. 'I returned home a few days ago from Rome', he wrote with a breathtaking thoughtlessness to her again from Venice in the weeks before *Manfred* appeared, 'but wrote to you on the road – at Florence I believe – or Bologna . . .'

> I have received all your letters – I believe – which are full of woes – as usual – megrims and mysteries – but my sympathies remain in suspense – for – for the life of me I can't make out whether your disorder is a broken heart or the ear-ache – or whether it is *you* that have been ill or the children – *or* what your melancholy – & mysterious apprehensions tend to – whether to Caroline Lamb's novels – Mrs Clermont's evidence – Lady Byron's magnanimity – or any other piece of imposture; – I know nothing about what you are in the doldrums about at present – I should think – all that could affect *you* – must have been over long ago – & as for me – leave me to take care of myself – I may be ill or well – in high or low spirits – in quick or obtuse state of feelings – like everybody else – but I can battle my way through – better than your exquisite piece of helplessness GL or that other poor creature George Byron.[102]

The key to that letter lies in the drum roll of cities with which it opens, because perhaps more important than anything else in the slow but inevitable estrangement of Byron and Augusta was the fact that while her life had contracted through poverty and loneliness to the domestic drudgery of Newmarket and St James's, Byron's was taking on a new lease. In his earlier letters he would berate her for any real or imagined neglect of him, but if he never ceased to love or demand *her* love with all his old imperiousness, his correspondence is full of a thousand other things in which she could play no role – of Claire Clairmont and the Alps, of mistresses and rumours of mistresses, of Venice and Ravenna

A sense of belonging:
St Peter's Croft, the Milbanke family pew.

FARE THEE WELL.

FARE thee well! and if for ever—
  Still for ever, fare *thee* well—
Even though unforgiving, never
  'Gainst thee shall my heart rebel.
Would that breast were bared before thee
  Where thy head so oft hath lain,
While that placid sleep came o'er thee
  Which thou ne'er canst know again:
Would that breast by thee glanc'd over,
  Every inmost thought could show!
Then, thou would'st at last discover
  'Twas not well to spurn it so—
Though the world for this commend thee—
  Though it smile upon the blow,
Even its praises must offend thee,
  Founded on another's woe—
Though my many faults defac'd me,
  Could no other arm be found
Then the one which once embraced me
  To inflict a careless wound?
Yet—oh, yet—thyself deceive not—
  Love may sink by low decay,
But by sudden wrench, believe not,
  Hearts can thus be torn away;
Still thine own its life retaineth—
  Still must mine—though bleeding—beat,
And the undying thought which paineth
  Is—that we no more may meet.—
These are words of deeper sorrow
  Than the wail above the dead,

Both shall live—but every morrow
  Wake us from a widowed bed.—
And when thou would'st solace gather—
  When our child's first accents flow—
Wilt thou teach her to say "Father!"
  Though his care she must forego?
When her little hands shall press thee - -
  When her lip to thine is press'd—
Think of him whose prayer shall bless thee—
  Think of him thy love had bless'd,
Should her lineaments resemble
  Those thou never more may'st see—
Then thy heart will softly tremble
  With a pulse yet true to me.
All my faults—perchance thou knowest—
  All my madness—none can know;
All my hopes—where'er thou goest—
  Wither—yet with *thee* they go—
Every feeling hath been shaken,
  Pride—which not a world could bow—
Bows to thee—by thee forsaken
  Ev'n my soul forsakes me now.
But 'tis done—all words are idle—
  Words from me are vainer still;
But the thoughts we cannot bridle
  Force their way without the will.
Fare thee well!—thus disunited—
  Torn from every nearer tie—
Seared in heart—and lone—and blighted—
  More than this I scarce can die.

PUBLISHED BY J. JOHNSTON, CHEAPSIDE.

The Separation, a Sketch from the private Life of **Lord IRON** who Panegyrized his Wife, but Satirized her Confidante !!

Escape not exile.
'Oh! What a snug little Island,
A right little, tight little Island.'

Ada: 'The impression she generally makes upon strangers is that of
a lovely child. . . The pertinency
of her remarks and the accuracy
of her descriptions are sometimes
beyond her years'.

Right One cage exchanged for
another: Aged nineteen, shortly
after her marriage to Lord King.

Below 'The greatest of all mercies
has been her disease – weaning
her from temptation & turning
her thoughts to higher and better
things.' On her deathbed,
sketched by her mother.

'Unreasonable – most excited – most irritated':
Medora Leigh, *c.* 1843, aged about twenty-eight.

Medora's last home, Lapeyre, on the banks of the River Sorgue, near St Affrique. TOMBE DE MEDORA LEIGH (FILLE DE LORD BYRON) the sign announces.

'I must thank you for the greatest gift that a human being can make to his fellow, the means of intercourse with a great soul – Robertson's.'
Rev. Fredrick Robertson

Inseparable even in death: the coffin of Augusta, next to that of George Leigh, in the catacomb, Kensal Green; and – a hundred yards away – the grave of Lady Byron.

'Yet, though dull Hate as duty
    should be taught,
I know that thou will love me;
    though my name
Should be shut from thee,
    as a spell still fraught
With desolation, and a broken
    claim;
Though the grave closed between
    us, – 'twere the same,
I know that thou will love me'

Left Prophesy fulfilled:
Byron and Ada, Hucknall.

and Pisa, of Ada and the birth of his illegitimate child Allegra, of Teresa Guiccioli, Italian politics, *Don Juan* and, finally, of Greece. 'I have never ceased nor can cease to feel for a moment that boundless attachment which bound & binds me to you,' he wrote almost savagely from Venice in May 1819 – that word 'bound' taking on a Dante-esque note of eternal punishment,

> which renders me utterly incapable of *real* love for any other human being – what could they be to me after *you?* . . . we may have been wrong – but I repent of nothing except that cursed marriage – & your refusing to continue to love me as you had loved me – I can neither forget nor quite forgive you for that precious piece of reformation. But I can never be other than I have been – and whenever I love anything it reminds me in some way of you . . . it is heart-breaking to think of our long Separation – and I am sure more than punishment for all our sins – Dante is more human in his 'Hell' . . . Circumstances may have ruffled my manner – & hardened my spirit – you may have seen me harsh & exasperated with all things around me; grieved and tortured with *your new resolution,* – & the soon after persecution of that infamous fiend who drove me from my Country and conspired against my life – by endeavouring to deprive me of all that could render it precious – but remember that even then *you* were the sole object that cost me a tear? and *what tears!* do you remember *our* parting? When you write to me speak to me of yourself – & say that you love me – never mind common-place people & topics – which can be in no degree interesting – to me who see nothing in England but the country which holds *you* – or around it but the sea which divides us. – They say that absence destroys weak passions – & confirms strong ones Alas! *mine* for you is the union of all passions and affections – Has strengthened itself but will destroy me – I do not speak of *physical* destruction – for I have endured & can endure much – but of the annihilation of all thoughts, feelings or hopes – which have not more or less a reference to you & to *our recollections*[103]

Byron was neither imagining nor exaggerating; his sense of desolation at the thought of Augusta was real. So, too, was his fear of losing her love. These feelings were, though, only half the truth. 'Speak to me!' Manfred demands of the implacable spirit of Astarte, 'Speak to me!' but as the years of exile stretched out it was increasingly Byron who was silent. Fifteen letters from him to her in the first months of exile; eleven in 1817, just two in 1818. For all its passion, the letter from Venice was the first Byron had written to Augusta in over eight months. 'I have been negligent in not writing, but what can I say?' he began defensively,

> Three years absence – & the total change of scene and habit make such a difference – that we have now nothing in common but our affection and relationship.[104]

'My dearest A.,' – he wrote almost exactly two years later from Ravenna, six months after his last six-line business note,

> What was I to write about? I live in a different world. – You knew from others that I was in tolerable plight – and all that. However write I will since you desire it.[105]

For Augusta, however, that desire had become more a reflex than the consuming need it had once been. After the exhausting months of the separation and the summer of 1816 her life had settled into a quieter rhythm. She still occasionally saw Annabella, and sent on Byron's letters – including that long 'Maniac' declaration of love – but for both the intensity of their relationship had inevitably slackened to a warier stand-off. With the fading threat to Ada, Augusta was less necessary to Annabella than she had first been, and for the time being, at least, her capacity for self-justification was appeased.

In her own way, too, Augusta had also got what she wanted out of the desperate spring and summer of 1816. She and her family had survived. With the eventual sale of Six Mile Bottom and their move to apartments in St James's in 1818 even the Leigh finances had taken a less parlous turn. Her husband was as useless as he had ever been, the small pension granted them by Lord Liverpool's government was invariably late, her boys were rapidly growing up in their father's image, her second daughter, Augusta Charlotte's mental abnormalities were becoming more pronounced, but these were the domestic problems for which Augusta, with her inexhaustible good humour and bewildering belief in providence, was well designed to cope.

The past too was losing its dangers. A letter from Byron still stirred her to a confused anxiety, but only his sporadic threats to return to England could cause real panic. She had survived the third canto of *Childe Harold*, with its celebration of her love; she had survived even *Manfred*, and if the Lamb family continued a campaign of hostility that stretched back to the notorious occasion at Lady Jersey's, a promise of safety seemed to lie in the fact that Annabella had become godmother to her youngest child, Emily.

If Augusta had survived though, the sad truth is that when she bought security with her complicity in Annabella's tyranny she effectively destroyed something in herself that never recovered. It might be absurd to expect or want anything more of a woman who had already given so much to Byron, but in trading love for respectability in the way she did in the first months of his exile, she lost an honesty and integrity that left her with little more than the farago of pieties, deceptions, compromises, and evasions with which she tried to prop up a shabby and uncertain middle age.

Even Annabella and Byron's grandson recognised that the more honest and least destructive answer would have been for her to follow Byron into exile. 'A real reformation', Lord Lovelace, wrote of Augusta in Astarte – the fascinating judgement of a man on whom heterodoxy had been forced by first-hand experience of the misery and corrosive consequences of his grandmother's brand of moral orthodoxy,

> according to Christian ideals would not merely have driven Byron and Augusta apart, but expelled them from the world of wickedness, consigned them for the rest of their lives to strict expiation and holiness. But this could never be; and in the long run, her flight to an outcast life would have been a lesser evil than the consequences of preventing it. The fall of Mrs. Leigh would have been a definite catastrophe, affecting a small number of people for a time in a startling manner. The disaster would have been obvious, but partial, immediately over and ended . . . She would have

lived in open revolt against the Christian standard, not in
secret disobedience and unrepentant hypocrisy . . . Judged
by the light of nature, a heroism and sincerity of united
fates and doom would have seemed beyond all comparison
purer and nobler than what they actually drifted into. By
the social code, sin between man and woman can never be
blotted out, as assuredly it is the most irreversible of facts.
Nevertheless societies secretly respect, though they excom-
municate, those rebel lovers who sacrifice everything else,
but observe a law of their own, and make a religion out of
sin itself by living it through with constancy.[106]

There is another point, too, because for all her vacillations and
her lack of 'centre', the paradox of Augusta's life is that it was
only in her complete self-abandonment to Byron that she achieved
her fullest and most vivid realisation. In his Stanzas to Augusta
he had addressed and claimed her as his 'other half', and in
cutting herself off from him she cut herself off from that part of
her nature that no other person or love could keep alive, from
what Henry James – with her in mind – would later call that 'deep
participating devotion', that 'unspeakable intensity of feeling . . .
identity of sensation, of vibration'[107] that had raised a very ordinary
woman to the heights of generosity and moral courage she
attained.

It is not surprising that James should be both moved and
shocked by Augusta's history. Three years after the death of his
own sister, he began, in a suggestive coincidence, to plan a short
story on the theme of sisterly love while in his carriage on the
way to dine with that same Lord Lovelace. That evening he was
shown for the first time the – then – secret letters between Augusta
and Byron. There would be, though, he noted in that engagingly
'ninnyish' way of his, nothing of the 'nefarious – abnormal –
character'[108] in his treatment of the theme.

The story was never written, but even so that 'nefarious' did
neither himself nor Augusta any real justice. The 'nefarious', the
'abnormal', were irrelevant to Augusta's love for Byron. It was the

most generous, most natural, most moral relationship of her life and if his ideas had ever got beyond those first brief notes James must have come to realise that. No one either could have done finer justice to the strange greatness of Augusta's sacrifice or the withering consequences of reneging on it. No one either could have been better equipped than the creator of Gilbert Osmond and Madame Merle to chart the refinements of mental cruelty that had reduced Augusta's life to the emotional lie it became.

If James 'on' Annabella and Augusta is the book we need, it is in another novel, sent by John Murray to Augusta after the birth of her last child, Emily, in 1819, that Augusta herself might have recognised the most poignant commentary on her loneliness. Given, too, the element of guilt in her inconsolable grief at the news of Byron's death at Missolonghi – the Bible she had given him eight years earlier still in his possession, her name one of the few intelligible words of his last incoherent ramblings – it was the text by which she might have harshly judged herself. 'Do you claim that for your sex?', Captain Harville asks of Anne Elliot at the end of Jane Austen's *Persuasion*, when the two are arguing the respective strength of male and female loyalty. 'Yes', she replies,

> 'We certainly do not forget you, so soon as you forget us. It is, perhaps, our fate rather than our merit. We cannot help ourselves. We live at home, quiet, confined, and our feelings prey upon us. You are forced on exertion. You have always a profession, pursuits, business of some sort or another, to take you back into the world immediately, and continual occupation and change soon weaken impressions . . .
>
> 'I should deserve utter contempt if I dared to suppose that attachment and constancy were known only by women . . . I believe you equal to every important exertion, and to every domestic forbearance, so long as – if I may be allowed the expression, so long as you have an object. I mean, while the woman you love lives, and lives for you. All the privilege I claim for my own sex (it is not a very enviable one, you need not covet it) is that of loving longest, when existence or when hope is gone.'[109]

AN INSTRUMENT OF DESTRUCTION

If ever a death marked a beginning rather than an end it was that of Byron at Missolonghi in the April of 1824. Over the last months of his life his battle for Greek freedom had already begun to thaw public opinion in England, and his death not only completed the metamorphosis from pariah to hero, but radically shifted public perceptions of widow and sister that the separation scandal of 1816 had seemingly set in stone.

Where once Annabella had been swept along on the tide of national indignation after the collapse of her marriage, she was now required to pay the price of England's soul-searching. She still had her loyal supporters in immediate family circles, but as composers set his verse to music and his friends paid court to his 'sweet sister', the 'Clytemnestra' who had driven him into exile was made to feel all the chilly loneliness of the moral high ground she had occupied unchallenged for the last eight years.

It was a deeply disturbing experience for Annabella, still more so as over the years of his exile there had been less and less to sustain her fragile recovery but the consciousness of her own rectitude. In its first months the battle for Augusta's soul and the possession of Ada had generated their own sense of purpose, but the fruits of victory on both scores was a loneliness and lack of direction that insidiously fed the doubts and unhappiness that Byron had left to her.

Almost from the start, too, her loneliness and aimlessness had a physical dimension, as she began the nomadic existence that would characterise the next forty years of her life. On her return from Lowestoft in the summer of 1816 she had stayed briefly at Harrow and in London, but once she had seen Augusta again

and resumed a limited friendship there was nothing to keep her
there or prevent her return to family life and Kirkby.

The problem for Annabella, however, was that an unbridgeable
gulf now separated her from her pre-married self, and she could
no more stay at Kirkby than she could have returned to Piccadilly.
Even during the separation crisis there had been tensions between
Annabella and her mother, and with continuing disagreements
over the renewed contact with Augusta it was soon clearly 'essential to the comfort of all parties', as Annabella put it, 'that my
mother and I should have separate establishments.'[110]

In April 1817 Annabella took a house in Hampstead, but while
for the first time since the separation her life took on some of
the trappings of normality, her preoccupations remained with the
past and not the future. In the middle of June she left her new
home again with Ada and a companion, and leaving her child
with her parents made a slow progress north to Seaham and on
to Scotland, feeling better than at any time since she first became
'Lady B' as she told Therese Villiers – so much so 'that I begin
amongst the associations of my native shore to fancy myself Miss
Milbanke again.'[111]

But wherever she went, and whomever she met – her lawyer,
Lushington, Mrs Minns, the maid who accompanied her on the
Halnaby 'treaclemoon' – there were inevitable reminders that
'Miss Milbanke' had disappeared into 'Lady B' forever. During
the Lowestoft journey the crowds had come to look at Byron's
daughter Ada, but even without that curiosity of warring heredity
in tow Annabella must have been conscious that her one claim
on anyone's attention lay in her name and history. 'I can safely
say that my heart ached for her all the time we were together',
Walter Scott, whom she visited in Scotland, wrote to Joanna
Baillie, one of Annabella's fiercest champions,

> there was so much patience and decent resignation to a
> situation which must have pressed on her thoughts, that to
> me she was one of the most interesting creatures I had seen
> in a score of years. I am sure I should not have felt such
> strong kindness towards her had she been at the height of

her fortune, and in the full enjoyment of all the brilliant
prospects to which she seemed destined.[112]

The dignity and poise were touching – especially in front of someone so naturally sympathetic to Byron as Scott – but back again
with her parents and Ada at Kirkby it was harder to preserve
appearances. In a diary entry from this period she confessed how
frightened she was to go into the 'dark' alone, and yet Annabella
had never lacked the kind of pride that serves for courage and
by the following spring she was again ready to face those places
most intimately associated with her loss.

It was almost as if she felt she had to test herself against the
reality of the emptiness ahead, to take, as it were, full and complete stock of what she had lost when she left Byron, and in the
May of 1818, she paid her first and only visit to the family home
at Newstead that had at last been sold. 'Just come from Newstead',
she recorded on 22 May – an account that must surely owe something to Lizzy Bennett's visit to Pemberley in *Pride and Prejudice*,
a novel Annabella greatly admired,

> The sunshine, the blue lakes, the appearing foliage of the
> remaining woods, the yellow gorse over the wild wastes gave
> a cheerful effect to the surrounding scenes. My feelings
> were altogether those of gratification. In becoming familiar-
> ised with the scene I seemed to contemplate the portrait
> of a friend.
>
> I entered the hall – and saw the Dog; and then walked
> into the dining-room – not used by Ld B. as such. He was
> wont to exercise there. His fencing-sword and single sticks
> – beneath the table on which they stood, a stone coffin,
> containing the four skulls which he used to have set before
> him, till (as he told me himself) he fancied them animated.
>
> I saw the old flags which he used to hang on the 'Castle
> walls' on his birthday. The apartments which he inhabited
> were in every respect the same – he might have walked in.
> They looked not deserted. The Woman who lived in his
> service regretted that the property was transferred. He
> should have lived there, particularly after he was married
> – but his Lady had never come there, and 'she, poor thing!

Is not likely to come there now,' compassionately and mys-
teriously. She said that he was 'very fond of Mrs L —, very
loving to her indeed,' as if this were the only part of his
character on which she could dwell with commendation,
for she drew a very unfavourable comparison between him
and G.B. in regard to charity.[113]

If the memory of Byron still carried with it a romantic aura,
however, her daughter, Ada, provided a permanent reminder of
her need to resist its allure. On the previous year's tour to Seaham
she had recorded her memories of a shoreline she had last walked
with Byron, and however desperate her talents as a versifier there
is no mistaking her resolution.

> But tho' tis not Memory's powers that fail,
> I see these moments as thro' a veil;
> The veil of sorrow hath passed between
> And dimmed the hues of the distant scene . . .
> Ada! Wilt thou by affection's law,
> My thoughts from the darken'd past withdraw –
> Teach me to live in that future day
> When those hands shall wipe those tears away
> Which flow, as I think on the craggy brow
> Where I stood . . . that form is before me now!
> *That* eye is beholding the waters roll;
> It seems to give them a living soul;
> *That* arm by mine is trembling prest,
> I cherish the dream, he *shall* be blest!.
> Again must I break from the magic bond,
> Which Memory fastens with links too fond?
> Had I been happy I might have wept,
> The resisting nerve of my soul had slept;
> But I must not soften beneath the spell,
> Nor pause o'er the spot where the tear-drop fell![114]

'Where there is leisure for fiction', Johnson robustly – and wonderfully wrong-headedly – declared, 'there is little grief'[115], and
the element of emotional narcissism at the heart of Annabella's
misery has always provided her critics with the ammunition they
need. It is certainly true that the figure of Ada could always be

more easily evoked *in absentia* than when she was around, but if her daughter remained an abstraction rather than a reality to Annabella, a call to duty rather than affection, it would be a mistake to underestimate how powerful a motive that was.

With every communication from Byron, too, with each threat of his return, every scrap of gossip from Geneva or Venice, each new piece of verse – the third canto of *Childe Harold, Manfred, Don Juan* – this sense of duty became more acutely defined. Through the years that followed her visit to Newstead, Ada provided in a sense the solitary thread of continuity in Annabella's life, giving the only genuine purpose to an increasingly peripatetic existence that took her to Seaham and from Seaham to Leamington and on to London, Hampstead, Tunbridge Wells and Hastings, while all the time – like some hideous family secret – the portrait of Byron in Albanian dress hung behind a green curtain at Kirkby to remind her of what she was protecting their daughter from.

While it was a duty Annabella never shirked, however, it was one that seemed to have brought her almost no pleasure, and the more successful she seemed in educating the 'Byron' out of her daughter the less she found to love. It was true that in Ada she could control his one legitimate child, but in some perverse way 'legitimacy' seems to have been hedged about for her with all the irony it has in *Lear*, a kind of second best state of loveless domesticity that robbed her own daughter of the glamour that time and again drew Annabella to the Byrons.

The misfortune of Ada's short and troubled life was, in fact, that as a Byron she could never be trusted by her mother, and as a Milbanke could never be loved. From her earliest childhood to her deathbed she was watched over with a pathological fear for signs of incipient 'Byronism', and yet the truth of it was that the traits Annabella disliked in her daughter as she grew up – her secretiveness, her emotional instability, her wilfulness, even, ultimately, her guilt-ridden sexuality – were precisely those that made Ada her mother's rather than her father's child.

Annabella was far too imperious to brook her own character in a daughter, but even if they had been temperamentally suited, it is unlikely that her small sum of maternal instincts would have survived the misery associated with memories of Ada's birth. In the early months of her pregnancy she might have clutched at the hope that a child would win Byron over, but once that illusion was destroyed Ada was always too intimately associated with her own rejection, too bitterly equated with the physical and mental suffering of her married life, ever to have the romantic appeal of the full-blown Byron for her.

But if Annabella could not love her – or inspire love – she was too fond of control to allow Ada to become emotionally dependent on anyone but herself. 'I am sorry that I must take the apparently harsh measures of dismissing the nurse', she had written to her mother as early as September 1817, the first in an insistent pattern of responses to any challenge to her dominance of Ada,

> for I am deeply impressed with the painful & pernicious consequence of presenting myself to Ada in the same secondary part which I have been obliged to play . . . It is a fact too well known, and too bitterly felt by myself that she never saw me without beginning to cry – No wonder when Mamma was made the constant bugbear.[116]

Perhaps none of this would have mattered much if Byron had lived, but when in May 1824 his cousin George – now the 7th Lord – travelled down to Beckenham to break the news from Missolonghi, Ada was all that she had left. For the last two years of Byron's exile communication with him had been limited to enquiries over the child, and with even Augusta now beyond Annabella's reach the misery and hopelessness of the first weeks of the separation returned with a force that she had not felt in eight years.

However different their responses, her situation was, in its way, oddly similar to that in which Shelley's death had left his emotionally estranged widow two years earlier. In her later fiction Mary Shelley would write with a confessional poignancy of a remorse that is frozen by death, and when Byron's servant Fletcher visited Annabella in July he left her convulsed with the same feelings,

the self-control and dignity that had so impressed Scott shattered
on the reality that any romantic illusions of reconciliation had
died with Byron

There had not even been a last word for her, hard as she
begged Fletcher to recall one, and the choice of Augusta and
her children as Byron's heirs further accentuated her sense of
estrangement. He had made no secret of his plans for the Leigh
family when he had drawn up his will just after his marriage, but
even though the deaths of Lord Wentworth that same summer
and of her mother in 1822 had left Annabella a wealthy woman,
so public an exclusion could have only one effect.

In more subtle ways, too, Byron's death confirmed a shift in
the balance of power between her and Augusta that had been
coming for some years. In the first months after the separation
she had held Augusta completely at her mercy, but for all her
pleasure in the exercise of power, Annabella could scarcely censor
Byron's letters without confronting the bruising truth that in
Byron's love Augusta had the only thing that she herself wanted.

If that thought alone was bitter enough, it was Annabella's
misery, as she brooded on her marriage, cut off from either the
grief or the celebrity of her husband's death, that in Augusta's
third daughter she had already begun to find the physical embodiment of everything she herself had lost. She had first seen the
infant Medora Leigh on her wedding visit to Six Mile Bottom in
1815, and though it was the older Georgiana Annabella had seen
most of, it was always and dangerously Medora – or Libby as she
was more commonly known – to whom she was attracted. 'Saw
A.L.'s children', she had noted in her journal as early as Sep-
tember1820, juxtaposing the sense of life and possibilities immi-
nent in their lives with the melancholy of her own,

> felt the most tender affection for – [Medora]. What is the
> reason?
> September 17th, Sunday. Walked early to look at my old
> house in Piccadilly – saw into the room where I have sat
> with him, and felt as if I had lived there with a friend long
> since dead to *me*.[117]

It needs stressing again that there is no conclusive evidence one way or the other for Medora's paternity, but nothing could better illustrate the power of Byronic myth over objective reality than Annabella's obsession with the child. It is almost certain that her belief that Medora was Byron's dated to her meeting with Caroline Lamb after the separation, but Annabella could never have admitted as much even to herself, and in the more exotic legend she made of her life, its most vivid proof had come at Six Mile Bottom when she saw the tenderness on his face as he looked at 'his' daughter.

The sight of Byron with Medora on that bridal visit – apocryphal or not – became a pivotal moment for Annabella that linked past and future in a single moral crusade. No one would ever replace Byron or Augusta in her imagination, and yet as Annabella grew older she came to find in Medora a child who by virtue of her vulnerability and pedigree answered to all the conflicting needs of her own loneliness – the daughter Ada could never be, the ultimate fix for her Byronic addiction, and above all, moral 'cause' and weapon of revenge wrapped in one toxic package.

For a child who was to carry such a burden of expectation, the little that is known of Medora's earliest years is disappointingly ordinary. She was just two when Byron went into exile and only ten at his death, the fourth of Augusta's seven children and Colonel Leigh's favourite – 'the loveliest Infant I ever saw'[118] Annabella brutally told her own daughter, Ada – with nothing more sinister than a look of Byron as a baby and the chaos of life at Six Mile Bottom to overshadow her future prospects.

Nor was it anything more romantic than the chronic state of the Leighs' finances that in the year after Byron's death, indirectly brought Annabella into Medora's life. In the will that Byron had signed in the summer of 1815 he had done everything he could to secure Augusta's and her childrens' futures, but for all the resentment it would generate, the terms of the bequest and the burden of existing debts had left the Leighs as desperately off as ever.

With £60,000 of the inheritance tied up for her lifetime in Annabella's marriage settlement, Augusta had all the discomfort of cutting the widow and rest of the family out of the will, with none of the financial rewards the sale of Newstead should have brought. It had been rightly assumed by Byron that the Wentworth fortune would secure Ada's future, but if Annabella could comfortably afford her public magnanimity at her own exclusion, Byron's separation of fortune from title made Augusta an enemy of the 7th Lord she could have done without.*

It is richly typical of Augusta's fortunes that her one prospect of financial security ended up causing nothing but misery, and when the biographical fall-out of Byron's death began, the gap between the two sides inevitably widened further. In the immediate aftermath of Byron's death Augusta and his friends must have hoped that in burning his memoirs they could silence rumour, but as Medwin, Dallas, Lady Blessington, Millingen, Hunt, Kennedy and the rest rushed in to fill the gap it was only a matter of time before a truce that had survived since Annabella and Augusta's first meeting after the separation was finally shattered.

In the end it would be the controversies raked up by Tom Moore's biography – and Annabella's answering pamphlet – brought out six years after Byron's death, which would lead to open rift, but though neither party saw it, the seeds had already been sown. In the year after Byron's funeral there had been only limited contact between Annabella and Augusta, but when a distant cousin of the Byrons' proposed to Georgiana Leigh in 1825, financial necessity and a habit of dependence that she had never quite shaken off made sure that the first person to whom Augusta appealed was Annabella. 'The young Man is studying the Law & has the talent to make the most of his profession', Augusta announced, in a letter that is so symmetrically and almost miraculously wrong-headed that it shows better than anything else the state to which the moral bullying and equivocation of the last ten years had brought her. He, she continued

---

* In order to compensate the new Lord Byron for his 'disinheritance', Annabella also made over to him her marriage jointure of £2000, a gesture that secured his loyalty to her for life.

is exceedingly clever & in other respects the only person I
know *worthy* of Georgey ... I've seen much of him since
from liking him & finding him so far superior to the *common
herd*, but without the slightest idea till lately that Georgey
was likely to attract him or indeed any body – She is such
a *quiet* being – with very sound & excellent sense & good
judgement, but not brilliant in any way, & I should have
said too *awkwardly shy* to be admired. As far as one can
judge, it promises all the happiness *this* world can give – &
in case of anything happening to me, it wd ensure a sort
of protection to her sisters.[119]

From her own experience Augusta had a horror of long engage-
ments, and with the lovers looking like ghosts, as she told Annabella, and George Leigh, who was violently opposed to the
wedding, temporarily out of the way she was determined to press
forward with her plans. For some reason that has never really
been clear Annabella was reluctant to be seen openly helping the
couple, but she had never forgotten Byron's injunctions to be
'kind' and using the name of one of her future travelling com-
panions, a Miss Chaloner, she advanced the £2000 needed for
the marriage. 'A line – dearest A to tell you our Marriage thank
God! Is happily over', Augusta wrote to her after it had taken
place on 4 February 1826 at St James's Piccadilly, with only herself
and Medora from the family there,

> & in parting with dearest Georgey I feel I could not to
> ANYONE in the world with such perfect confidence *as* to
> Henry Trevanion. I have seen him *daily hourly* for three
> months – in Moments of Sickness, Sorrow, anxiety & sus-
> pense – all most trying predicaments to the Lords of the
> Creation – & which Shew the *real* Character – & his has
> only *risen* in my estimation!
>
> I cannot express *all* I feel to you for your kindness on
> this occasion to which we owe *so* MUCH! But indeed I *am*
> grateful – so are they –[120]

It is psychologically fascinating that at seventeen Georgey – a
'ringer' for Augusta in so many ways – also shared her mother's
attraction to the standard Byronic 'model'. At the time of their

wedding Henry Trevanion was still talking of a legal career for himself, but by temperament and ambition he was a poet *manqué* and not a lawyer, a feebly imitative peddler of Byronic guilt with a strange by-line in religiosity – a Byron gone Celt as it were – with nothing of the energy or talent of his inheritance and everything of its self-indulgence and sexual fecklessness.

The susceptibility of both mother and daughter to this type of man would seem to be an insistent reflex of heredity, but Trevanion's own motives in marrying Georgey are probably more complicated. It is only too possible that he shared the tribal narcissism of so many of the Byrons, and yet if his single volume of verse is anything to go by, the attraction was more pose than 'fatality', a conscious determination to live up to the challenge of his birthright, arrogating to himself everything that was closest to Byron in an assertion of equality that seems closer to the possessive psychology of an Edward Trelawny than it does to the helpless compulsion of Augusta. 'The Giant Minstrel ceased to sweep Childe Harold's Harp', he revealingly addressed one poem, signalling his obsession with the Byronic inheritance.

> At length the harp a maiden takes –
> We start – and Memory weeps to hear;
> As Feeling to the touch awakes
> The Music distant echo makes
> To music felt more near.[121]

It was not often that Augusta defied her husband, and still rarer that George Leigh was right about anything, but in trusting her daughter to Henry Trevanion she made the one cardinal error of her life. For the first two years of the marriage, however, the only public strains seemed the traditional Leigh problem of money, but when in 1829 Georgey was expecting her third child and her fifteen-year-old sister, Medora, was sent to stay with them at Bifrons, the great barrack of a house Lady Byron had lent the couple outside Canterbury, a new episode in the Byron saga began.

*   *   *

One of the great frustrations of this part of the story is that the only account we have of events is that written by Medora herself fourteen years after they occurred. There are a handful of Trevanion's and Georgey's virtually illegible letters to Annabella surviving among the Byron papers, but for any consecutive narrative we are dependent on the 'Autobiography' posthumously published after everyone involved with it who might have challenged Medora's version of things, was dead.

'I am the fourth child of a family of seven', Medora began it, narrating her sufferings with such a lobotomised calm – such a complete absence of conscience or moral consciousness – that they read more like the bloodless synopsis for some Lefanu novel than intelligible autobiography.*

My eldest sister, Georgiana, married Mr. Henry Trevanion, a distant cousin, in 1826, when I was eleven years old. The marriage, which had the approbation of no one except my mother, did not turn out very happily, owing to the small- ness of fortune, and the uneven temper of both parties. I was frequently called in to keep them company, and in March, 1829 (after they had been married three years), it was decided that I should accompany them to a country house which had been placed at their disposal by my aunt Annabella, Lady Byron, during the time of my sister's approaching confinement. The house was in the neigh- bourhood of Canterbury. The last injunctions and admon- itions I received from my mother on starting, were to devote myself in all things to please my brother-in-law, Mr. Trev- anion; to get rid of the dislike I entertained for him, and to cease ridiculing him, as I had been in the habit of doing. I was urged more particularly to this course of behaviour in consideration not alone of his delicate health, but of the poverty which made him peculiarly sensitive. I promised compliance, and accompanied them to the country, as my mother and sister had arranged. My sister's illness, before

---

* The manuscript on which it was based had been in the possession of a man called only 'Mr. S.' in the introduction, a London solicitor named Thomas Smith who had befriended the twenty-eight-year old Medora in 1843, persuading her to write down an account of her history in an attempt to escape her financial misery.

her confinement, was the occasion of my being left much
alone with Mr. Trevanion. Indeed, I found myself thrown
entirely upon him for society. I was with him both in-doors
and out, by day and by night, and was frequently sent by
my sister into his bedroom on errands, after every one else
in the house had retired to rest. Some months passed in
this manner, during which Mr.Trevanion took advantage
of my youth and weakness, and effected my ruin, and I
found myself likely to become a mother, by one I had ever
disliked.[122]

If it is hard to understand their subjection to a man they both
despised, the explanation probably lies not so much with Trevanion himself, but with the Leighs and their chronic vulnerability
to the dismal tyranny of the 'professional' male inadequate of
which he was so perfect a type. In his volume of poetry published
in the year after his marriage Trevanion had self-consciously
staked his claim to the Byron mantle, but in his mix of emotional
incontinence and moral cowardice the Byron that Medora's
seducer comes closest to is not Augusta's brother but – libertine,
charmer, sponge and dependent – her father, 'Mad Jack'.

The romantic appeal of this kind of figure to Augusta, who as an
orphaned child had secretly cherished the image of her disgraced
father, is unsurprising, and in a more febrile, unstable form there
was clearly the same tenderness in the young Medora. 'I remember when a child to have been so much affected and horror struck
with the fate of the Wandering Jew', she later recalled, tracing
her own intense sympathy for the suffering and dispossessed in
every form – from orphans to hunted murderers – to the strange
meld of images that had filled her childhood nights,

> the loneliness of his fate – the everlastingness of this world
> to him – & the uncle who lived and died (I was taught) –
> deprived of all he loved with none but strangers to love or
> care for him all worked together (a strange confusion) &
> many nights have I cried myself to sleep.[123]

It would have gone against Medora's whole nature, though, to
accept responsibility, and in the years ahead, she blamed not just

Georgey, but also Augusta, who, in the spreading fallout of her hatred, was accused of conspiring in her ruin. In her different accounts of these intrigues Medora would later claim Augusta had traded her for Trevanion's favours, and even if the only source for this assertion was Trevanion himself that would never be enough to protect Augusta from the stigma of the charge.

And if it seems beyond belief that Georgey and Medora were the bait dangled by their mother before Trevanion, as Medora claimed, between such Gothic extravagance and a belief in Augusta's total innocence lies a wide expanse of grey that was her natural habitat. At the time that Trevanion arrived in London Augusta was probably as vulnerable as at any period since the separation, and in her Byron cousin she clearly saw a kind of mirror image of what Annabella would want in Medora – the son that her own loutish boys were not and, more importantly, the reincarnation of the brother at whose funeral Trevanion had been his family's representative.

Whatever the degree of Augusta's complicity in her daughter's seduction, however, the only concern at Bifrons as Medora approached her term, was secrecy. Pleading poverty as an excuse for leaving the country, Georgey asked Augusta's permission to take Medora with them for 'H's amusement'. 'The permission was obtained without much difficulty', Medora recalled in the Autobiography,

> & when within four months of my confinement I accompanied them to Calais – The misery I suffered contributed to bring on a premature confinement which took place clandestinely in the house. My child lived & was taken care of by the Medical Man who had attended me . . .[124]

In later life Medora came to believe the baby had been stolen by Lady Byron, but in fact it did not survive long, and three months after the birth, the trio returned to England, Georgey and Trevanion to an aunt's house in Cadogan Square, Medora to her mother's apartment at St James's Palace. Even in Medora's version of these events Augusta clearly had no idea of what had happened

in France, and when Trevanion again became a daily visitor at
St James's, Augusta and Georgey were equally happy to leave the
two alone together. 'During the whole autumn & winter', Medora
went on, blameless as ever in her own eyes,

> I was constantly & daily left in H's society & often till a late
> hour of the night ... & early in the following year I found
> myself likely again to become a Mother. When by H's
> entreaties & prayers I consented to confide in my Mother,
> or rather to seek her assistance – for which purpose I copied
> & signed a letter he wrote to her charging her with all she
> had exposed me to & invoking her assistance – she burnt
> it as soon as read – was kind to me at first but became most
> cruel afterwards to me – though to H. the only difference
> she made was to increase her kindness.[125]

It is hard to imagine how Augusta could have been blind either
to Medora's physical state after her return from France or to
Trevanion's attentions, but there was no faking her shock. 'It
would be impossible for me in the *first* instance to speak to you
my dearest', she wrote immediately to him, the first of two notorious letters that eventually found their way to Annabella – letters
that, whatever gloss one puts on them, mirror the 'labyrinth', as
she called it, of pieties, penitence, and delusions Augusta found
herself wandering lost in during the years after Byron's death,

> Without such emotion as would be painful to us both – and
> I therefore take up my pen, but only to break the ice!
>   You know how I have loved and regarded you as my own
> Child – I can never cease to do so! to the last moment
> of my existence you will find in me the tenderness, the
> indulgence of a Mother – can I say more? If I could, tell
> me so! Show me only how I can comfort and support you
> – confide in me, dearest – too much suffering has been
> caused by a want of confidence. What *might* not have been
> prevented could I have known, guessed, even *most*
> REMOTELY suspected! – but I would not breathe a word
> if I could help it to give *further* pain! ...

I am convinced, dearest, that as I have opened my heart and feelings to you, you will comfort me! I need not point out to you the means! Your own heart will dictate them – and as you are most dear! MOST dear! *Much*, MUCH is in your power.

Heaven bless, comfort and guide you![126]

'Your note just received is to me *inexplicable!*' she wrote again the next day,

> *When* and *how* have you '*witnessed my acting upon a system of distrust?*'
>
> When you answer this, I may be able to meet your accusation – certainly a most unjust one! I will not say *unkind*, for I can make allowances for the effects of your present state of mind upon feelings so sensitive as yours! Dearest – I wish I *could* comfort you!
>
> I was so completely worn out last night from the effort I made to subdue my feelings and to appear cheerful before both the subjects of my agonising solicitude, that I *could not* write to you after you left me – if I had, I might have caused you pain from the uncontrollable state of my feelings . . . Dearest, do not mistake me by supposing that I have so little consideration for the weakness of human nature as to think of 'a TOO *precipitate* execution of my purpose' – a purpose on the accomplishment of which depends my only hope of consolation! You say, *you do not respect me* – you would still *less* respect me if I did not entertain such a hope, and do my utmost by the most judicious means I can think of to accomplish that on which the *eternal* welfare of that unhappy Being depends! And the PRESENT welfare – (nay, I may say *existence* and *sanity*) of so many others depends! . . . Consult dearest G. on the *most judicious means* of proceeding in such a cruel predicament. I have explained my ideas to her on some minor points of *prudence*, which are perhaps more essential than you think for – it is a hateful word where more important interests are at stake, but where the ruin of many may be the alternative of its observance it becomes a serious consideration.
>
> Now Dearest – let me implore of you to be comforted –

to do your utmost to make the best of circumstances – to trust in my affections. That you are tried, SEVERELY tried, I feel – and I pray God to support you and comfort you and guide you! And I feel confident he will never abandon you if you trust in Him!

Do not accuse yourself, dearest, and make yourself out *what you are NOT!*[127]

At the same time Augusta wrote to Medora.

I cannot describe with what pain I observe much that is passing before me; and, my beloved and unhappy child, I implore you – *on my knees I implore you!* To use every *effort of your soul* to cope with those temptations which assault you! . . .

Reflect that you are – no, not now – Great God avert it! That (how shall I write it) you have committed *two* of the most deadly crimes! Recollect who you have injured! – and whom you are injuring – not only your own Soul, but that of another, you think *more* dear than yourself. Think *whom* you have deprived of *his* affection! Think of the others upon whom *shame* and *disgrace* must fall, if even now you are not *outwardly circumspect* in your demeanour! Think of his Family – of *yours* – of your unmarried and innocent sister – of the broken heart of your Father, for that THAT would be the result, I am *convinced* – you know not his agonies for the loss of that poor Angel who was from cruel circumstances comparatively an alien to him – think what *this* would be! – and more than that, of the DREADFUL consequences to HIM – to *another still more* – that no time or place would shield him from their vengeance! Think of what might and *most undoubtedly* WOULD be the consequences even in THIS world! And think of those more important interests, the *eternal* ones of all those Beings dear to you.[128]

Although these letters would come back to plague Augusta, they seem to have had no immediate effect, and when Trevanion and Georgey moved to Colerne, near Bath, Augusta was impotent to stop Medora joining them. If Medora is to be believed Augusta had done her best, in fact, to persuade her to have her child destroyed, but even in the chaos of the Leigh household there was no permanently disguising a second pregnancy, and when Georgey threatened to return alone to St James's, Colonel Leigh had to be told. 'In June of the same year', Medora recalled,

> Colonel Leigh unexpectedly arrived at the country house, preceded by an attorney and sheriff's officer. These parties having gained admittance, Colonel Leigh drove up to the door in a travelling carriage. His old coachman was on the box, and a woman, intended to represent a lady's maid, sat inside. What ensued was great misery to me. I then believed, *though I had been told the contrary by my sister and her husband*, that Colonel Leigh was my father. I wished to spare him the knowledge of my shame. We were never, any of us, taught to love and honour him. But, strange to say, I was his favourite child, and had greater influence over him than any one when he was violent, and would have done anything to hide his faults or spare his feelings.[129]

However naturally violent George Leigh was, a terrified Augusta had clearly persuaded him to see the necessity of discretion, and Medora was able to win herself ten minutes alone with Trevanion before she joined Leigh in his carriage. She had only agreed to go in the belief that she would be returning to her mother's apartments, but on their midnight arrival in London she was transferred instead to a hackney coach 'somewhere near Oxford St'. 'We were driven I know not whither', Medora continued her story, more Lefanu-like than ever,

> until we arrived at a house where I was given into the charge of a lady. The windows of the room into which I was put were securely nailed and fastened down, and there were outside chains and bolts, and other fastenings to the door. There was every show and ostentation of a prison. During my confinement in this place, Colonel Leigh came to see me three times, when I declined to see him any more. My mother came once. Some religious books were sent to me by one of my aunts, I forget which.[130]

The house where Medora was held was in Lisson Grove – 'a private lunatic asylum' in Charles Mackay, her editor's, gloss – to the west of the Regent's Park. In the few minutes conversation she had managed with Trevanion he had promised to follow her to London, however, and after two weeks imprisonment Medora saw him and Georgey driving past her barred window. For the next fortnight the same pattern was repeated almost every day.

> Notes were sewed in my linen when it came from the wash, I did not know by whom, but I suspected by my sister. By this means I was enabled to understand the signs he made to me when he drove past the house. One day the lady to whose care I had been entrusted told me that if I liked to walk out of the house nobody would stop me, and showed me how to remove the chains affixed to the door. I did not hesitate in any choice between two evils, but at once put on my bonnet, followed her instructions, and found Trevanion outside waiting for me. We left the street with all possible haste and secrecy, which we might have spared ourselves, as nobody attempted to follow us.[131]

The evidence for the next stages is fragmentary, and after the strange gothic dramas of Lisson Grove, we have only the skeleton of what Charles Mackay called 'the saddest story . . . that was ever laid to the scrutiny of a harsh and unforgiving world.'[132] For the first two years after escaping George Leigh's control and abandoning Georgey, Medora and Trevanion lived on the Normandy coast under the names of Monsieur and Madam Aubin, but as her health declined and it seemed that she would never 'bear a living child', his interest died and he agreed to the separation she claimed she had always wanted.

During these first, nomadic years of Medora's exile, between July 1831 and June 1833, as she and Trevanion drifted from Normandy to Brittany, her mother had no idea of where she was or even whether she was still alive. In a deposition Augusta later made for Annabella she wrote that she had received news of her daughter's condition for the first time in 1833, and that after every plea for her to come home had been 'resolutely and contemptuously refused', agreed an allowance of £60 on condition that Medora should leave Trevanion and take refuge in a convent.

Medora – a Catholic since 1831 – had already, in fact, entered a convent in Treguier in September 1833, but discovering within days of her arrival that she was once again pregnant, left before Augusta's offer reached her. United again with Trevanion, the couple moved first to Carhaix and then in the following year to a decrepit old chateau near Plouneour Menez. There, in May 1834 – after living together as brother and sister as she put it without a shade of irony – she gave birth to the child Trevanion had always craved. 'Henry at this time gave himself up wholly to religion and shooting', Medora added, 'I to my child.'[133]*

The respite was only temporary, however, and as Trevanion brought a second mistress into the house, Medora's health began to fail. By the spring of 1838, it seemed that she had not long to live. 'The hardships I had endured caused me to fall dangerously ill', she wrote,

> and after some days my life, contrary to all expectation, was saved, though I was declared to be in a consumption, without hope of living beyond a few months. The medical man who attended me was very kind, and the little experience of kindness which I had during my lifetime, made me, at his solicitation, confide to him my real history. I asked his aid to free me from the cruelty of one whom I had never really loved, and who by his conduct every day convinced me more and more of his worthlessness. My greatest wish was to die away from him. Through Mr. C's [Victor Carrel] means I wrote to my mother, and my aunt, Lady Chichester, informing them of my position, and imploring the means to free

---

* Augusta has often been criticised for her inertia, but it needs remembering that she was already trying to look after not just her own family but Georgey and her three children too. 'Her income is £800 per annum', Mrs Villiers later wrote in her defence to Annabella, giving a vivid insight into the background to all Augusta's dealings with Medora during these years,

> Out of this she has to board her husband when at home, and her son Henry always, to maintain herself, Emily, and her servants entirely. She gives her eldest son George £100 per annum – her son Frederick has never cost her less (if so little) as £200 per ann: and she has *entirely* to provide (as far as she can) for the wants and really necessaries of Georgiana Trevanion and her three growing up daughters.[134]

myself. I obtained £5, left Trevanion's roof, and went to the neighbouring town, where I continued to receive most affectionate letters from my mother, but very little money.[135]

With a new reign and Annabella's cousin – William Lamb, the second Lord Melbourne – Prime Minister, even the Leighs' pension had been stopped, and if there was little money going to Medora, that was because there was none to give. As Byron's heirs, however, there was the prospect of the £60,000 tied up for Annabella's lifetime in her marriage settlement, and with every bulletin coming from France sounding as though it might be the last, Augusta executed a Deed of Appointment in Medora's favour for £3000 to protect the future of her three-year-old child, Marie.

It was that Deed of Appointment – an act of generosity on the mother's part but a sniff of independence to the daughter – that over the next years finally and permanently metamorphosed Augusta in Medora's eyes from 'Dearest kindest Mama'[136] to the hyena she became. Within months of its execution Medora had tried to sell the reversion on the Deed, but so long as her mother held the original she was helpless. 'I endeavoured to persuade her to allow me regularly £120 per annum', Medora remembered, with her characteristic disregard for the realities of her mother's desperate finances,

> the small sum I could live on in a very cheap place. She promised, but did not perform; so that after a year and a half I found I should be compelled, as I was advised to do, to sell the reversion to £3000 which I had, with some difficulty, obtained as a provision for my child, after my death, if I did not wish to be forced to return to Mr. Trevanion. During some months the correspondence between myself and my mother continued as affectionate as ever, I endeavouring all the while to obtain from her the means of existence, and she retaining the Deed. At length I wrote to my aunt, Lady Chichester, who had sent me the £5, begging her influence to obtain the Deed for me, and to Sir George Stephen, to whom I had applied to sell the reversion, stating that I was sure my aunt, Lady Noel Byron, would use any influence she might possess with my mother,

to induce her to give up to me that which was my right.[137]
In one respect, at least, Medora was right about her aunt:
Lady Byron was never going to pass up the chance of so
perfect an opportunity of revenge.

THE END OF THE AFFAIR

Even if Medora was unaware of it, her aunt had, in fact, known her story ever since she had first gone to live with Georgey and Trevanion at Bifrons nine years earlier. Old friends in the neighbourhood had kept Annabella abreast of the scandal, and through her old ally George Byron, she had provided the money that took them to Calais at the time of Medora's first confinement.

On the face of it this might seem an act of spontaneous generosity – the fulfilment of her pledge to Byron – but a coincidence of dates and the involvement of anyone so antipathetic to Augusta as George Byron, suggest there were other motives involved. From her first sight of Medora, Annabella had felt a bond that gave Byron's injunction to 'be kind' a special force, and yet if that certainly played its part, the controversy in the same year over Tom Moore's biography makes her assistance seem as much an act of revenge on her as a kindness to her daughter.

The row over Moore's book could not, either, have come at a worse time. In the previous year there had been a bitter argument over the trusteeship of the Byron marriage settlement, and if the dispute was ostensibly a legal one, both Annabella and Augusta knew that the real issues were questions of freedom and control that went to the heart of their relationship. For almost a decade Annabella had felt her grip on Augusta gradually weakening, and the anger with which she had rounded on her when Augusta contested her choice of trustee is an index of the frustration she felt. 'I have had a great deal to annoy me lately', she wrote to one of her confidantes at the end of 1829,

> Think of Mrs Leigh's having, after all my endeavours to
> serve her, accused me of the unfriendly conduct. She can-

not, I think, believe what she says, after all the reason to know how sacred I have held the promise to be 'kind still to Augusta'. I grieve that she deprives me of the opportunities of *acting* up to it in future. It is impossible for me to admit of personal intercourse with her after such wilful misconstructions.[138]

'I can forgive and do forgive freely,' Augusta wrote in her turn, after Annabella had demanded not just her complete submission, but an admission that she had always acted in Augusta's best interests,

all and everything that has agonised, and I may say all but destroyed me. I can believe that you have been actuated throughout by a principle which you thought the right one, but my own self-respect will never allow me to acknowledge an obligation where none has been conferred.[139]

This was an 'insolence' that Annabella could not forgive. Later that same year Augusta sent Ada prayer books for her birthday. 'I had them nicely bound,' she wrote to Byron's old friend Hodgson,

and *Ada*, in old English characters, engraved on the back, and wrote her name and date inside, put them up directed 'To the Hon. Miss Byron, with every kind and affectionate wish', and wrote over this, 'With Lady Byron's permission.' In another outside envelope directed them to Lady B., sent them booked by coach; and have never heard one word since.[140]

It is hard to know if either Augusta or Annabella quite recognised what they were shedding, or, in the genuine anger on both sides, whether they could even remember the intensity of need and affection that had once bound them, but it is doubtful. It was impossible of course for either woman to give up the other without a spasm of pain, and yet it had been so long since the honesty and generosity had seeped out of the relationship, that for both of them its death seems more a release than a tragedy.

More than twenty years would pass before they met again at Reigate, and for Annabella in particular, the break should have been an opportunity to recover something of the emotional balance that had been lost at the separation. In the last years before their break she had continued the nomadic course begun in 1816, moving from one rented house to another in a restless search for peace and health, from Tonbridge and Brighton to Canterbury, Dover, Switzerland – rather like Seaham, only bigger as she wonderfully put it – Italy, Canterbury again, Swansea, Clifton and the West Country.

This restlessness would never completely cease, but for the first time now in more than a decade the Byrons were not the all-engrossing presence in her life, and in 1832, at the age of forty, she moved with Ada to a house called Fordhook, to the west of London, where the educational interests that she had originally shown in 1818 bore their first real fruit. In the 1820s Annabella had involved herself with both prison reform and the burgeoning co-operative movement, but it was only with the Industrial School, inspired by Swiss educational reformers, which she founded at Ealing Grove in 1834, that she could immerse herself at last in a world immune to the aristocratic, destructive energies of Byronism.

With maturity, too, had come a calm and reserved dignity – at least where Augusta was not involved – that could inspire the same kind of chivalrous response Annabella had elicited from Scott sixteen years earlier. 'Her manner', Thomas Campbell admitted, might be 'cool, but is modestly and not insolently cool'. 'I look', he wrote in the *New Monthly Magazine* when Tom Moore's biography had ignited the old controversies over the separation again,

> with wonder and even envy at the proud purity of her soul and conscience, that have carried her exquisite sensibilities in triumph through such poignant tribulations.[141]

For partisan or enemy alike, however, as Campbell's eulogy underlines, it was still her history and *name* that made her interesting. 'I don't know if you have seen the last brochure', *Noctes Ambrosianae* described a portrait of her done at this time, milking the Byron memories as if there were no other terms of reference for a woman establishing her own formidable reputation in the world of early nineteenth-century philanthropy,

> It has a charming head of Lady Byron, who, it seems, sat on purpose – a most calm, pensive, melancholy style of

native beauty, and a most touching contrast to the maids of Athens and all the rest of them.[142]

'Her complexion seemed to me rather dark for an English-woman', another observer noted at the end of the decade, harking back to the same theme,

> marble-like, quite colourless, but her features were faultless, and her expression was sedate, serene, with hardly a trace of grief long since buried.[143]

In a sense they were right, too, because while the period that followed the break with Augusta was marked by some of her most productive work, it was never enough to fill the cravings of her passionate and possessive nature. There can be no question of the seriousness or success of her philanthropy, but Annabella was herself the first to recognise that in some vital way it was little more than a substitute to her for what she had lost.

And as long as she had Ada at home – sixteen when they moved to Fordhook, and an increasingly alienated, unstable and secretive adolescent – Annabella could never free herself of her obsessive fear of the Byron inheritance. In 1823 Byron had written to Augusta for information on the character and appearance of the daughter he had last seen as a baby, and the description Annabella reluctantly furnished gives an interesting insight into the child that heredity and discipline were making of the seven-year-old Ada. 'Ada's characteristic is cheerfulness, a disposition to enjoyment', Annabella wrote,

> this happy disposition was only partially interrupted when at the most oppressive period of her illness, under which she was patient and tractable. The impression she generally makes upon strangers is that of a lively child. Of her intellectual powers observation is most developed. The pertinency of her remarks and the accuracy of her descriptions are sometimes beyond her years; she is by no means devoid of imagination, but it is at present chiefly exercised in connection with her mechanical ingenuity ... With respect to her temper, it is open and ingenuous – at an earlier age it

threatened to be impetuous, but is now sufficiently under control.[144]

There are elements here – the nature of her imagination, the fondness of mechanical pursuits – that would serve equally well for a description of the adult Ada, but if the note of sanguine confidence in that last sentence was genuine, Annabella was deluding herself. 'About Ada', she wrote to a friend in 1830, seven years after her pen portrait for Byron,

> Her prevailing, indeed besetting fault at this time is a disposition to *conversational litigation* – I can give it no other name – and she goes to law with me still more frequently than with anyone else. It is very necessary that this habit should be checked, both as disagreeable and inconsistent with feeling of respect. When represented to her she admits the fact; but she does not *strive* to correct the fault. In one of her letters to you I saw that she gave herself credit for being more influenced by a sense of a duty than by the expectation of approbation or censure. I cannot say that there is much evidence of the former *unconnected* with the latter.[145]

In its own less schematic, intellectually rigorous way, in fact, there is something redolent of the upbringing of J. S. Mill about Ada's childhood, and something not dissimilar in its consequences. There was never at any time in Ada's life the full and articulate realisation of things that Mill so memorably recorded in his autobiography, and yet in its own fashion her whole existence was a conscious or unconscious protest against control, an emotional and physical refusal to bow down to repression that manifested itself in the anger, illnesses, rebellions and deceptions which punctuated her childhood and adult years.

In Ada's own memories, her mother's ruthlessly controlled regime of nurses, governesses, 'furies' and 'spies' took on a nightmarish quality, and there is evidence enough that the placidity of which Annabella boasted had always come at a heavy psychological price. Among the surviving papers from Ada's early years are letters and narrative fragments suggesting a longing for escape, but if the fantasies of flight that haunted Ada's imagination seem revealing enough by themselves, the illness that struck her down in 1829 points to an even deeper psychological malaise.

It is impossible to be sure of what was wrong with her, but with Annabella's and Ada's own subsequent history in mind, a condition that began with an attack of measles and left the child on crutches for the best part of three years was almost certainly psychosomatic. 'At this time she never slept in her bed', her mother's friend, Sophia De Morgan, recalled, in an account that brings out just how temperamentally fragile the adolescent Ada had become,

> but wrapped herself in a rug or blanket outside the bed or on a sofa ... She had strange fancies about eating, which Lady B told me were a repetition of her father's – indeed all these whims, & others which I have now forgotten were, her mother told me, simply inherited ...[146]

It was an illness, too, as this account unwittingly suggests, that had been stalking Ada all her life, because at its root was a confusion of identity that went back to the first time she had asked about her father. In later years Annabella would always claim that she had never prejudiced her against Byron, but Ada's first tentative attempts to understand who she was – to recover that Byronic inheritance she became so vividly, almost mystically, aware of as an adult – was met with such a 'fearfully stern and threatening manner', that it produced a feeling of guilt and 'dread towards her mother which continued till the day of her death'[147].

And if there were times when, as she later confessed to Annabella, she hated her, the 'furies' were always there to enforce the natural guilt of a child unable to love its mother. 'My dear Ada,' her governess wrote to her in 1833,

> You have a parent to whom you have at times behaved in a manner unbecoming the child of so invaluable a mother ... Do not, then, lose the time that is now afforded to you, in doing anything you can to lessen the sufferings and encrease the comfort of your inestimable mother ... In your dear and excellent mother you have (in my opinion)

all that can be offered as an ex[am]ple short of the character of our Saviour, and she is always with you.[148]

Up till the age of sixteen, however, Ada's rebellion was largely
confined to the unconscious protest of her body, but in 1833 the
rumbling discontents finally burst out in an act of defiance that
for the first time openly exposed the yawning gap between appearance and reality in her upbringing.

The details of the incident are still uncertain, but sometime
round this period Ada fell in love with a tutor hired to teach her
shorthand. By her own later admission they had sexual relations
that stopped only short of 'complete penetration'[149], and when
the pair were discovered and the tutor sacked, Ada ran after him
in an attempt to elope that was not thwarted until his family
contacted Annabella and had her daughter taken home.

There is understandably little evidence of this episode amongst
Annabella's papers, but while she might successfully suppress it,
it brought home to her just how fragile her control of Ada was.
In one of the curious anomalies of Ada's character, however,
rebellion would invariably be succeeded by bouts of contrition
and 'self-reform', and the months that followed this aborted
elopement ushered in probably the most stable years in her whole
fraught relationship with Annabella. 'Her daughter is now about
sixteen', a visitor to Fordhook, Francis Trench, wrote of her,
oblivious to any tensions between daughter and mother or the
miseries implicit in his description of the adolescent Ada Byron,

> with a fine form of countenance, large expressive eyes, and
> dark curling hair. Her features bear a likeness to her
> father's, but require some observation before it appears
> strongly. Then, I think, it does. At present her health is
> delicate, and she is obliged to use crutches.[150]

In May 1833, the seventeen-year-old Ada was presented at court,
and within two years this promise of social and emotional con-
formity was confirmed by her engagement to the 8th Lord King.
The two had probably first met through a Cambridge contemporary of his at the home of the great mathematician Mrs Somerville,
and by June 1835 he had proposed and been accepted, writing

to her from his Somerset 'hermitage' 'in a state of continued intoxication of delight'[151] that must have offered Ada her first real glimpse of an escape route from the emotional constrictions of Fordhook.

But if Ada was above all 'grateful'[152] to William King, as she told him in her first letter, she might well have taken alarm from her mother's delight and relief at the news of the engagement. For all her egalitarian and radical pretensions Annabella had always been serenely conscious of the advantages of rank and wealth, and in the thirty-year-old, impeccably earnest, improving landowner with estates in the West Country and Surrey, she thought that she had at last found the perfect gaoler for her emotionally wayward daughter.

And in spite of Ada's apparent willingness to reform, Annabella's suspicions and fears went too deep for a marriage to do anything more than signal a shift rather than a suspension of vigilance. For nineteen years she had watched for every symptom of emotional or moral excitability in her daughter, and if Ada had dreamed that marriage was her release from the disciplines of childhood, then the first letter of her new life should have sounded a bitterly prophetic warning. 'Had I felt less towards my Son,' Annabella wrote to her the day after the wedding,

> I could have *given* my blessing – but he will feel assured of it – and in your own happiness mine *must* be secured whether absent or present. Dear little Canary bird, may the new 'cage' be gladdened by your notes.[153]

As far as Annabella was concerned, in fact, Ada's marriage simply represented an opportunity to co-opt her devoted and tractable son-in-law as a new partner in her life's crusade. In later years events would turn her affection for William King to a vengeful and contemptuous hostility, but through these first years of the marriage they were happy to watch together over Ada's moral welfare as fellow trustees, monitoring her emotional temperature and health, controlling her reading, friendships, servants and children, equally ready to prescribe claret or mathematics as the danger seemed to demand.

Even in the first heady days of this alliance with her son-in-law, however, there was an emotional void in Annabella's life that Ada could no more fill than could the school at Ealing or her work for the Hastings Co-operative. On the surface of it the years immediately after Ada's marrriage were some of the most sanely content of Annabella's life, but when in 1840 she received through the solicitor, Sir George Stephen, a letter from the child she believed Byron's incestuous daughter she was as vulnerable as she had ever been to its dangerous appeal. 'On Sir George Stephen forwarding my letter to Lady Byron', who was at the time visiting Paris, Medora wrote of the first extraordinary contacts with the aunt who had paid for her flight to the continent with her sister and Trevanion ten years earlier,

> I received a most kind and affectionate letter from Lady Byron, and money, with offers of protection for myself and child, and the power of quitting a neighbourhood which was most painful to me. This was in August, 1840. I willingly and joyfully accepted these offers, and accompanied a medical gentleman whom Lady Byron had sent, and met her at Tours, where it was first thought I should reside. Lady Byron, however, proposed that I should accompany her to Paris, and remain with her for a time. I did so, being desirous of attending to the least wishes of one towards whom I had reason to feel so grateful.
>
> At Fontainebleau, where she was detained by illness, *Lady Byron informed me of the cause of the deep interest she felt, and must ever feel, for me. Her husband had been my father.* She implored and sought my affection by every means; and almost exacted my confidence to the most unlimited extent. I was willing and anxious, in any and every way I could, to prove my gratitude and the desire I so sincerely felt to repay by my affection and devotion any pain she must have felt for circumstances connected with my birth and her separation from Lord Byron. Her only wish, she said, was to provide for me, according to Lord Byron's intentions respecting me, and according to my rank in life. She evinced much anxiety for my health and comfort, expressed indignation for all I had suffered, spoke of the comfort I would be to

her, and of the necessity that I should be a devoted child
to her. There was a Chancery suit begun against my mother,
to obtain possession of the Deed.[154]

For ten years since their argument over the marriage trusteeship,
Annabella had been brooding over Augusta's 'ingratitude', and
it was soon clear that she had found the instrument of revenge
she wanted. As late as 1838 Medora had been affectionately
addressing her mother as 'My own Dearest kindest Mamma', but
now with a new patroness to placate she was shrewd enough to
see that the symbiotic demands of revenge and justification could
only be satisfied in one way.

There was nothing Medora Leigh was not prepared to say
against Augusta, and nothing Annabella was not ready to believe,
or pass on to a growing circle of confidantes that soon included
her own daughter. Throughout Ada's childhood Annabella had
always been ruthless in keeping the Leighs at arm's length from
her, but under the excitement of the new cause she now claimed
from Ada on Medora's behalf the rights of a 'sister'.

It was a curious sisterhood – as odd in its way as that of Augusta
and Annabella – but for the time at least both were willing
initiates. 'I have formed a very favourable opinion of her', Ada
wrote of Medora to her husband from Paris, where in the spring
of 1841 she had gone to join her mother and Medora.

> She impresses me with the idea of *principle* very strongly;
> and I find from the Hen, [the Lovelace family name for
> Annabella] (who has now communicated to me *everything*),
> that her sincerity & perfect *truthfulness* have been tested
> very completely. I have heard altogether a history *most shock-
> ing*. The whole of it must be made known to you, but this
> can be done only in conversation.
>
> As for the ruin of Medora, it was effected by the *united
> efforts* of the Mother; the Sister; Mrs. T; and Mr. T. himself;
> and by means of drugging the victim, who found herself
> ruined on coming to her senses. Under the circumstances,
> Medora herself (who always particularly *hated* Mr T) must

be considered absolutely guiltless. She emancipated herself
as soon as possible from Mr T.; but owing to the cruel
conspiracy against her, she was in a manner *forced* to remain
in his power during two or three years.[155]

It is to this period that we owe the most lurid extravagances of
Medora's history, as piece by piece – the drugging and rape, the
collusion of Augusta, her affair with Trevanion, the corruption
of one daughter, the pimping of the next – the thin, dreary
story of Trevanion and Medora took on its definitive shape in
Annabella's vengeful imagination. 'Think of Mrs L. sending word
to Mr.T. that her other daughter Emily was *ready* for him whenever
he chooses to come to England', Ada wrote to her husband in
April 1841, adding one final grace note to the score of Augusta's
crimes,

> which being outlawed, he luckily cannot do! What a *Monster*
> of iniquity! And how her wretched children, who are all
> victims one way or others, are to be pitied – I hope you
> burn these letters.[156]

It is hard to see how even Annabella could have brought herself
to believe a story so utterly at odds with any of the known facts,
but for her it became part of a wider delusion that had been
growing with the years, belated proof of the wickedness of the
woman who, in her distorted memory, had deliberately kept Byron
from reconciliation. 'Yet alas! It is *nothing* to what I have learned
of circumstances now many years passed away!' Ada repeated this
received version of Augusta's wickedness,

> So iniquitous & villainous a tale could never have entered
> into the imagination of any but the wretched actors them-
> selves.
>
> How comes it that my Mother is not either dead, mad
> or depraved? *This* is the question that must suggest itself as
> most obvious.
>
> A new language is requisite to furnish terms strong
> enough to express my horror & amazement at the appalling
> facts ! That viper – Mrs. L. – crowned all by *suppressing*
> letters of my Mother's to my father when he was abroad

after the separation, & *forging others* in their place! *She monster!*[157]

With such a history for justification, it was not just a matter of pleasure but duty to keep Medora away from the woman who had polluted the child's life at source. In the first months after her intervention Annabella made sure that there was no direct contact with Augusta, but when in the spring of 1841 she received a letter from London pleading for information about her daughter, all the bottled resentment of a decade's silence burst out. 'I am to be considered responsible for the safety and comfort of your daughter Elizabeth Medora', Annabella wrote,

> Her malady, the effect of physical & mental suffering com-
> bined, can be retarded, in the opinion of the physician &
> surgeon whom I have consulted, only by extreme care and
> by her avoiding all distressing excitement. The former I
> can secure, but not the latter – I would save you, if it not
> be too late, from adding the guilt of her death to that of
> her birth. *Leave her in peace.*[158]

There is no minimising Annabella's malice towards Augusta, nor the injustice with which she persecuted her, but it is impossible to follow her involvement in Medora's story and not recognise its more poignant sub-text. 'I am particularly happy just now', she had written from Fontainebleau to Lady Olivia Acheson after her first meeting with Medora, giving frightened expression to all those more generous and fearful instincts that were tangled up with the desire for revenge,

> Feelings that have long lain, like buried forests, beneath
> the moss of years, are called forth, and seem to give happi-
> ness to one for whom I have something like a mother's
> affection. This is a little gleam in my life – it will not last,
> but its memory will be sweet. The object of my affection is
> marked for an early grave.[159]

It was not the prospect of Medora's death that clouded this happi-
ness, though, but as letter after letter makes plain, the fear of one more rejection at the hands of the Byrons. 'Do you remember

Dear E' [Medora had become Elizabeth by this time], Annabella asked a year later, by which time the underlying strains of their relationship were already taking their toll,

> that I asked you early in our acquaintance not to use affec-
> tionate expressions towards me? I then felt the possibility
> of a change in your feelings. You did not regard my request,
> and I suffered myself to believe that you had conquered
> the early impressions to my disadvantage which were made
> upon your mind, and were able to love me. But I ought
> not to have let you deceive yourself and me (much pain
> would then have been spared) and should not have
> accepted your expressions of entire confidence and
> affection.[160]

'From some of your recent letters', she continued the theme in a second letter,

> you have appeared to suppose, contrary to my repeated
> assertions, that I wished for *expressions* of affection. Far from
> it. My bitter experience of them in your family has made
> me almost shrink from them . . .[161]

The relationship was perhaps more complex than this suggests, however, because if Annabella had allowed herself to be emotionally ensnared, the same was true of Medora. Her main concern was always with the Deed and the independence it could give her, but from the day she came under Annabella's care parts of her nature that had been virtually extinguished were suddenly, confusedly and painfully brought back to life.

It is in fact only from this period, when Medora was twenty-eight, that we can gain any sense at all of the personality that lay behind her *Autobiography*. The strongest impression the published version of the story produces is of a self-justifying selfishness, but in the letters she wrote to Annabella over the next two or three years – literally hundreds of them, many six, eight pages long – one gets for the first time some glimpse of a complex nature that from earliest adolescence had been warped by events and expectations beyond its control.

They are extraordinary letters, written in a hand that changes not just from letter to letter, but from paragraph to paragraph, vivid, restless, impulsive and contradictory, humble and self-justifying by turn. They are the letters of someone who feels everything with a frightening immediacy. They often seem written under the influence of alcohol. They are full of the moment – of flowers coming into bloom and dying, of weather, shifting clouds, sunsets, pets, servants, and strangers – and all felt and *lived* with an empathetic intensity that hovers on the edge of mental imbalance.

Above all, though, in her correspondence with Annabella, one can begin to see the appalling cost of the life of sexual and emotional abuse that she had suffered from the age of fifteen. They are not letters that can make one *like* Medora any more than the autobiography does, but for all their self-dramatising egotism there is a terrible pathos in their cry for a lost innocence, a shocking and unanswerable validity in both their infantilism and rage against the childhood she had never had.

She addressed Annabella as 'Mama', as 'Pip', as 'Pippin', as 'My old Porpoise', and signed herself 'your loving child', 'your own dear child'. She berated herself for being a bad child. She pleaded forgiveness for her temper, her hatreds. 'Oh I have been a good child tonight', she told her, 'I have been kind and gentle as you like me.' 'If you only take care opening this' she sent off another letter, 'you will find such a nice kiss.' 'My dearly beloved Porpoise' she wrote to her, in a letter which fuses all these emotions into one,

> My mother is sixty years old tomorrow – how well I remember my anxiety to procure her violets for that day – now it can pass by occasioning *only* a shudder of horror – almost fear – why was I born to love so dearly . . . Forgive me if I am naughty I do not mean it, your child.[162]

For all the genuine emotional needs the relationship satisfied on both sides, however, there was always going to be enough of the warder in Annabella's attitude to create its own inevitable tensions. While they were in Paris together Medora had been welcomed into the family as Ada's 'sister', but back in England and installed at Moore Place – the new house Annabella had bought near her son-in-law's Surrey estate – a certain ambiguity entered into her status, leaving her stranded somewhere between celebrity victim and 'madwoman in the attic', a charge too romantic to be abandoned and a weapon too inherently unstable to be deployed with any security. 'I find the mind in the state you described', reported Annabella's friend Mrs Jameson – a kind of Grace Poole at Moore Park to Medora's dark skinned, dark eyed hispanic-looking Bertha Mason,

> Unreasonable – most excited – most irritated – changing however from storm to sunshine at every moment . . .
> There is the wish to be & do right – with an utter blind-ness to the right – which is inexpressibly painful to contem-plate . . . I am at moments embarrassed and provoked as with a perverse but charming child – & when I think that this child is a woman –[163]

Mrs Jameson had a put her finger on it with that last remark, because at the age of twenty eight, with a seven-year-old daughter of her own, Medora was in no mood to endure the control that had blighted Ada's childhood. In the early days of dependency it may have suited her to pander to Annabella's emotional and moral demands, but as she sensed the power inherent in her birthright it was her financial 'rights' as Byron's child and not moralising charity she demanded.

For all Medora's desire for independence, however, the final crisis in their relationship was emotional and not financial. She had originally turned to Annabella in an attempt to secure the Deed designed to guarantee Marie's future, but when in May 1842 Augusta at last backed down rather than face the inevitable scandals of a court hearing, Medora reacted with a fury not even Mrs Jameson could have predicted.

Medora's response to her victory is still difficult to understand, but over the last year she had felt both the frustrations and the power of her position too vividly to be placated by anything short of her mother's humiliation. It is impossible to know if she had come to believe the stories she had told against Augusta in France, but whether she did or not she was no longer prepared to be the mere instrument of someone else's revenge and in a bizarre twist rounded on the patron who had financed her legal battle. 'In May, 1842', she wrote of Annabella in her *Autobiography*,

> my long anxiety in the matter of the Chancery suit was ended. The suit was concluded in a way, without consultation with me, which showed that all that had been promised to me, unsolicited and unsought, was not sincere, and that I had been in a manner sacrificed in my mother's interest.[164]

'You cannot imagine the scenes of fury she exhibited', Annabella later wrote to Selina Doyle,

> I had *never* seen anything like it – She told me I was her bitterest enemy and threatened every kind of revenge – I not having from first to last uttered an unkind word to her ... She obliged me to quit my house some weeks before she left England, by rendering it intolerable to me – but I loved her still.[165]

That last phrase was not simply for show, but after two volatile years there was a recognition on both sides that their friendship had exhausted its usefulness. At the beginning of July Annabella offered Medora an annual income of £150 if she would live quietly abroad with her daughter Marie, and after contesting every condition in a bid for more money, a defeated Medora finally gave way to terms that left her securely in Annabella's financial control and the Deed in the safekeeping of Lord Lovelace. 'After consulation with Ada and Lord Lovelace', Medora recalled a year later, conveniently forgetting the rage with which she had turned on Mrs Jameson on her last day or the threats to Ada that she would throw herself 'down the throat' of the first man who would marry her,

> it was thought best I should leave, and Ada promised, and I thought I might trust to such, to watch over and protect

me, assuring me her mother was deeply attached to me. I trusted to this, and left England on Friday evening, the 2nd of July, 1842. And partly in order to prove to Lady Byron my earnest wish to leave her still, and on my maid's solicitation on account of their importance, in the event of my death, left a box of letters and papers with Lady Noel Byron's housekeeper, to be given to Lady Byron on her return to Moore Place; and the Deed of appointment to Ada on her leaving me at 6 o'clock that evening, to be deposited with Lord Lovelace's papers at Ockham.[166]

Even at the death, though, their relationship was shot through with other emotions, and by the sense of a shared enmity stronger than any internal feuds. Before leaving for France Medora went up to London to have a daguerreotype taken for Annabella, and driving to Ada's house in the north-west corner of St James's Square, saw her mother for the last time. 'Dearest Pip, I have this instant met my Mother', she wrote to Annabella, in a hand that over the course of the letter degenerates with rage and drink into virtual illegibility,

I instantly recognised her – she is unchanged in face – & turned my head as if waiting for William who was ringing at the door. She could not have seen my face – my veil being down – & I saw her before she saw me . . . She turned round & looked at the carriage – for I observed her from the little back window – probably from curiosity or thinking it might be you. She was followed by a dirty-looking rascally kind of servant out of livery who was playing with his glove, & was dressed in a dark muslin gown with white pattern, & black silk shawl with long fringe and gathered round her as if she was afraid of losing it & a straw bonnet trimmed with white satin ribbbons. Her large eyes are ever & indeed *unchanged*, her walk is most altered & looks WICKED. Oh, were there a thing I had hoped to be spared it was this . . .

This has shocked me – pained me, but it is over. I have drunk quantities of wine since, & now there is nothing left for me to suffer that I dread. Oh how dearly fondly I loved her, & had she only stifled the existence her sin gave me – but God *is* there – & I will do my best to bear as I have ever done but it is so long, so constant – God forgive her. Oh how horrible she looked – so wicked – so hyena – like – That I could have loved her so! Bear in mind one feeling the sight of her has given me yet more strongly – if for my good or that of Marie – intimidate her – she will grovel on the ground, fawn, lick the dust – all – all that is despicable & bad . . . Oh could I only have loved the memory of my mother, but had death passed over me the chill – the horror – could not have been so great. Pity & forgive me if I involuntarily pain, I do not mean – but I *do* suffer.

Dearest Pip, I have come up to-day early on purpose to get you a Deguerotype done of me – I have heard you say that it would please you to have one – but the Sun is clouded over but you shall have one & as little ugly as possible. I do not contradict what you say about affection – time will best show you. I no more wish for a 'farewell than you' – we have parted – if we meet not again here we shall only meet in happiness hereafter & if we *do* meet again as we *shall* when I am happy and well – we shall not be the sadder for having had an agony less.[167]

If Annabella looked at this letter and saw what a good job she had done with Medora, she ought to have been shrewd enough to know that there was no way she could ultimately control a woman capable of such hatred. In the bargaining that preceded Medora's departure, she had insisted that Medora should be dependent on her alone, but within months Medora had reneged on that and almost every other clause of their agreement, abandoning the anonymity of the provinces for Paris where she canvassed financial and legal help, before returning to England the following year to get her own hands on the Deed. 'In the summer of 1843', Charles Mackay began his introduction to the published version of her *Autobiography*, completely ignorant of that streak of self-destructive wildness that had become a mania of defiance in Medora, twenty-seven years after the separation of Lord and Lady Byron, and nineteen years after the death of Lord Byron at Missolonghi, there arrived in London from Paris and the South of France, where she had resided for some time previously, a young lady, with a pretty little daughter, nine or ten years old . . . She was good-looking rather than eminently handsome, had dark eyes and hair, and a dark complexion, and was altogether a very lively and agreeable person. She was not, however, in strong health, and worst of all to her at the moment, she was without the means of subsistence for herself and daughter, the little girl Marie, to whom she was passionately attached, and whom she had brought with her from Hyeres. She had come to England to urge a claim which she had, or fancied she had, upon the generosity and kind feeling of Lady Byron; and her expenses from Paris to London had been defrayed by Captain De B[arralier], a gallant veteran of the British army, who had served through the Peninsular war in the 71st Regiment, and had received several severe wounds at the battle of Waterloo, for which he enjoyed a pension of £100 per annum. This officer had long been resident in the South of France, had found Miss Leigh in Paris in a state of utter destitution, had heard her sad story, had relieved her to the extent his limited means allowed, and had defrayed the charges of her return to England, in order that she might plead her cause in person with her wealthy and powerful relatives, and especially with Lady Byron, who had long treated her with motherly affection, and paid for her maintenance, but had suddenly withdrawn her favour, and left her and her child to perish of neglect and hunger.[168]

For all the violence and hatred with which she could turn on people, there was a pathos and plausibility about Medora that could impress strangers, and the English solicitor, Thomas Smith, to whom Barralier introduced her, proved no less vulnerable than the Waterloo veteran. On 21 July, Smith went to see Annabella's old lawyer from the separation battle, but Lushington was as ready now as he had been then to defend his client's interests, and nothing Smith could say could bridge the gap between Anna-

bella's insistence on controlling the Deed and Medora's equal
determination to have her fate in her own hands

It was an impasse to which there was no solution, because contrition had ceased to be enough, and Medora was not ready to submit to the absolute tyranny that was Annabella's immovable
position. 'You have but *one* course to pursue', Ada had warned
Medora in March, in a letter that with its unpleasant echoes of her
own mother's emotional and moral bullying is 'Milbanke' all over,

> submission to your benefactress; and if you have one spark
> of good feeling or of prudence, you will at once recognise
> your rash and ungrateful conduct and regret for it . . . Do
> not make *me* regret that I have not myself been what, let
> me tell you, many in my particular position would have
> been, viz: esteeming it *much* to behave to you with conde-
> scension and toleration, and beyond all measure and
> reason, to extend to you *affection* and *equality* of intercourse.
> Remember what you were at Paris – Grateful for any coun-
> tenance from me. You had scarcely dared to hope it.
> Remember too that there are circumstances, disgraceful
> circumstances, connected with your *birth and position*, which,
> with many in my relationship to you, would have made you
> an object of contempt.[169]

The threat was useless. For thirty years Annabella had tried to
control the Byrons in one incarnation or another, but whether it
was a matter of incestuous genes or not she had found in Medora
the phenomenon in its most virulent and untramelled form, a
life-force ready to consume itself in its own defiance, a reckless
independence of spirit and will that in the end is Medora Leigh's
most valid claim to the Byronic lineage the world had foisted on
her.

Given the fierce defiance of Medora and the obstinacy of Annabella, there is an inevitability about the rest of the negotiations
that is so deeply rooted in the characters of the two women that
the only surprise is that the final split did not happen earlier.
Through the end of July and the beginning of August, Smith did
all he could to find some way out of the impasse, but while Annabella was prepared on Lushington's advice to buy off Medora's

servants when they threatened to go public with her story, all contact with Medora herself was over.

Medora had fatally overplayed her hand. Even as late as the spring of 1843, when Annabella sent her old friend Dr King to Paris in an attempt to induce reason, she could still have had £300 a year in return for her submission. Now she had nothing. She had alienated, too, anyone who might possibly help. One final savage letter to her mother was her last contact with either Augusta or Annabella. After that, there was nothing left for her to do but raise what money she could on the Deed that had at last been given to her, and leave England.

The rest of her story, too, has the same air of inevitability about it, and for all its poverty and obscurity, a sadly Byronic fitness. From the age of fifteen Medora's existence had been shaped by perceptions of her birth, and exile was simply the logical conclusion of that, the inevitable destiny of a girl who for all her vividness of being had primarily existed as the construct of others' imaginations – the heroine of a Byronic drama, the solipsistic product of the bloodline, the violent, unstable embodiment of Byronic sin in all its forbidden glamour – that had to be wooed, watched and finally banished to the obscurity of a foreign grave.

The end was not long in coming either. Two years later while working as a servant in Saint-Germain-en-Laye, she became the mistress of a French hussar called Jean-Louis Taillefer, and was soon pregnant. Moving near to his native village in the south, she gave birth to a son in 1847 under her old name of Madame Aubin, and on Taillefer's discharge from the army the following year, married. But Medora was no more born for respectability than she was for security. Almost exactly a year later she went down with smallpox, and died on 28 August, 1849, aged thirty-five, leaving behind her a husband, two children and a strong-box of papers which – in a strangely circular irony – went the same way in her solicitors' fire that Byron's memoirs had gone at John Murray's almost forty years earlier.

She has, however, left a mark on her adopted country. A reliable oral tradition preserved for a generation the memory of a popular and exotic figure in her husband's village, and at the entrance to the tiny hamlet of Lapeyre, huddling in a bend of the River Sorgue a few kilometres to the south of St Affrique, a sign now announces without any equivocation the 'TOMBE DE MEDORA LEIGH, FILLE DE LORD BYRON'.

The *tombe* itself lies across the river, shallow and fast here except for the deep pool below the bridge, where the woman who believed herself Byron's daughter did her washing. It is on a hillside overlooking the grey spire of the XII century church and terracotta roofs of the village. The earth of the cemetery has been banked, and buttressed at the front with a stone wall, but the graves still lie on a gentle incline, the rows of dead seemingly tilted towards their old homes in the valley below.

There is something unmistakable about every country's cemeteries, and it would be hard to imagine anywhere less English, or a scene more remote from the big, bleak skies and flat expanses of Newmarket, where Annabella first saw Medora in 1815. At one end of the graveyard the ruins of an old church tower rise from a cluster of tall cypresses and fruit trees, and behind it is a tiny chapel, the beaded skeletons of funeral wreaths mouldering in the quiet cool within.

There is nothing to disturb the peace of Medora's grave except the noise of the river and the sound of the Angelus bell floating across the valley from the village church. She lies towards the southern end of the small cemetery, her grave marked by a stone cross cannibalised from the old church, and a newer plaque recording her name. It is less confident than the notice at the road side, but in its blend of English and French, of speculation and fact, it does – quite literally – set in stone a self-fulfilling myth of alienation that links the end of this thirty-five-year-old exile to another death among strangers a generation earlier at Missolonghi. 'Elisabeth Medora Leigh-Byron', it reads.

Epouse Taillefer
28 Aout 1849
"Strangers not regardless pass
Ling'ring like me to gaze and sigh 'Alas'"

Gordon Lord Byron.

A PREPARATION FOR INVISIBILTY

At the time that the news of Medora's death reached England in the autumn of 1849, Annabella was fifty-six years old, a mother of a successfully married daughter, the grandmother to three children, and her eye already fixed on the world to come. For as long as her daughter or son-in-law could remember her health had been a source of endless worry and talk, and although she still had another ten years to live, her appearance was already beginning to hold out to her admirers some ethereal suggestion of the 'other side'. 'Her form was slight', Harriet Beecher Stowe wrote of her first sight of her, just a few years after this,

> giving an impression of fragility; her motions were both graceful and decided; her eyes were bright, and full of interest and quick observation. Her silvery-white hair seemed to lend a grace to the transparent purity of her complexion, and her small hands had a pearly whiteness. I recollect she wore a plain widow's cap of a transparent material; and was dressed in some delicate shade of lavender, which harmonised well with her complexion.
>
> When I was introduced to her, I felt in a moment the words of her husband:-
>
> 'There was awe in the homage that she drew;
> Her spirit seemed as seated on a throne.'
>
> Calm. Self-poised and thoughtful, she seemed to me rather to resemble an interested spectator of the world's affairs, than an actor involved in its trials.[170]

'I sit as God', one less charitable observer, quoting Tennyson, put it, 'holding no form of creed But contemplating all'[171], and there had always been those who found this Olympian certainty less than attractive. As early as the separation Byron's great champion Hobhouse had declared that she was simply a woman that no man could have lived with, and over thirty years later neither age nor illness had done anything to slacken her minute control over the lives of those around her. 'I found Lady Byron in her sick-room', Mrs Stowe described another meeting with Annabella, brilliantly – if accidentally – capturing the mix of tyranny and untouchable certitude that characterised her last years,

> that place which she made so different from the chamber of ordinary invalids. Her sick room seemed only a telegraphic station whence her vivid mind was flashing out all over the world.
>
> By her bedside stood a table covered with books, pamphlets, and files of letters, all arranged with exquisite order, and each expressing some of her varied interests. From that sick-bed she still directed, with systematic care, her various works of benevolence, and watched with intelligent attention the course of science, literature, and religion; and the versatility and activity of her mind, the flow of brilliant and penetrating thought on all the topics of the day, gave to the conversations of her retired room a particular charm ... All the new books, the literature of the hour, were lighted up by her keen, searching, yet always kindly criticism ... Her opinions were always perfectly clear and positive, and given with the freedom of one who has long stood in a position to judge the world and its ways from her own standpoint.[172]

With so much of Annabella's energies also absorbed in monitoring the lives of the Lovelace family, and a fresh emotional outlet for her opening up in Brighton with her friendship with Frederick Robertson, it is doubtful how much the death of Medora impinged. Among her papers is preserved a letter from Medora's daughter from Toulon in 1843, but whether Annabella retained any memory of the endearments penned in a painfully neat child's hand, they were not enough to extract an answer when an orphaned Marie added herself to the list of Leighs who had written to Annabella for help.

From at least the 1830s Annabella had been perfecting the tactic of leaving any unwanted letter unopened, and any plea that was connected with Medora seems to have gone straight into the Dead Letter Office that she had made of her mind. In a letter she wrote three years before her own death she confessed her failure to be of any help to those she had loved, and yet if that moment of almost Byronic insight is worth cherishing, a list of victims the length of her lifetime underlines the ruthlessness with which she visited her own inadequacies on those she knew that she had failed.

In 1849 the violent rupture with her son-in-law and daughter was still nearly two years away, but Byron, Augusta, Medora, Marie, Mrs Jameson – the list could go almost indefinitely – were among those from whom she withdrew her love or affection. During the Brighton years that began around the time of Medora's death the friendship of Frederick Robertson briefly filled this void, but when in a characteristic gesture of self-dramatising humility, she found herself only four years later walking behind the coffin of her last 'soul mate', all that remained was the preparation for posterity of her 'history' that would become the final 'duty' of these last years.

With her manic hoarding of letters and evidence since the time of the separation, her whole life had in a sense been a preparation for this, but it was Robertson's sympathy that gave her intentions coherent shape. From the earliest conversations with him she had found a willing listener, and as she unfolded the story of her marriage and Medora's life, a plan was born for Robertson to tell Annabella's history.

Given the ultimate integrity of Robertson, it is doubtful that this could ever have emerged in any shape that would have satisfied Annabella, but the alliance did produce one concrete outcome. When Annabella had parted with Medora in 1843 she had severed relations with all the Leighs, but as she rehearsed again for Robertson's benefit the miseries of her long infatuation with the Byrons, the lure of old affections and the chance of extorting one last confession out of Augusta proved too hard to resist.

Augusta had, in fact, written to Annabella in 1848, begging for financial help, but the letter had been returned unopened, with a note that any future communication should go to her lawyer. Over the next few months desperation had forced Augusta to try again, but with Medora's accusations still fresh in mind, there was no budging Annabella and a humiliated Augusta was forced to turn to the grandson of Byron's old guardian and satirical butt, Lord Carlisle.

Augusta's pathetic attempts to awaken Annabella's sympathy show the levels to which poverty had reduced her, but in the Leigh household there was worse to come. During the 1840s the disintegration of her family had continued along its old predictable lines, with her sons turning out everything they had always promised, Georgey estranged from her mother and only her youngest daughter, Emily, of any comfort to Augusta.

Punctuated by long bouts of torpor and depression, George Leigh, too, had continued his feckless path to the grave, his long career with the turf climaxing when he was arrested for debt on the racecourse at Newmarket. There is a poignant entry in Augusta's commonplace book that suggests how attritional the effects of life with him must have been, but whatever his failings, loyalty and affection were so deeply ingrained in her character that his death in May 1850 proved a decisive blow.

For over forty years she had been covering for him, begging for him, and pandering to his temper, and yet if George Leigh had done nothing else he had given the purpose and focus to life Augusta had always needed. With his death it was at last possible to make economies that had been out of the question during his lifetime, but with no one to look after there was no one to live for and Augusta's health suffered the collapse that would lead ultimately to her death.

By the end of 1850 she was beyond looking after family affairs, and in the February of the following year, with 'ruin staring us in the face', her daughter Emily approached Lushington in one last attempt to enlist her godmother's support. 'My Mother has been trying for some time to enable her to make an arrangement with creditors', she wrote with the mix of subservience and fear that had come to mark the Leighs' dealings with Annabella,

There is no channel that she has not tried. But Alas! all to no purpose & I now turn to Lady Byron as our last & only hope ... Nothing would have induced me to make this application but my unhappiness at seeing My Mother in this wretched state & health ... I should feel so grateful if you would have the kindness to communicate it to Lady Byron as I fear from her not having answered my letters she was displeased but the recollection of her kindness to me when a child at Brighton induces me to hope she would forgive my appealing to her.[173]

This plea arrived at a time when Annabella's dialogue with Robertson had stirred all her old, ambivalent feelings about Augusta, and, giving only the post-office at Brighton as her address, she set out the terms on which they might meet. Over the next weeks letters went backwards and forwards between Brighton and London refining the place and rules of engagement, with an exhausted and bewildered Augusta – the black-edged mourning paper of her letters as prophetic as it was commemorative – reluctant to have a witness to their meeting and Annabella adamant. 'I can give no better proof of my wishing to see you', Augusta at last wrote, caving in as she had almost always done before the implacable will of her 'sometime sister',

than by the sacrifice of my own feelings in consenting to see any third person during any part of our interview which must be of a painful nature & may be the last we may ever have in this world – however such are your terms, & be it so.[174]

The letter has a faint but recognisable fatalism about it, and even if Augusta had guessed Annabella's full intentions, she would probably have made no attempt to escape. There was one further delay due to illness but on 8 April she left her daughter, Emily, and her maid, behind, and boarded the train at London Bridge for Reigate and the fly waiting to take her to the White Hart, a sick woman of sixty-seven held together by nothing more than a deluded confidence in a providence about to desert her.

Because if neither Augusta nor Annabella could have pulled

back from that final meeting, its failure was just as certain. In the days before Reigate Annabella had worked herself up to a pitch of nervous excitement, and with her burning belief that Byron would have returned to her had he lived, nothing Augusta could say could ever make up for the life that had ended with the separation.

But if Annabella believed, when she left Reigate with Robertson in the train for Brighton on that Tuesday in 1851, that she could erase Augusta from her mind as easily as she had Medora, she was mistaken. It was characteristic that the last letter she ever received from Augusta should be returned unopened, but when two months after the meeting she received a letter from Augusta's daughter, Emily, she could no more resist its claim on her kindness than she had been able to nearly forty years before.

'I saw death in her face at once'[175], Annabella had said after meeting Augusta at the White Hart, and she had been right. Augusta had returned from their meeting in a state of emotional and physical collapse, and by June the end was certain enough for her to make her will. 'Fairly worn out with trouble & anxiety'[176], her daughter reported, her illness had turned to dropsy. Down at Moore Place, Annabella gave instructions that she was to be kept informed, and at the beginning of October wrote to Emily with a last message for her mother. 'About a week ago I felt so great a desire to send her a message', she told Robertson,

> that after fully considering what might be the effects I determined to disregard all but those which it might possibly have upon herself – I wrote to ask the daughter to whisper two words from me – words of affection long since disused.'[177]

On 5 October Emily wrote back. 'She desires me to say', she answered on her dying mother's behalf,

> that the tears which refused to flow from sorrow were produced by the joy of hearing 'Dearest Augusta' from you – that they were her greatest consolation – her voice has grown so weak and thick that it is with difficulty that I can make out what she says – she said a great deal more to me

that I could not hear distinctly – I dare say that she will mention the subject again.[178]

She never did – 'A *second* message lost'[179] was Annabella's wry response, the first being from Missolonghi in April 1824 – and a week after Emily wrote to her again from the apartment in St James's that had been Augusta's only refuge. 'My dear Aunt,' she wrote a brief note early on Sunday, 12 October 1851,

> Poor Mamma died this morning after three having suffered most dreadfully since yesterday afternoon – it is indeed a most happy release but her loss can never be made up to me.[180]

'I feel it every moment & hour of the day', she wrote again, when she was more able to compose herself, sending her black-edged letter, in its black-edged envelope with its black sealing wax and penny red stamp to her aunt at Moore Place,

> & yet it is a merciful release [from] her sufferings that have been dreadful . . . It is a great consolation to me that I have always been with her & that she died with her dear hands in mine & that she said I had always been such a comfort to her.[181]

This death bed reconciliation was perhaps Annabella's first unalloyed gesture of generosity towards Augusta in almost forty years, but it was no more than tacit acknowledgement of what their friendship had meant. In the aftermath of Augusta's death she would inevitably retreat from any public admission of such a truth, but a letter to Emily the following year probably comes as close to the complex reality of her feelings as a lifetime's self-justification could allow. 'I found that Mrs Villiers had touched in conversation with you on my conduct towards your mother', she wrote on 2 July 1852,

> Before my marriage, when your mother was a stranger to me, I resolved to be to her as an own sister. Mine is not a nature in which affection *can* fade away. Nearly forty years have shown this in regard to *her*. She was throughout the object of my unvarying devotedness. It was her infatuation

(pardon the word) not to recognise in me her truest friend ...

I failed in other attempts to serve her & her children, but there never was a time when her welfare was not my first object. I could not give up the *rights* of others or my own, & I was in consequence forced into an *apparently* unfriendly position but the closing of her life & my previous wish for an interview with her, must prove that my affection had withstood every trial; – all; – and your expression as the effect of my last message upon her afforded me the consolation that she was at last sensible how truly I had loved her.[182]

The death of Augusta in October 1851 could not have come at a worse time for Annabella, because it coincided almost exactly with a double-blow that rammed home the hollowness of all her 'victories'. For the best part of forty years she had done her best to redeem the Byron bloodline from itself, and if she had failed with the Leighs she had at least been able to console herself with the fiction that she had saved Ada from her inheritance.

She had felt sure enough of this to mark her daughter's first Christmas as a married woman by trusting her with the portrait of Byron in Albanian costume that had hung behind the curtain at Kirkby, and Ada's support during the Medora saga had seemed to endorse her judgement. In her son-in law, William King – now the Earl of Lovelace – Annabella had also found a supporter ready to cede her all the influence she could want. During the 1840s she had virtually run his domestic and public life for him, overseeing his children and his children's tutors, his speeches in parliament and his philanthropies at home, his improvements to his country estates and his place in town – in all things, as she announced with barely the slightest trace of irony, '*the Omnipotent.*'[183]

With the swings of mood to which Ada had always been subject, there were times when she savagely resented this interference, but between her ambivalent attitude towards motherhood and ill health, she, too, put up little resistance. Throughout her childhood she had been subject to bouts of mysterious illness, and these had continued into married life, with sporadic and grotesque attacks of swelling and nervous paralysis – heightened by a regime of opium and laudanum – violently punctuating the chronic miseries of asthma and anorexia.

But illnesses apart, Ada was unfitted by temperament and intellect for domestic life, and happy to leave its tedious details to her mother and husband. From her earliest days she had shown an aptitude for science, and if she was never the figure in the history of Babbage's inventions legend has made of her, she had become a mathematician of real talent, with a passionate desire for intellectual fulfilment and a mystical belief in her own genius that makes her father's claim to be Napoleon's equal seem modest:

> I do not believe, that my father was (or ever could have been) such a *Poet* as I shall be an Analyst (& Metaphysician).[184]

'I believe no creature ever could will things like a Byron', she wrote again, striking that note of enthusiasm and excess her mother had spent her life trying to eradicate,

> And perhaps that is the bottom of the genius-like tendencies in my family. We can throw our *whole life* and *existence* for the time being into whatever we *will* to do and accomplish.[185]

As her sense of her powers had grown, even her illnesses seemed providential. 'With all my wiry power and strength', she wrote,

> I am prone at times to bodily sufferings and peculiarities of my physical constitution. They have taught me, and continue to teach me, that which I think nothing else could have developed. It is a force and control put upon me by Providence, which I *must* obey. And the effects of this continual discipline are mighty. They *tame* in the best sense of that word, and they *fan* into existence a pure, bright holy, unselfish flame within that sheds cheerfulness and light on many.[186]

*   *   *

Increasingly bored with her husband, impatient of the constraints of rank, and only sporadically interested in her children, her life took on a frenetic urgency the constant threat of illness only intensified. During the early years of marriage there had been periods of acute depression in which she felt herself no more than a 'walking intellect', but as Lovelace took his refuge in estate improvements and the approbation of Annabella, Ada found in the friendships of scientists and the risks of the turf the excitement and *life* her whole upbringing had tried to stifle.

With a devoted son-in-law, one of her old 'spies' still reporting, and a controlling say in all the Lovelaces' affairs, only Annabella's faith in her own judgement could have blinded her to the danger. In the 1830s she had confidently prescribed mathematics as a 'cure' for Ada's imagination, and although she might dislike men like Babbage and her other new friends on social grounds, she seemed utterly blind to the intoxicating possibilities of the world they had opened up for Ada.

Her disillusionment was abrupt, and came from an unexpected quarter, when on an extended tour of the northern counties, Ada wrote to her mother with the news that she had visited Newstead for the first time. Over thirty years earlier Annabella had made the same pilgrimage to the Byron family home, but while she had been happy enough to allow herself the luxury of a versifying melancholy she could not bear the place to have the same impact on Byron's daughter.

It might have been better and cleaner in the long run if Annabella had known that Ada had arranged with its new owner to be buried beside her father in the family vault at Hucknall, but even in her ignorance her anger had all the furious implacability of wounded feelings. In her own eyes she had always done her best to protect Byron's memory for his daughter, but when Ada wrote of her gradually thawing feelings for the '*Mausoleum*' of her race – of the way in which images of melancholy and death had changed to 'resurrection'[187] – it seemed as though all the suffering and moral struggle of Annabella's life was being thrown in her face. 'I was his best friend', she wrote back in a letter stiff with resentment and threat,

It often occurs to me that my attempts to influence your
Children favourably in their early years – will be frustrated
& turned to mischief, – so that it would be better for them
not to have known me, – if they are allowed to adopt the
unfounded popular notion of my having abandoned my
husband from want of devotedness & entire sympathy – or
if they suppose me to have been under the influence, at
any time, of cold, calculating, & unforgiving feelings, –
such having been his published description of me, whilst
he wrote to me privately (as will hereafter appear) 'I did –
do – and ever shall – love you.'[188]

Although it was the reports of Newstead that upset Annabella at
the time, Ada's news of the great Voltigeur's success at Doncaster
in one the most famous of all horse races hid a more desperate
threat to her mother's regime. It is not possible to say when Ada
had begun to gamble heavily, but by the time that Voltigeur
completed his extraordinary St Leger/Doncaster Cup double in
1850 she was an addict, immersed in the clandestine world of
the Victorian turf, deep in debt and – abetted it would seem by
Babbage – as supremely confident as any self-respecting punter
would be of mathematical systems that would get her out of gaol.

A fascination with gambling always seems to require some
explanation – as if it were not the most natural, intellectually
stimulating and satisfying of all human activities – but in Ada's
case it probably does. Through the early years of the 1840s she
had enjoyed the most fulfilling period of her life, and yet there
seems to have been a restless dissatisfaction that craved some
more lurid outlet than a life of intellectual bohemianism, a need
for stimulus – her father's old battle cry – that must have seemed
in the face of worsening health its own proof to her that she was
alive.

Lovelace had known for some time that she was gambling,
without ever having any idea of the stakes involved, but when the
small syndicate to which she belonged sustained massive losses
on the 1851 Derby, secrecy became impossible. Through her
various contacts Ada managed to borrow her own share of the
debt, but under the pressure of blackmail from another member

of her consortium she had no choice but to turn for help to her husband.

After years of anxieties, she was also seriously – probably terminally – ill again, as an examination conducted by the family doctor, Laycock, in the month after the Derby confirmed. There had seemed a brief hope in 1850 that her health might recover, but even though she was not told the likely prognosis she was already consciously living her life with the sense that she might not have long. 'I'd rather', she wrote, with a genuinely Byronic bravado, to a friend,

> have 10 or five what I call *real* years of life, than 20 or 30 such as I see people usually dwelling on, without any spirit.[189]

The last person Ada wanted to see in such circumstances was Annabella, but Lovelace's response to any domestic or public problem was to consult his mother-in-law, and on 19 June 1851 he went to Leamington Spa, where she was nursing her own ill-health. He took with him a diagnosis of cervical cancer from Ada's doctor, but if Annabella seemed bizarrely unmoved by Laycock's grim prognosis the revelations of Ada's gambling provoked an anger that eclipsed even her Newstead bitterness.

Coming only two months after the last abortive meeting with Augusta at Reigate, the news seems to have almost unhinged Annabella. It would have been bad enough for her to have been excluded from her daughter's confidence, but as with Medora almost a decade earlier she found herself confronting, in the spectre of Byronic 'sin' triumphant, the failure of her whole life's work.

It was, though, oddly, Lovelace himself who bore the brunt of her bitterness, and with his revelations her affection and trust turned into an immediate and implacable hostility. In Annabella's eyes he had not only failed Ada but betrayed *her* too, and letter after bewildered letter from him did nothing more than give her the chance to crystallise her fury into a moral indignation from which there could be no retreat.

It was the first time that Lovelace had felt the full force of a personality that had been petrifying with age and the almost unopposed exercise of her own will. To the end of her life Annabella retained an extraordinary ability to inspire devotion in her friends, but when 'the devil of the North Pole was upon her', as one Esher acquaintance put it, 'she was stern, unyielding, and unforgiving in her hate.' 'The touch of her hand', at such times, William Howitt wrote in the *Daily News* in 1869, 'was like that of death; in her manner was the silence of the grave.' A 'woman of the most honourable and conscientious intention', he remembered her,

> she was subject to a constitutional idiosyncrasy of a most peculiar kind, which rendered her, when under its influence, absolutely and persistently unjust . . . Through this the changes in her mood were sudden, and most painful to all about her. I have seen her of an evening in the most amiable, cordial and sunny humour, full of interest and sympathy; and I have seen her the next morning come down as if she had lain all night not on a feather-bed, but on a glacier – frozen as it were to the very soul . . .[190]

'There was a strong vein of eccentricity in her character', Robertson's biographer, Frederick Arnold, recalled, pushing Howitt's observations a step further,

> She would take violent and unreasonable prejudices. She was capable of a very strong tinge of bitterness. She would show great and lavish kindness, and the kindness, without any reason would be capriciously withdrawn. Indeed one of her medical friends who had watched her very narrowly has declared that in his judgement her mental balance was impaired.[191]

To Lovelace's credit, after years of doing what he was told, he refused to allow Annabella to confront Ada personally, but with the cancer now clearly terminal some kind of rapprochement was inevitable. Through the second half of 1851 Ada managed with the help of laudanum to maintain some semblance of independence, but when at the beginning of 1852 her condition declined sharply neither she nor Lovelace any longer had the strength to hold out.

It was the opportunity Annabella had been waiting for, and by the end of May she was at her daughter's bedside, in control of her debts, her medication and her conscience. Over the previous weeks Ada had been brought to admit some of her losses to Annabella's lawyer, but it was the catharsis of personal confrontation, confession and remorse that her mother demanded and Ada found herself as powerless before her as she had been as child.

Within days the details of Ada's gambling began to emerge – the scale of the losses, the secret pawning of the Lovelace jewels, the paste replicas made to replace them – and with every confession Annabella's sense of divinely elected purpose increased. It had been typical of her disbelief in any but her own illness that the first news of Ada's should leave her unmoved, but as the cancer spread, and with a kind of horrific symmetry inexorably destroyed Ada's womb, her mother saw with all the blinkered certainty of Annabella Milbanke her own appointed role in an illness sanctioned by heaven.

There may perhaps have been deaths more lingering, more excruciatingly painful, more emotionally disturbing than that of Ada, but the presence there for week after week through the summer of 1852 of Annabella gives it a horror all its own. From the moment that Ada's husband had revealed his wife's gambling he had been cut off as if he was almost not there, and in an atmosphere of unsuppressed hostility Annabella sat at her daughter's side, surrounded by a sea of mattresses on which the tortured Ada would throw herself, the 'angel of mercy' of Annabella's acolytes revealed in all the retributive and unbending rigour of Victorian moral tyranny. The 'greatest of all mercies', shown her, she wrote of what she called the 'blessing' of Ada's cancer, in September,

> has been her disease – weaning her from temptation, & turning her thoughts to higher and better things.[192]

There are certain historical habits of thought and feeling that in spite of all effort remain beyond grasp, and no movement of imaginative sympathy can take one into the mind of Annabella as she sat at her daughter's deathbed. It was one thing for her fellow 'souls' to see Ada's agonies as a redeeming mercy of God sent to break a rebellious spirit, but as her mother watched over her last interminable days, and one by one the broken confessions of excess and sexual infidelities came out, consuming teller and hearer in the same misery of blighted faith and memories, it beggars belief that she can have escaped her own part in Ada's tragedy.

Because it was not just the destructive work of cancer Annabella was witnessing, but the physical devastation of a lifetime's campaign of emotional suppression and control. As a child Ada had fantasies of flying, and was afraid to sleep within the prison of a fourposter, wrapping herself in blankets on the floor. Now she had nightmares of being buried alive. As the illness dragged on, and she lay there, compulsively fiddling with a handkerchief, – 'spreading it, measuring it, & waving it about with her hands'[193] – it was her constant refrain that they should make no mistake over her death. Her husband was moved by her courage, but the simple truth was she was broken. As the bullfinch sang in its cage, Ada's groans filled the room, a repentant sinner brought back to her mother's faith. Her punishment at God's hands, the proud, materialist mathematician, told Annabella, would last a million years. It had been revealed to her in a dream.

If this was Annabella's victory, however, it was a pyrrhic one, as empty as every other in her struggle against Byronism. As her daughter rambled of her sins and God's punishment it might have seemed that she had won her back, but as she learned for the first time now that Ada would be buried with her father, her coffin next to his in the Byron crypt at Hucknall – the prophecy of *Childe Harold* fulfilled – Annabella must have recognised a gesture of rejection too complete and symbolic to escape.

As she sat there, sketching Ada's face as it lay sunk in a pillow, the hard, ugly lines of the drawing petering away into nothing, a thin, disembodied hand seeming all that is left of her daughter's tortured form, it is hard to believe that she could not also see there the mirror of her own life. For more than forty years she had tried to project her own emotional and sexual longings onto one external threat or another, but in the shattered body of a daughter she had so successfully created in her own image it was as if she was at last brought face to face – Dorian Grey like – with the reality of her own inner world.

By the end, too, Ada's pain was such that not even Annabella could extract any emotional or spiritual comfort from it. On 26 November she confessed to a friend that some respite was needed if Ada was to *feel* as she should, but the only respite open to her daughter now was drug-induced, and on the next evening she finally slipped insensibly away, after all her agonies dying at last with something of the quiet of the young Paul Dombey, whose end – the figure of his father just beyond his fading gaze – Dickens himself had been asked to read to Ada at her death bed.*

And it is, in the end, in the literature of the nineteenth century and not in medical case notes so typical of an age buckling under the pressure of its divided identity that we can best feel the tragedy that reached its grim conclusion with Ada's death. In the text books of hysteria her symptoms and those both of Annabella and Medora can be found time and again, but in the generation before Freud it was left to the great novelists to recognise the full, destructive horror that lay at the heart of Annabella's story.

It is hard to pick up a nineteenth-century novel and not find a trace of Byron in some form, but in less obvious ways his wife's history made an equally profound impression. In her posthumous 'Vindication' of Lady Byron, Mrs Stowe claimed that anyone who wanted to understand Annabella's sufferings need only read *Romola*, but a striking coincidence of dates suggests that it is rather in *Middlemarch* and Dorothea Brooke's resurrection from the

---

* Dickens had first met Ada in 1843, when she had been wary that he only wanted to know her because of the Byron connection. Judging from dinner guest lists in Forster's biography, he often subsequently saw her – certainly often enough for her to ask him to come when she was dying and for him to hurry to comply

emotional and sexual trauma of marriage, that George Eliot gave her own answer to the moral death Annabella had brought on herself.*

It is a sobering thought, in fact, that to the nineteenth-century writer with the most profoundly *moral* sense of life and art, the story of Annabella's revenge seemed too shocking to be allowed into the light of day. 'It remains a grievously pitiable thing to me', Eliot wrote to Sara Hennell, when Annabella's carefully controlled version of her story, with its insistent theme of self-justification and vengeance finally became public in 1869,

> that man or woman who has cared about a future life in the minds of coming generations should have deliberately, persistently mingled with that prospect the ignoble desire to perpetuate personal animosities, which can never be rightly judged by those immediately engaged in them. To write a cruel letter in a rage is very pardonable – even a letter full of gall and bitterness, meant as a sort of poisoned dagger. We poor mortals can hardly escape these sins of passion. But I have no pity to spare for the rancour that corrects its proofs . . . chuckling with the sense of its future publicity.[195]

It was probably always Annabella's fate to fall short of George Eliot's standards of humanity, and yet it is also possible that with her generosity of mind Eliot could simply not bear the human reality that faced her in Annabella's story. In Dorothea Brooke she created and then redeemed a heroine with the same priggish and evangelical narrowness as the young Annabella Milbanke, but the desolate truth is that outside the life-enhancing world of Eliot's imagination it is hard to think that anyone could have

---

* George Eliot began the restructuring of *Middlemarch*, for the first time sketching in the character of Dorothea, almost to the day that the controversy over the Byron marriage burst again on nineteenth-century England in 1869. It is quite possible that the process was an unconscious one, but as her letters show, Annabella and the separation story were at the front of her mind as she fleshed out her modern day St Theresa. Another member of the Byron family also provided the inspiration for *Daniel Deronda*. In the autumn of 1872 George Eliot was in Hamburg, and was upset to see 'Miss Leigh, Byron's grandniece', gambling, 'her fresh face among all the hags and stupid men around her'[194] – the spark for the character of Gwendolen Harleth.

recovered the trust or suppleness of spirit that Annabella lost when she lost Byron.

While George Eliot in the end shied away from the full tragedy of Annabella's life, there is one novelist who did not, and in the character of Miss Havisham, Dickens has left a portrait that might stand as the obituary notice for Annabella Byron. There is no more question that Dickens knew of her story than that Eliot did, and with his profound sense of the relationship of the inner and outer life, and intuitive sense of the pathology of emotional disorders, the man who sat at Ada's deathbed need have looked no further for his inspiration.

It is difficult to believe, in fact, that with the evidence of what Annabella had done to her daughter and to herself, he did not have her in his mind when only weeks after Lady Byron's death he began *Great Expectations*. The genesis of any character in a novel is a complex and uncertain business of invention and borrowing of course, but if the external trappings of Miss Havisham's character come from any number of sources, the *emotional* truth is the truth of Annabella's life. The woman who sat 'corpse like' among the decay of Satis House, her 'withered bridal dress . . . grave clothes', her yellowing veil a shroud, the clock and watch stuck for ever at the same time, is the Annabella Byron who clung obsessively to the humiliations of her own wedding day. The woman who used and perverted her adopted child Estella to take her revenge on the world that had rejected her, is the same Annabella who turned Medora against her mother. 'What have I done?' Miss Havisham demands of Pip (coincidentally the Byron nickname Medora revived for Annabella) when she at last sees the human destruction a lifetime of obsession and revenge has caused: 'I knew not how to answer, or how to comfort her', Dickens's narrator recalls in one of the supreme passages of human understanding in English fiction,

> That she had done a grievous thing in taking an impression-able child to mould into the form that her wild resentment, spurned affection, and wounded pride, found vengeance in, I knew full well. But that, in shutting out the light of the day, she had shut out infinitely more; that, in seclusion,

she had secluded herself from a thousand natural and heal-
ing influences; that, her mind brooding solitary, had grown
diseased, as all minds do and must and will that reverse the
appointed order of their Maker; I knew equally well. And
could I look upon her without compassion, seeing her punishment in the ruin she was, in her profound unfitness for
this earth on which she was placed, in the vanity of sorrow
which had become a master mania, like the vanity of penitence, the vanity of remorse, the vanity of unworthiness,
and other monstrous vanities that have been curses in this
world?[196]

If there had ever been a stage, however, when Annabella could
have asked herself Miss Havisham's question and answered it with
any honesty that had long since passed. At the time of Ada's death
she made the best public face she could of her daughter's choice
of burial place, but as she moved back to Brighton and resumed
the rhythms of her old life again, prosecuting her feud with Lovelace with an icy determination, that last, symbolic rejection
became just one more detail that had to be rewritten for the
posthumous legend she was determined to leave.

It was one of the ironies of Annabella's history, in fact, that
through all her long 'preparation for invisibility', as she phrased
it, no one could have been more concerned with the verdict of
this world. Throughout her life she had obsessively hoarded every
scrap of evidence that might bear on her reputation, making
notes and depositions in a hand that only ever wavered under
the most intense emotional strain, copying letters and minut-
ing conversations, filling notebook after notebook – little red,
green, and marbled covered monuments to mania – with observations, judgements, character analyses, morality lessons, auto-
descriptions, pen-portraits, religious scruples, and fantasies of
deluded self-justification.

The death of Robertson in 1853, at the Byronic age of thirty-six,
robbed her of the collaborator she would most have wanted to
put this mass into order, but in the same year Annabella first met
the woman with whom her revelations will always be associated,
the novelist and abolitionist, Harriet Beecher Stowe.

Although in one sense Annabella could have found no more disastrous confidante than a woman as entirely innocent of the workings of English social life as Mrs Stowe, there was no one more prepared to see her struggle in the terms she wanted it. In her childhood fantasies Annabella had dreamed of herself at Thermopylae or 'with Howard in the cheerless dungeon', and the author of *Uncle Tom's Cabin* was ready to champion her in the same terms, portraying her as the spiritual companion of Clarkson and Wilberforce, of Francis Xavier, Fenelon and the protestant martyrs, her life torn between a Christ-like love for the wayward souls who had wronged her and a final duty – 'no matter at what expense to her own feelings' – to denounce corruption. 'By nature and principle truthful', Mrs Stowe wrote of her, when almost ten years after her death she went public with Annabella's version of her marriage, passed from one soul mate to another like some Olymypic flame of moral truth,

> she had the opportunity of silently watching the operation of a permitted lie upon a whole generation. She had been placed in a position in which it was necessary, by silence, to allow the spread and propagation through society of a radical falsehood. Lord Byron's life, fame, and genius had all struck their roots into this lie, been nourished by it, and had derived thence a poisonous power.
>
> Was this falsehood to go on corrupting literature as long as history lasted? Had the world no right to true history? Had she who possessed the truth no responsibility to the world? Was not a final silence a confirmation of a lie with all its consequences?
>
> Lady Byron has been falsely accused of having ruined *the* man of his generation, and caused all his vices and crimes, and all their evil effect on society. She submitted to the accusation for a certain number of years for reasons which commended themselves to her conscience; but when all the personal considerations were removed, and she was about passing from life, it was right, it was just, it was strictly in accordance with the philosophical and ethical character of her mind, and with her habit of considering things in their widest relations to the good of mankind, that she

should give serious consideration to the last duty which she might owe to abstract truth and justice in her generation.[197]

It was not only her version of her marriage story she entrusted to Mrs Stowe, but the image of herself in old age that she wanted perpetuated for posterity. Until the end of her life Annabella remained as alert as ever to the practical aspects of things, and yet the picture she left was of a woman who had already abandoned this earth, all inessentials distilled away to leave only that terrible creation of the Victorian mind – the all-seeing, all forgiving angel of compassion and death, hovering somewhere between the next world and this in sexless and untouchable serenity. 'To talk to her seemed to the writer of this sketch', Mrs Stowe wrote,

the nearest possible approach to talking with one of the spirits of the just made perfect . . . We have already spoken of that singular sense of the reality of the spiritual world which seemed to encompass Lady Byron during the last part of her life, and which made her words and actions seem more like those of a blessed being detached from earth than of an ordinary mortal. All her modes of looking at things, all her motives of action, all her involuntary actions of emotion, were so high above any common level, and so entirely regulated by the most worthy causes, that it would seem difficult to make the ordinary world understand exactly how the thing seemed to lie before her mind. What impressed the writer more strongly than ever was Lady Byron's perfect conviction that her husband was now a redeemed spirit; that he looked back with pain and shame and regret on all that was unworthy in his past life; and that, if he could speak or could act in the case, he would desire to prevent the further circulation of base falsehoods, and of seductive poetry, which had been made the vehicle of morbid and unworthy passions.[198]

There is, in fact, something absolutely seamless in Annabella's descent to the grave, in the unchanging internal and external rhythms, the mental obsessions, the invalidism, the constant, restless wandering. For a time after Ada's death in 1852 she had taken apartments in Dover Street in London, but after that it was back to the old vagrant pattern, moving between Brighton and Hastings, London, Esher, Ham, Richmond, and finally London again, where at 11 St George's Terrace, on 16 May 1860 – one day short of her sixty-eighth birthday – the end finally came.

With her was her friend, Mrs Barwell, and her devoted granddaughter, Lady Anne King. She had been suffering from bronchitis for weeks, complicated at the last by pleurisy, but death itself was quiet, Annabella slipping gently and calmly from sleep into the sleep of death, as her grandaughter wrote gratefully to Mrs George Lamb. Shortly after, Annabella's grandson, Ralph, arrived, and the family sent for the Pre-Raphaelite sculptor, Thomas Woolner. The next day Woolner described the scene that met him. 'I had to go and see a Cast taken of the left hand of Lady Byron, wife of the poet; he wrote to Tennyson's wife,

> The summons said it was essential an honourable man should do it, or I should not have been troubled. I do not much like taking casts of any one dead, but could not refuse in this case, as I know so many of their friends. But I was glad I did go, for a nobler sight I never saw – she looked as if she was living, and had just dropped to sleep, and as proud as a queen in her splendour . . . She seemed to have been almost adored by those around her.[199]

EPILOGUE

EPILOGUE

I t is fitting that Annabella's febrile wanderings should only end
with death, because her kind of chronic restlessness – Tolstoy
movingly portrayed it in old Prince Bolkonski – is a frequent
symptom of terminal illness, and her whole widowhood had been
little more than one long dying. In a perceptive obituary Harriet
Martineau linked her bedouin life to the traumas of her marriage
home with Byron, and if this outer life does offer any clue to her
inner state then something in Annabella as surely died with her
marriage as it did in Miss Havisham on her wedding day.

'Is her memory to be regarded with the deepest horror or
the most profound compassion?'[1] John Paget demanded when
Annabella's story was finally published in 1869, but Dickens had
already answered that question ten years earlier. In her *Lady Byron
Vindicated* Mrs Stowe did her best to co-opt Annabella for the
cause of women's freedom, but while there are certainly other
economic and social patterns of nineteenth-century feminist history to which her life belongs it is the insights that Dickens offers
that take us to the heart of her tragedy.

It is right that the decisive word on Annabella should be with
him, too, because no novelist was better equipped to see not just
the consequences of repression but also the relationship of the
individual to the whole. There is such an outlandish quality to
the sufferings of Miss Havisham that she seems to come from a
planet of her own, but what Dickens saw was that the gothic horror
of her bridal chamber and the physical and mental aberrations

of a Jaggers or Wemmick are all of a piece in a society that has suppressed and warped its most generous instincts.

And that in the end is the fascination and importance of Annabella Byron, because her story is in miniature the story of the age; her descent from the passionate possibilities of her youth to the chillier virtues of justice and charity, the classic movement of the century. In a moment of savage disillusion Byron once labelled her 'the moral Clytemnestra of her lord'[2], and yet if this is a Greek tragedy it is a very English one, and Annabella a Clytemnestra of the sort Lord Leighton might paint, the embodiment of an England – the England of Lawrence's timeless battle of the community and the individual – that had come inexorably into its own with the Victorian era.

It is this, too, that gives such a monitory quality to her life, because the price she paid when she killed off in herself all those finer impulses, is just that which Europeans like Mazzini recognised England had paid when it drove Byron into exile. In her own warped and obsessive way, Annabella went on loving him until the end of her life, and yet it was a Byron of her own invention she always wanted, the outsider reabsorbed into the fold, the man who had lived with such vivid and dangerous intensity 'purified and ennobled,' 'the shadows of earth for ever dissipated', 'the angel in him,' as she expressed it to Mrs Stowe, 'made perfect according to its divine ideal.'[3]

It was only nine years after Annabella's death that Mrs Stowe published *Lady Byron Vindicated*, and yet it is no exaggeration to say that the row she started is still not over. In the months after the separation the rumours of incest had been common currency in aristocratic London, but when Mrs Stowe's revelations and Medora's *Autobiography* were published in the same year, the story broke on a mid-Victorian England that had buried those scandals beneath memories of Greek liberty and Missolonghi. 'Who that has a spark of generous feeling', George Eliot had asked fourteen years earlier in her great essay on the Evangelical Dr Cumming,

> that rejoices in the presence of good in a fellow-being, has
> not dwelt with pleasure on the thought that Lord Byron's

unhappy career was ennobled and purified towards its close
by a high and sympathetic purpose, by honest and energetic
efforts for his fellow-men? Who has not read with deep
emotion those last pathetic lines, beautiful as the after-
glow of sunset, in which love and resignation are mingled
with something of a melancholy heroism? Who has not
lingered with compassion over the dying scene at Missolonghi – the sufferer's inability to make his farewell messages of love intelligible, and the last long hours of silent
pain?[4]

To George Eliot it seemed unbearable – in fact wicked – that Mrs
Stowe should shatter this image of Byron, and the public response
was even more extreme. It is typical that in a fit of xenophobic
snobbery it was Mrs Stowe who bore the brunt of national anger,
but when the dust had settled, all those who did not believe that
she had simply misunderstood, or that Annabella was deranged,
took out their disillusionment on Byron's widow in full measure.
She was 'an absolute moral monstrosity, an anomaly in the types
of female hideousness.' 'It is said', declared *Blackwood's* – her
champion back in 1819,

> that there are some poisons so subtle that they will destroy
> life, and may yet leave no trace of their action. The mur-
> derer who uses them may escape the vengeance of the law;
> but he is not the less guilty. So the slanderer who makes
> no charge; who deals in hints and insinuations: who knows
> melancholy facts he would not divulge; – things too painful
> to state; who forbears, expresses pity, sometimes even affec-
> tion, for his victim . . . is far more guilty than he who tells
> the bold falsehood.
> Lady Byron has been called

> 'The moral Clytemnestra of her lord.'

The 'moral Brinvilliers' [the notorious 17th century French
murderess who in one year killed her father, sister and two
brothers and – famous for her charity – was said to try out
her poisons on the sick in hospitals] would have been a
truer designation.[5]

There can be few women who have received the posthumous mauling that Annabella Byron has suffered, but if England shot the messenger that does not mean that it did not listen to the message. In the century and a half since Mrs Stowe's *Lady Byron Vindicated* there is scarcely a calumny that has not been piled on Annabella's head, but if nobody has ever thanked her for destroying Byron one only has to stand in the church at Hucknall where this book began to recognise the triumph of her bloodless vision over a tougher reality.

'And all men kill the thing they love'[6], – the line has the same swelling insistence in this context as in Wilde's Ballad – and if there is anywhere to feel how England has traditionally done that best, the place is St Mary's, Hucknall. This is not the only country that knows how to deal with its rebels of course, but there can be nowhere else that combines ruthlessness and re-assimilation with the same certainty of touch, demonising and then sanitising into posthumous harmlessness its aberrant genius – reabsorbing Shelley as the ineffectual angel of Victorian myth, the pariah Wilde as the author of *The Ideal Husband*, the blazing 'Pilgrim of Eternity', that Shelley dubbed Byron, as the simple Christian 'pilgrim' of Canon Barber's version.

The church – famous and visited for only one thing – is a hymn to this instinct for re-absorption. Near the porch, a small exhibition now preserves fragments of Byron's coffin and other memorabilia. At the west end, a Byron funeral hatchment hangs. On the south wall of the chancel, a tablet to Byron's memory records, all scandal hushed, that it was placed there by his sister. A medallion portrait – face in profile, hair curled, open neck – shows the ideal of what a poet *should* look like. In the floor is set a single slab of black marble, a gift of the King of Greece, with Byron's name and dates, surrounded by a hero's wreath.

What more perfect revenge could there be? Even Byron's corpse, hacked and battered by the doctors at Missolonghi, has shared in the same metamorphosis, brutal reality subsumed into the demands of Christian-classical mythology. What has happened to the disfigured and unrecognisable face that Hobhouse could scarcely bring himself to look at? Where in the idealising account of Canon Barber – the 'custos of the body' as he called himself – are the crushed skull, the skeletalised limbs, the severed foot lying in the corner of his coffin? Where, for that matter, the 'unusually pronounced sexual organ' privately noted by one of his churchwardens that June evening in 1938?

The cloven footed, priapic satyr of Byronic legend still has its place in popular demonology of course, but in its own way, that myth is no more threatening than the embalmed and ennobled corpse of Canon Barber's fiction. For the nineteenth century the gothic trappings of Byronism at least masked a real urgency of concern, but that anxiety has long since evaporated to leave the Byron of contemporary popular culture – the Byron routinely dragged up among the usual suspects at any identification parade of Don Juans or sexual deviants – with about as much historical solidity or danger about him as Bram Stoker's vampire.

'Byron, thou should be living at this hour!'[7] Auden invoked him on the eve of the Second World War – as Lawrence had done the aristocratic outsider on the eve of the First – but no generation has ever really wanted him as he *was*. In the same way that every age comes up with its own Shakespeare, so too it invents its own Byron, but it is always a Byron that is smaller and more manageable than the original, a writer of lyrics in one generation or letters in another, the author of the 'Hebrew Melodies' or *Beppo*, the champion of political and sexual freedoms or a psychological case study.

Byron, though, is more serious than that. If he was right about England, England too was right about him, right that it could not afford to hold him. For a couple of years his contemporaries imagined, like Annabella, that they could enjoy the frisson of Byronic romanticism without any of its consequences, but as events rammed home that he had *meant* what he said they were left with nothing behind which to hide. They could take the libertine, Francis Jeffrey admitted. They could even take the atheist. What they could not take was the brilliant, unremitting stare that Byron turned on all their beliefs, illusions and self-deceptions. 'The reveller may pursue his orgies,' Jeffrey wrote in the *Edinburgh Review*, with all the desolation of a man who has heard the echo in the Marabar Caves, and the wanton display her enchantments with comparative safety to those around them . . . But if the priest pass from the altar, with exhortations to peace and purity still trembling on his tongue, to join familiarly in the grossest and most profane debauchery . . . our notions of right and wrong are at once confounded – our confidence in virtue shaken to the foundations – and our reliance on truth and fidelity at an end for ever.

This is the charge which we bring against Lord Byron. We say that, under some misapprehension as to the truth, and the duty of proclaiming it, he has exerted all the powers of his powerful mind to convince his readers, both directly and indirectly, that all ennobling pursuits, and disinterested virtues, are more deceits or illusions – hollow and despicable mockeries for the most part, and, at best, but laborious follies. Love, patriotism, valour, devotion, constancy, ambition – all are to be laughed at, disbelieved in, and despised! . . . Thus all good feelings are excited only to accustom us to their speedy and complete extinction, to the staple and substantial doctrine of the work – the non-existence of constancy in women or honour in men, and the folly of expecting to meet with any such virtues, or of cultivating them, for an undeserving world; – and all this mixed up with so much wit and cleverness, and knowledge of human nature, as to make it irresistibly pleasant and plausible – while there is not only no antidote supplied, but every thing that might have operated in that way has been anticipated, and presented already in as strong and engaging a form as possible – but under such associations as to rob it of all efficacy, or even turn it into an auxiliary of the poison.[8]

There is always so much sense in what Jeffrey writes of Byron – and such a palpable openness to his qualities – that it is hard to understand why he did not see that Byron was himself the 'antidote'. It would be hard to think of another satirist who fed so voraciously off himself as Byron did, but in an odd way it is that very egotism his critics railed against that is the guarantee of a shared humanity that ultimately roots even his most savage satire in a sense of common frailty.

In the end, though, it is not the quality of self-knowledge which distinguishes Byron – nor even the exuberance and fun with which he could go on looking at the world's follies – but something more profound. In the greatest of all English tragedies Shakespeare constructed a universe of faithlessness and cruelty and found within it the courage to *live*, and that essentially is what Byron did – saw humanity and his own character with all the clarity of *Lear*, saw life with its lies and deceptions, its cruelties, injustices, absurdities, abuses and hypocrisies, and discovered within *himself* the grace and bravery to live it with the intelligence and decency he showed in Greece.

It is easier, though, to fall back on other myths, and idealised hero or demonised caricature, Hucknall seems to have him both ways. On a cold, drizzling day in the early December of last year, the church was shut for lunch to pilgrims. At the far end of the High street, though, down from Byron Carpets, along the same route that his black-plumed funeral carriage was drawn in 1824, the Byron Cinema – Bingo twice a week – was showing *The Exorcist*.

It had a nice irony to it. It is not finally, though, at Hucknall but further south in west London's Kensal Green cemetery that one can fully count the cost of Annabella's crusade against the Byrons. It is where Augusta lies, and where no more than a hundred yards from her, Annabella was buried.

The way to approach that grave is from the main entrance of the cemetery, at the west end. As one goes through John Griffith's massive classical gateway, the path forks to left and right, the left hand path leading, as a contemporary noted with satisfaction,

> to the abodes of the Turks, Jews, Infidels, Heretics and 'unbaptised folk' and the right hand after passing among the beautiful and consecrated graves of the faithful, leads to the Episcopal chapel. This chapel is a beautifully executed work, in the same style as the entrance buildings and is fitted up in excellent taste.[9]

It is down in the massive, barrel-vaulted catacomb beneath this chapel, that Augusta lies. With the encroaching pieties of old age she would probably have been pleased to find herself there, but there seems something very forlorn about her coffin, tucked away on the bottom shelf next to that 'precious piece of helplessness' George Leigh, the wood beginning to disintegrate, a plain lead coffin plate the only identification, and above her head – as crushing a weight in death as in life – the great and uncompromising mass of religious and social orthodoxy enshrined in the grim doric of Griffith's chapel.

It is hard not to feel that Byron's Astarte – his Zuleika – would be happier among the Turks and infidels, but there are no such doubts as one stands by the grave of Lady Byron a minute's walk to the east. About twenty yards from where she is buried is the tomb of the hated Hobhouse, but there is a kind of inviolable self-sufficiency about Annabella's plain grave that no contagion can disturb. It is a single, flat stone. On it – the Anne of Anne Isabella Byron misspelled – is her name and dates. That misspelling, though, is the only liberty. Next to her, like the slaves of some despot slaughtered on her death, lie the family of her lawyer Lushington. All around, too, monuments are collapsing in the heavy clay, marble columns and Egyptian obelisks falling, Ozymandias-like, into yawning graves. But not hers. Even its iron railings, fencing her off from the world around, have survived. 'Let the English take care', Chateaubriand warned, 'if they break the mould of the man – Byron – who had made them revive, what will remain?' What remains – and standing there on the white cliffs of Dover, child in her arms, Albion's daughter on perpetual guard, what always remains – is Lady Byron.

ENDNOTES

Abbreviations in endnotes:

Ada: Moore, D. L., *Ada, Countess of Lovelace, Byron's legitimate daughter,* London, 1977

Astarte: Lovelace, R. M., *Astarte: a fragment of truth concerning George Gordon Byron,* New York, 1921

Blessington: Lovell, J. (ed.), *Lady Blessington's Conversations of Lord Byron,* Princeton, 1969

Byron (McGann): Byron, (ed. McGann, J. J.), *Lord Byron: the complete poetical works,* Oxford, 1980

BLJ: Marchand, L. (ed), *Byron's Letters and Journals,* London, Vols 1–12, 1973–82

Byron, Lady, *Auto-Description,* 1831: Byron Lovelace Papers, Bodleian Library, Byron, Lady, *Auto-Description,* 1831

Elwin (LBF): Elwin, M., *Lord Byron's Family, Annabella, Ada and Augusta, 1816–1824,* London, 1975

Elwin (LBW): Elwin, M., *Lord Byron's Wife,* London, 1962

Gunn: Gunn, P., *My Dearest Augusta,* London, 1968

Mayne: Mayne, E. C., *The Life and Letters of Anne Isabella, Lady Noel Byron,* London, 1929

Medora (Mackay): Mackay, C. (ed), *Medora Leigh; a history and an autobiography,* London, 1869

Stowe: Stowe, H. B., *Lady Byron Vindicated,* London, 1870

PART I

1 Lawrence, D. H., Pheonix: The Posthumous Papers of D. H. Lawrence, Ed. Edward McDonald, London, 1936. *Study of Thomas Hardy,* pp. 398–516

2 Nicholson, Andrew (ed), *Lord Byron, the complete miscellaneous prose,* Oxford, 1991, p. 97

3 Barber, T. G., *Byron and Where he is Buried,* Hucknall, 1939, pp. 136–7

4 *Blackwood's,* 1825, quoted in Stowe, p. 315

5 BM Add Ms 31038

6 Byron (McGann) Vol 2, p. 180

7 Carlyle, T., *The Love Letters of Thomas Carlyle and Jane Welsh,* London, 1909, p. 366

8 quoted in Elwin (LBW), p. 63

9 Trelawny, E. J., *Recollections of the Last Days of Shelley and Byron,* London, 1858, pp. 222–4

10 *Byroniana,* London 1834, p. 111

11 *The Quarterly Review,* XXVII, quoted in Redpath, T., *The Young Romantics & Critical Opinion 1807–1824,* London, 1975, p. 191

12 Stowe, p. 80

13 *Blackwood's,* 1819, quoted in Stowe, p. 314

14 Wilde, O., (ed. Fong, B. & Beckson, K.), *The Complete Works of Oscar Wilde,* Oxford, 2000, Vol I, p. 196

15 Lawrence, D. H., *op. cit.,* pp. 398–516

16 Lawrence, D. H., *ibid.*

17 Byron (McGann), Vol I, p. 107

18 Trelawny, E. J., *Records of Shelley, Byron and the Author,* London, 1878, Vol I, pp. 30–1

19 Stowe, p. 128

20 Stowe, p. 290

21 Stowe, p. 300

22 Stowe, *ibid.*

23 Lovelace Byron papers, Bodleian Library, Byron, Lady, *Auto Description,* 1831

24 quoted in Mayne, p. 9

25 Byron, Lady, *Auto-Description,* 1831

26 Byron, Lady, *Auto-Description*, 1831, quoted in Mayne, pp. 4–5
27 Lamb, C., *Glenarvon*, London, 1995, pp. 29–30
28 Byron, Lady, *Auto-Description*, 1831, quoted in Mayne, p. 15
29 quoted in Goldring, D., *Regency Portrait Painter, the life of Sir Thomas Lawrence, PRA*, London, 1951, p. 262
30 Byron, Lady, quoted in Mayne, pp. 36–7
31 Byron, Lady, quoted in Mayne, p. 38
32 Byron, Lady, *Auto-Description*, 1831, quoted in Mayne, p. 39
33 Marchand, L. (ed), *Byron's Letters and Journals*, London, 1973–82, Vol 4, pp. 182–3
34 Morgan, Lady, *Lady Morgan's Memoirs*, London, 1882, Vol II, p. 200
35 Lovell, J. (ed.), *Lady Blessington's Conversations of Lord Byron*, Princeton, 1969, pp. 132–3
36 Lamb, C., *op. cit.*, pp. 10–11
37 BLJ, Vol 2, pp. 175–6
38 BLJ, Vol 2, p. 218
39 BLJ, Vol 2, p. 199
40 Byron, Lady, quoted in Mayne, pp. 48–9
41 BLJ, Vol 2, pp. 226–7
42 Gronow, Captain, *Reminiscence of Captain Gronow*, Frome, 1984, Vol 1, p. 150
43 Medwin, T., *Conversations of Lord Byron; noted during a residence with his lordship at Pisa*, London, 1824, p. 88
44 Cecil, D., *Melbourne*, London, 1955, p. 80
45 Blessington, p. 149
46 BLJ, Vol 2, p. 238
47 BLJ, Vol 2, p. 233
48 BLJ, Vol 2, p. 242
49 BLJ, Vol 3, p. 32
50 Hayman, R., *Nietsche: A Critical Life*, London 1980, p. 35
51 Lawrence, D. H., *op. cit.*, pp. 398–516
52 BLJ, Vol 3, p. 225
53 BLJ, Vol 3, p. 204
54 Lawrence, D. H., *op. cit.*, pp. 398–516
55 BLJ, Vol 3, p. 69
56 Lawrence, D. H., *op. cit.*, pp. 398–516
57 BLJ, Vol 3, p. 69

58 Lawrence, D. H., *op. cit.*, pp. 398–516
59 Medwin, T., *op. cit.*, p. 69
60 *The Town and Country Magazine*, January 1779, quoted in Gunn, p. 11
61 Osborne, Lady M., quoted in Gunn, P., *op.cit*, p. 38
62 BLJ, Vol 3, p. 32
63 Byron (McGann), Vol IV, p. 40
64 BLJ, Vol 5, pp. 273–4
65 BLJ, Vol 3, p. 68
66 Byron (McGann), Vol III, p. 120
67 quoted in Astarte, p. 263
68 Byron (McGann), Vol 3, p. 120
69 BLJ, Vol 3, p. 205
70 Byron (McGann), Vol III, p. 159
71 Byron, Lady, quoted in Mayne, p. 48
72 BLJ, Vol 4, p. 36
73 BLJ, Vol 4, p. 39
74 Byron (McGann), Vol 3, pp. 359–60
75 BLJ, Vol 3, p. 179
76 BLJ, Vol 4, p. 45
77 BLJ, Vol 4, pp. 110–11
78 BLJ, Vol 4, p. 104
79 Stowe, p. 121
80 Byron, Lady, quoted in Mayne, pp. 57–8
81 Byron, Lady, quoted in Mayne, pp. 57–8
82 Byron, Lady, quoted in Mayne, p. 73
83 Byron, Lady, quoted in Mayne, p. 58
84 BLJ, Vol 3, p. 99
85 BLJ, Vol 3, p. 174
86 Moore, T., *The Letters and Journals of Lord Byron, with notices of his life*, Paris, 1829, Vol 1, p. 581
87 Byron, Lady, quoted in Mayne, p. 111
88 quoted in Eisler, B., *Byron*, New York, 1999, p. 447
89 Byron, Lady, quoted in Mayne, p. 408
90 quoted in Gunn, p. 265
91 Byron, Lady, quoted in Mayne, p. 406

PART III

1 Keynes, G. (ed), *The Complete Writings of William Blake*, London, 1957, p. 75–6
2 Byron, Lady, quoted in Mayne, p. 409

3 Byron, Lady, quoted in Mayne, p. 408

4 Byron, Lady, *Memorandum of my interview with Mrs Leigh at Reigate*, Lovelace Byron papers

5 Byron, Lady, quoted in Mayne, p. 409

6 Byron, Lady, quoted in Mayne, p. 410

7 Byron, Lady, quoted in Mayne, p. 403

8 Leigh, A., quoted in Gunn, p. 262

9 Robertson, F., quoted in Arnold, F., *Robertson of Brighton, with some notices of his times and contemporaries*, London, 1886, pp. 184–6

10 Byron, Lady, quoted in Mayne, p. 399

11 Arnold, F., *op.cit.*, p. 155

12 Byron, Lady, quoted in Ada, p. 297

13 quoted in Stowe, p. 287

14 Byron, Lady, quoted in Elwin (LBW), p. 250

15 Martineau, H., quoted in Mayne, p. 287

16 Elwin (LBW), p. 254

17 Byron, Lady, quoted in Elwin (LBW), p. 254

18 Leigh, A., quoted in Gunn, p. 123

19 Byron, Lady, quoted in Elwin (LBW), p. 257

20 BLJ, Vol 4, p. 249

21 BLJ, Vol 4, pp. 252–2

22 BLJ, Vol 4, pp. 263–4

23 Bence-Jones, Dr., quoted in Elwin (LBW), p. 285

24 BLJ, Vol 4, p. 262

25 Byron, Lady, quoted in Elwin (LBW), p. 192

26 Byron, Lady, quoted in Elwin (LBW), pp. 294–5

27 BLJ, Vol 4, p. 285

28 *Ibid*

29 Leigh, Augusta, quoted in Elwin (LBW), p. 300

30 Byron, Lady, quoted in Mayne, p. 183

31 Byron, Lady, quoted in Mayne, p. 181

32 Ticknor, G., *Life, Letters and Journals of George Ticknor*, 1876, Vol 1, pp. 50–56

33 *Ibid.*

34 Byron, Lady, quoted in Mayne, p. 181

35 Byron, Lady, quoted in Mayne, p. 194

36 Lawrence, D. H., *op. cit.*, pp. 398–516

37 Byron, Lady, quoted in Mayne, p. 195

38 Barnard, Lady A., quoted in Stowe, p. 306

39 BLJ, Vol 5, p. 14–15

40 Byron, Lady, quoted in Elwin (LBW), p. 346

41 Byron, Lady, quoted in Mayne, pp. 200–1

42 Byron, Lady, quoted in Gunn, p. 154

43 Byron, Lady, quoted in Mayne, p. 203

44 BM Add MS 31037

45 *Ibid*

46 BLJ, Vol 5, p. 20

47 *Ibid*

48 Leigh, A., quoted in Elwin (LBW), p. 384

49 Leigh, A., quoted in Elwin (LBW), p. 428

50 Byron, Lady, quoted in Elwin (LBW), p. 426

51 Byron, Lady, quoted in Elwin (LBW), p. 456

52 *Ibid*

53 Byron, Lady, quoted in Elwin (LBW), p. 457

54 *Ibid*

55 Byron, Lady, quoted in Elwin (LBW), p. 459

56 Byron (McGann), pp. 386–8

57 Byron, Lady, quoted in Elwin (LBW), p. 463

58 Nicholson, Andrew (ed), *Lord Byron, The Complete Miscellaneous Prose*, Oxford, 1991, p. 95

59 Robinson, H. C., quoted in Stowe, p. 186

60 Wordsworth, W., quoted in Redpath, T., *The Young Romantics & Critical Opinion 1807–1824*, London, 1975, p. 199

61 Barnard, Lady A., quoted in Stowe, p. 306

62 quoted in Stowe, p. 80

63 Byron, Lady, *Auto-Description*, 1831

64 BLJ, Vol 5, p. 24

65 Byron, Lady, quoted in Ada, p. 141

66 Byron (McGann), Vol 2, p. 119
67 Polidori, J., *The Vampyre and other tales of the macabre*, Oxford 1997, p. 3
68 Marshall, J., *The Life and Letters of Mary Wollstonecraft Shelley*, Vol 2, pp. 113–14
69 Byron (McGann), Vol 3, pp. 380–2
70 Byron (McGann), Vol 3, p. 383
71 Byron (McGann), Vol 4, pp. 1–2
72 BLJ, Vol 5, p. 66
73 Byron (McGann), Vol 3, p. 64
74 Tennyson, A., in Ricks C. (ed) *The Poems of Tennyson*, Avon, 1969, p. 321
75 Lamb, Mrs G., quoted in Grosskurth, P., *Byron, the flawed angel*, London, 1997, p. 272
76 Byron, Lady, quoted in Elwin (LBF), p. 45
77 *Ibid*
78 Byron, Lady, quoted in Elwin (LBF), p. 54
79 Byron, Lady, quoted in Mayne, p. 181
80 Clermont, Mrs, quoted in Fox, Sir J., *The Byron Mystery*, London, 1924, p. 147
81 Byron, Lady, quoted in Medora (Mackay), p. 55
82 Byron, Lady, quoted in Medora (Mackay), pp. 54–5
83 BLJ, Vol 5, p. 66
84 Byron, Lady, quoted in Elwin (LBF), p. 30
85 Villiers, The Hon Mrs G., quoted in Elwin (LBF), p. 30
86 Byron, Lady, quoted in Elwin (LBF), p. 30
87 Villiers, The Hon Mrs G., quoted in Elwin (LBF), pp. 33–4
88 Byron, Lady, quoted in Elwin (LBF), p. 42
89 Byron, Lady, quoted in Elwin (LBF), p. 35
90 Leigh, A., quoted in Elwin (LBF), p. 42
91 Byron, Lady, quoted in Elwin (LBF), p. 33
92 Leigh, A., quoted in Astarte, p. 224
93 Byron, Lady, quoted in Astarte, pp. 247–8
94 Leigh, A., quoted in Astarte, pp. 249–50

95 Hobhouse, J. C., quoted in Grosskurth, P., *Byron, the flawed angel*, London, 1997, p. 27
96 BLJ, Vol 6, p. 232
97 Byron (McGann), Vol 4, p. 74
98 Villiers, The Hon Mrs G., quoted in Astarte, p. 69
99 BLJ, Vol 5, p. 91
100 BLJ, Vol 5, p. 115
101 BLJ, Vol 5, p. 190
102 BLJ, Vol 5, pp. 231–2
103 BLJ, Vol 6, pp. 129–130
104 BLJ, Vol 6, p. 129
105 BLJ, Vol 8, p. 139
106 Astarte, pp. 61–2
107 quoted in Edel, L., *Henry James, the middle years 1884–94*, London, 1963, p. 243
108 quoted in Edel, *op.cit*, p. 244
109 Austen, J., *Persuasion*, London, 1965, p. 238
110 Byron, Lady, quoted in Mayne, p. 267
111 Byron, Lady, quoted in Elwin (LBF), p. 161
112 Lockhart, J. G., *Life of Scott*, Edinburgh, 1839, Vol 5, p. 253
113 Byron, Lady, quoted in Mayne, pp. 277–8
114 Byron, Lady, quoted in Mayne, p. 272
115 Johnson, S., *The Works of Samuel Johnson*, London, 1825, Vol 7, p. 119
116 Byron, Lady, quoted in Ada, pp. 8–9
117 Byron, Lady, quoted in Mayne, p. 292
118 Byron, Lady, quoted in Ada, p. 373
119 Leigh, A., quoted in Gunn, pp. 225–6
120 Leigh, A., quoted in Gunn, pp. 226–7
121 Trevanion, H., *The Influence of Apathy*, London, 1829, pp. 122–3
122 Medora (Mackay), pp. 122–4
123 Leigh, Medora, Byron Lovelace Papers, Bodleian Library, Box 86, f.18
124 Medora (Mackay), p. 124
125 Medora (Mackay), pp. 125–6
126 Leigh, A., quoted in Mayne, p. 342

127 Leigh, A., quoted in Mayne, pp. 342–4
128 Leigh, A., quoted in Mayne, pp. 344–5
129 Medora (Mackay), pp. 126–7
130 Medora (Mackay), p. 128
131 Medora (Mackay), p. 129
132 Medora (Mackay), p. 119
133 Medora (Mackay), p. 131–2
134 Villiers, The Hon Mrs G., quoted in Mayne, p. 351
135 Medora (Mackay), p. 132
136 Leigh, Medora quoted in Mayne, p. 352
137 Medora (Mackay), pp. 133–4
138 Byron, Lady, quoted in Gunn, p. 233
139 Leigh, A., quoted in Gunn, p. 234
140 Leigh, A., quoted in Gunn, p. 235
141 Campbell, T., *New Monthly Magazine*, 1830, quoted in Stowe, p. 85
142 *Blackwood's* quoted in Arnold, F., Arnold, F., *Robertson of Brighton, with some notices of his times and contemporaries*, London, 1886, p. 163
143 Gallinge, Mr, quoted in Arnold F., *op.cit.*,p.169
144 Byron, Lady, quoted in Elwin (LBF), pp. 236–7
145 Byron, Lady, quoted in Ada, p. 31
146 de Morgan, S., quoted in Ada, p. 34
147 Woolley, B., *The Bride of Science: romance, reason and Byron's daughter*, London, 1999, p. 90
148 Briggs, Miss, quoted in Ada, pp. 47–8
149 Woolley, B, *op.cit.*, p. 120
150 Trench, F., quoted in Arnold, F., *op.cit.*, p. 170
151 King, Lord, quoted in Ada, p. 65
152 Byron, Ada, quoted in Ada, p. 66
153 Byron, Lady, quoted in Ada, p. 72
154 Medora (Mackay), pp. 135–7
155 Byron, Ada, quoted in Ada, p. 124
156 Byron, Ada, quoted in Ada, p. 125
157 *Ibid*
158 Byron, Lady, quoted in Mayne, p. 350
159 Byron, Lady, quoted in Mayne, p. 353

160 Byron, Lady, quoted in Mayne, p. 358
161 *Ibid*
162 Leigh, Medora, Byron Lovelace Papers, Bodleian Library, Box 86, ff.151–171
163 Jameson, A., quoted in Ada, p. 138
164 Medora (Mackay), pp. 137–8
165 Byron, Lady, quoted in Ada, p. 140
166 Medora (Mackay), p. 141
167 Leigh, M., quoted in Mayne, p. 360–2
168 Medora (Mackay), pp. 91–3
169 Byron, Ada, quoted in Ada, p. 172
170 Stowe, p. 135
171 Arnold, F., *op.cit.*, p. 193
172 Stowe, pp. 140–1
173 Leigh, Emily, quoted in Gunn, pp. 255–6
174 Leigh, A., quoted in Gunn, p. 259
175 Byron, Lady, quoted in Mayne, p. 408
176 Leigh, Emily, Byron Lovelace Papers, Bodleian Library, Box 85, f.3
177 Byron, Lady, quoted in Gunn, pp. 264–5
178 Leigh, Emily, quoted in Gunn, p. 265
179 Byron, Lady, quoted in Mayne, p. 414
180 Leigh, Emily, Byron Lovelace Papers, Bodleian Library, Box 85, f.18
181 Leigh, Emily, Byron Lovelace Papers, Bodleian Library, Box 85, f.22
182 Byron, Lady, Byron Lovelace Papers, Bodleian Library, Box 85, f.73
183 Byron, Lady, quoted in Ada, p. 152
184 Byron, Ada, quoted in Ada, p. 76
185 Byron, Ada, quoted in Arnold, F., *op.cit.*, p. 171
186 Byron, Ada, quoted in Arnold, F., *op.cit*, p. 173
187 Byron, Ada, quoted in Ada, p. 268
188 Byron, Lady, quoted in Ada, p. 271
189 Byron, Ada, quoted in Woolley, B., *op.cit.*, pp. 344–5
190 Howitt, W., *Daily News*, 2 September 1869

191 Arnold, F., *op.cit.*, p. 193
192 Byron, Lady, quoted in
    Ada, p. 312
193 Lovelace Journal quoted in Ada,
    p. 325
194 Eliot, G., (ed. Haight G), *The
    George Eliot Letters*, London, 1956,
    Vol 5, p. 314
195 Eliot, G., (ed. Haight G), *The
    George Eliot Letters*, London, 1956,
    Vol 6, pp. 371–2
196 Dickens, C., *Great Expectations*,
    London, 1965, p. 411
197 Stowe, pp. 245–6
198 Stowe, pp. 301–2
199 Amy Woolner, Thomas Woolner
    R. A., *Sculptor and Poet, His Life in
    Letters*, London, 1917

Epilogue

1 Paget, J., quoted in Stowe,
    p. 122
2 Byron, (McGann), Vol 4, p. 44
3 Stowe, p. 299
4 Eliot, G., *Selected Critical Writings*,
    Oxford, 1992, p. 148
5 *Blackwood's* 1825, quoted in Stowe,
    p. 122
6 Wilde, O., *op.cit.*, p. 216
7 Auden, W. H., 'Letter to Lord Byron'
    in *Collected Poems*, ed. E. Mendekon,
    London, 1976, p. 86
8 Jeffrey, F., quoted in Redpath, *op.cit.*,
    p. 289
9 Collison, G., *Cemetery Interment*,
    London, 1840, p. 157

SELECT BIBLIOGRAPHY

Arnold, Rev. Frederick. *Robertson of Brighton with Some Notices of His Times and Contemporaries*, London 1886

Barber, Rev, Canon T.G. *Byron and Where he is Buried*, Hucknall, 1939

Broughton, Lord [J.C. Hobhouse]. *Recollections of a Long Life*. 6 vols. Ed. Lady Dorchester, London, 1911

Eisler, Benita. *Byron, Child of Passion . . . Fool of Fame*. New York. 1999

Elwin, Malcolm. *The Noels and the Milbankes*. London 1967

Elwin, Malcolm. *Lord Byron's Wife*. London 1962

Elwin, Malcolm. *Lord Byron's Family*, London 1975

Fox, Sir John. *The Byron Mystery*, London 1924

Grosskurth, Phyllis. *Byron, The Flawed Angel*. London 1997

Gunn, Peter. *My Dearest Augusta*. London 1968

Knight, G. Wilson, *Lord Byron's Marriage: The Evidence of Asterisks*, London 1957

Lovelace, Ralph Milbanke. *Lady Noel Byron and the Leighs: Some Authentic Records of Certain Circumstances, etc.* Privately Printed, 1887

Lovelace, Ralph Milbanke. *Astarte: A Fragment of Truth concerning George Gordon Byron, Sixth Lord Byron. Recorded by his Grandson, Ralph Milbanke, Earl of Lovelace*. New York, 1921

Marchand, Leslie. *Byron, A Biography*, 3 vols. New York, 1957

Marchand, Leslie. (ed.) *Byron's Letters and Journals*, 12 vols. London, 1982

Maurois, Andre. *Byron*, New York, 1930

Mayne, Ethel Colburn. *The Life and Letters of Anne Isabella, Lady Noel Byron*, London 1929

Mackay, Charles. *Medora Leigh; A History and an Autobiography*, London 1869

McGann, Jerome J. (ed.) *Byron: The Complete Poetical Works*. 7 vols. Oxford, 1993

Moore, Doris Langley. *Ada Countess of Lovelace, Byron's Legitimate Daughter*, London 1977

Moore, Doris Langley. *The Late Lord Byron*, London 1962

Nicholson, Andrew. (ed.) *Lord Byron, The Complete Miscellaneous Prose*, Oxford 1991

Pierson, Joan. *The Real Lady Byron*, London 1992

Stowe, Harriet Beecher. *Lady Byron Vindicated, A History of the Byron Controversy*, London 1870

Woolley, Benjamin. *The Bride of Science, Romance Reason and Byron's Daughter*, London 1999

INDEX